CONTROLLING ACCIDENTS AND INSURERS' RISKS IN CONSTRUCTION: A FUZZY KNOWLEDGE-BASED APPROACH

CONTROLLING ACCIDENTS AND INSURERS' RISKS IN CONSTRUCTION: A FUZZY KNOWLEDGE-BASED APPROACH

IMRIYAS KAMARDEEN

Nova Biomedical Books
New York

For permission to use material from this book please contact us:
Telephone 631-231-7269; Fax 631-231-8175
Web Site: http://www.novapublishers.com

NOTICE TO THE READER

The Publisher has taken reasonable care in the preparation of this book, but makes no expressed or implied warranty of any kind and assumes no responsibility for any errors or omissions. No liability is assumed for incidental or consequential damages in connection with or arising out of information contained in this book. The Publisher shall not be liable for any special, consequential, or exemplary damages resulting, in whole or in part, from the readers' use of, or reliance upon, this material. Any parts of this book based on government reports are so indicated and copyright is claimed for those parts to the extent applicable to compilations of such works.

Independent verification should be sought for any data, advice or recommendations contained in this book. In addition, no responsibility is assumed by the publisher for any injury and/or damage to persons or property arising from any methods, products, instructions, ideas or otherwise contained in this publication.

This publication is designed to provide accurate and authoritative information with regard to the subject matter covered herein. It is sold with the clear understanding that the Publisher is not engaged in rendering legal or any other professional services. If legal or any other expert assistance is required, the services of a competent person should be sought. FROM A DECLARATION OF PARTICIPANTS JOINTLY ADOPTED BY A COMMITTEE OF THE AMERICAN BAR ASSOCIATION AND A COMMITTEE OF PUBLISHERS.

Library of Congress Cataloging-in-Publication Data

Kamardeen, Imriyas.
 Controlling accidents and insurers' risks in construction : a fuzzy knowledge-based approach / Imriyas Kamardeen.
   p. cm.
 Includes bibliographical references and index.
 ISBN 978-1-60741-368-4 (hbk.)
 1.   Construction industry--Insurance. 2.   Construction industry--Risk management. 3.   Construction industry--Accidents. I. Title.
 HG8053.7.K37 2009
 363.11'969--dc22
                                                                                    2009006349

Published by Nova Science Publishers, Inc. ✚ *New York*

To my wife, Nadia, and daughter, Mahdiyya

Contents

Preface

There has been a greater concern globally as to how to minimise construction accidents and their consequences on construction workers, contractors, clients, design and project management consultants, and insurance companies. This book introduces new strategies and models that will facilitate readers in the construction and insurance industries in revamping their existing practices towards minimising accidents, improving profitability, and alleviating liabilities. Some of the new elements introduced in the book are:

- New theoretical models for OHS risk assessment and workers' compensation insurance that address the shortcomings of the existing techniques;
- New strategies to foster stakeholder involvement in risk control;
- Pioneering the partnering arrangement in construction OHS management and insurance;
- New approach for insurance risk assessments using fuzzy technique; and
- Cost effective and easy to follow methodologies for the self-development of advanced knowledge based systems for practitioners in their vocations.

At the project level, these will lessen construction accidents and thereby safeguard the interests of construction workers, insurance companies, design and project management consultants, contractors and clients. At the corporate level, these will foster sustainable business reputation, goodwill, and growth. At the national level, these will reduce the social costs of construction, and will improve GDP growth.

One of the unique features of this book is its *cross-domain application*. The book integrates four domains, including occupational health and safety management in construction, workers' compensation system, insurance and risk management, and knowledge based systems to come up with new strategies and models. The structured integration of diverse disciplines in the book eliminates the confusions, challenges and difficulties facing practitioners, researchers and tertiary students in cross-domain applications. Another unique feature of this book is its equal emphasis on both strategic and operational measures of management. Most of the existing books on OHS and insurance in construction pitch the subject at site level. Nevertheless, this book discusses both strategic and operational level measures to mitigate accidents and their associated losses for stakeholders.

The book will appeal to a wide range of audience, including insurers, project managers and design consultants, OHS professionals, contractors, software vendors, researchers, academics, and tertiary students. The specific area that may appeal to each of these audiences is described below.

- Insurers – the premium rating model and the fuzzy KBS will benefit insurers significantly in re-engineering current practices towards minimising their financial losses and deficits;
- Project managers and design consultants – the risk assessment frameworks discussed in the book will be handy for these professionals for evaluating safety proposals in construction tenders;
- OHS professionals & contractors – the book discusses best practices and frameworks for hazards assessment and safety implementations in construction projects. These will be crucial for OHS professionals and contractors;
- Software vendors – the book explains the methods and steps in easy to follow steps for developing knowledge based systems for construction insurance. It will serve as a good reference material for software vendors who produce and commercialise knowledge based systems for the construction, risk management and insurance industries;
- Researchers – the book reports a pioneering research work in the field, and has established a strong platform for future research. Researchers could take the recommendations forward to create new ideas and findings; and
- Academics and tertiary students – this book will serve as a valuable text and reference book for tertiary students both at undergraduate and postgraduate levels in construction management, insurance, project management, business administration, OHS management, and knowledge based systems. This will also be a handy resource for academics for their teaching purposes.

This is a research-based book and chapters in the book are grounded on recent research and best practices. They demonstrate how innovative insurance and construction companies can exploit contemporary research to drive the re-structuring of poor practices that compromise their business sustainability. With diverse audiences in mind, the chapters are written in clear and easy-to-follow styles. The CD enclosed with the book contains the prototype of the KBS that the book discusses. Readers will appreciate this useful appendix of the book that underpins the practical implementation of new theories.

Acknowledgments

This book represents the composition of my ideas and efforts in addition to the support rendered by various people. I am greatly indebted to acknowledge all these invaluable pillars in making this book a success. I owe special thanks to Professor Low Sui Pheng of Department of Building, National University of Singapore who helped shape my ideas with his thoughtful comments and encouragement. I would like to thank the professionals from general insurance companies and construction companies in Singapore who voluntarily participated in the research study that underpins the contents on this book. Without their support, the research study would not have been possible. Thanks to my colleagues in the Faculty of the Built Environment, University of New South Wales, for your support and encouragement. Last but not least, I extend my appreciation to my wife, Nadia, for her unflinching support, encouragement and patience throughout my career.

Abbreviations

AU$	Australian dollar
BCA	Building and Construction Authority of Singapore
CAD	Computer-aided design
CAR	Contractors' all risk insurance
$CCI_{contractor}$	Claims control incentive for the contractor
$CLR_{contractor}$	Cumulative loss ratio for the contractor
CRH_{score}	Degree of hazard contributed by crane use
$CsiteH_{score}$	Degree of hazard contributed by works on contaminated sites
$CspaceH_{score}$	Degree of hazard contributed by works in confined spaces
DMH_{score}	Degree of hazard contributed by demolition works
EMR	Experience modification rating
EM_{score}	Adequacy score for emergency management system
ERD	Entity-relationship diagram
ERH_{score}	Degree of hazard contributed by erection works
EXH_{score}	Degree of hazard contributed by excavation works
FIS	Fuzzy inference system
FLH_{score}	Degree of hazard contributed by falseworks
GDP	Gross domestic product
GIA	General Insurance Association of Singapore
GUI	Graphical user interface
HSE	Health and safety executive
IPU	Intermediate processing unit
IRC	Intersection rule configuration
IT	Information technology
KBS	Knowledge based system
LTA	Land Transport Authority of Singapore
MF	Membership function
MOM	Ministry of Manpower, Singapore
MTH_{score}	Degree of hazard contributed by machinery and tools use
NCD	No claim discount

OHS	Occupational health and safety
PHI	Project hazard index
PSI	Project safety index
PSO_{score}	Adequacy score for project safety organisation
RAM_{score}	Adequacy score for risk assessment and management system
RFH_{score}	Degree of hazard contributed by roof works
S$	Singapore dollar
SI_{score}	Adequacy score for safety inspection system
SLH_{score}	Degree of hazard contributed by scaffolding and ladder use
SMD_{client}	Safety monitoring discount for the client
SM_{score}	Adequacy score for sub-contractors' safety systems
SMT_{score}	Adequacy score for safe use and maintenance of machinery and tools regime
SSCP 79: 1999	Singapore's Code of Practice for Safety Management for Consruction Sites
STC_{score}	Adequacy score for safety training and competency of people involved
SWP_{score}	Adequacy score for safe work practices
TAC	Total actual claims
UK	United Kingdom
URC	Union rule configuration
US	United States
US$	American dollar
VBA™	Visual basic for applications
WCH_{score}	Degree of hazard contributed by welding and cutting works
WCI	Workers' compensation insurance
WSHA 2006	Workplace Safety and Health Act 2006 of Singapore
XOL	Excess of loss reinsurance

Chapter I

Introduction

The Global Trend of OHS
in the Construction Industry

The construction industry is an integral part of the national economy of any country. It is of national significance because: (1) its contribution to gross domestic product (GDP) is relatively high, (2) it generates abundant employment opportunities, and (3) it creates a country's infrastructure and other industries in the economy, and these are the basis for a country's socio-economic development. For example, the UK construction industry, while boasting a GDP contribution of over 5%, is providing employment to around 2.5 million people (Business Monitor, 2008). Also, construction, dwellings and property made up 48% of Gross Fixed Capital Formation in 2006 (National Statistics, 2008). The Reserve Bank of Australia summarised that construction industry's share of GDP in the Australian economy is 7.5%, and the industry employs 940 000 people a year on average (RBA, 2007).

Despite the contributions to national economy, the construction industry has been characterised to have poor OHS performance records globally. In the United States, it was reported that the construction industry accounted for only 5% of the United States' workforce but claimed a disproportionate 20% of all occupational fatalities and 9% of all disabling injuries (National Safety Council, 1997). In Great Britain, construction accounted for 31% of all work-related deaths in 2002/03 (Haslam *et al.*, 2005). The Australian construction industry accounted for 9% of the workers' compensation claims when it employed approximately 5% of the Australian workforce (Dingsdag *et al.*, 2006). The incidence of workplace fatalities were 9.2 per 100,000 workers in construction, compared with the national average of 3.1 fatalities per 100,000 workers (NOHSC, 2005). The fatality rate is three times higher than the all-industries rate. On average, 49 construction workers have been killed at work each year (Fraser, 2007). The construction industry of Kuwait recorded 42% of all occupational fatalities (Kartam and Bouz, 1998), and the construction industry of Hong Kong accounted for more than one-third of all industrial accidents over the last 10 years (Tam and Fung, 1998). Singapore's construction industry, for only 29% of the total number of industrial workers, accounted for 40% of worksite accidents (Chua and Goh, 2004). Moreover, the analysis of worksite accidents by Singapore's Ministry of Manpower revealed that the construction industry recorded the highest accident frequency and severity among all the industries in Singapore (OSHD-MOM, 2006).

This situation has disadvantaged many parties involved in the construction of built facilities, including construction workers, insurance companies, clients, design and project management consultants, and contractors. The parties affected are as follows:

- Increased rate of construction accidents not only wipes out the profit margin of contractors but also degrades the quality of life of workers and their families. These skyrocket the social costs associated with occupational accidents, eventually affecting the GDP growth of the country. A recent study by the Health and Safety Executive (HSE), UK has found that accident costs on a construction site amounted to 9.5% of the tender price of the project being undertaken. The HSE has estimated that over 30 million working days are lost due to workplace accidents, and that when all the costs are properly taken into account, the total cost of work accidents and work related ill-health, to society as a whole, is likely to be between 10 and 15 billion pounds sterling a year - equivalent to between 1.75% and 2.75% of the GDP of the UK (IET, 2008). The US construction industry has recorded that the costs of accidents and injuries account for between 7.9% and 15% of construction costs (Everett and Frank, 1996);
- The insurance industries in many countries have been experiencing detrimental losses by workers' compensation insurance. For example, New South Wales is the largest workers' compensation market in Australia, but traditionally is one of the poorest performers from both profitability and unfunded deficit basis. It had accumulated a deficit of AU$2,353,000 until November 2005 (Burton, 2005). The industry statistics for year 2006 of the General Insurance Association of Singapore noted that workers' compensation insurance is the third largest class of insurance in Singapore. It continued to struggle in 2005 with an underwriting loss of S$7 million in the first half of 2005 compared to the same period in 2004, when it lost S$1 million. The incurred loss ratio has climbed from 72% to 80% (GIA, 2006); and
- An emerging trend is discernible internationally that OHS regulatory bodies are revising their Workplace Health and Safety Act to hold clients, design and project management consultants, and contractors accountable for any occupational accidents in their projects. The Ministry of Manpower, Singapore, for example, recently revised the Workplace Safety and Health Act to hold all the stakeholders along the construction supply chain accountable for occupational accidents (MOM, 2006). This critical revision to the Act exposes the stakeholders to the risk of court proceedings.

Hence, minimising accidents and injuries in construction is of critical essence to:

- Improve the GDP growth of a country;
- Safeguard the interests, and the quality of life and welfare of workers and their families;
- Minimise avoidable losses to the construction and insurance industries; and
- Protect construction professionals, clients and contractors from the risks of legal proceedings, fines and imprisonments.

The Drive towards Re-engineering Workers' Compensation Insurance for Improving Safety in Construction

Construction is one of the most dangerous and risky businesses; insurance is a keystone to eliminate most of the financial risks in construction business (Clough *et al.*, 2005). Bunni (2003) identified five types of insurance that are available to contractors for different risk nature; contractors' all risk insurance, general liability insurance, workers' compensation insurance (WCI), motor insurance, and marine transport insurance. Table 1.1 describes the types of risks covered by each class of insurance. Out of these five classes of insurance, providing an adequate WCI cover has been made mandatory by law in most countries for employers to engage workers under a contract of service. It is enforced to safeguard the interests of occupational injury victims, and to ease their employers' financial burden of compensating.

Table 1.1. Insurance in construction

Insurance class	Indemnity description
1. Contractors' all risk insurance	It covers physical losses or damages to works, plant, equipment and materials during the course of construction that are resulted by crises such as natural disasters, fire/explosion or collapse, etc.
2. General liability insurance	This indemnifies the contractor in respect of legal liability for damages arising from deaths or injuries to non-contracting entities or damages to non-contracting entities' properties due to a project. For example, damage to an adjacent property, injury to any third party due to an excavation work or damages to underground utilities may be indemnified with this insurance.
3. Workers' compensation insurance (WCI)	According to the Workers' Compensation Act, the cost of all the injuries and fatalities to workers resulting from construction activities should be borne by the contractor, irrespective of fault. Workers' compensation insurance is taken to transfer this financial risk to a professional insurer.
4. Motor insurance	Motor insurance provides financial protection when the contractor is legally obligated to pay for bodily injuries or property damages arising from the ownership, maintenance or use of covered vehicles. This includes liability coverage for over-the-road hazards for self-propelled motor vehicles used for the sole purpose of providing mobility to construction equipment such as pumps, cranes, air compressors, generators, etc.
5. Marine transport insurance	In international construction, marine transport insurance is required for protection against any losses resulting from ship crises when transporting by sea.

Source: Modified from Imriyas *et al.*, 2006.

Since WCI is compulsory for every contractor and no project can be started on site without procuring it, this book invokes to exploit WCI premiums for accident control. As per the proposed strategy, the premium amount for a WCI policy will significantly be influenced by the effectiveness of a contractor's safety management system, which needs to be assessed in real-time. If a contractor's real-time safety management system is robust, the contractor will get a cost effective insurance cover, which will enable the contractor to compete better in tenders. Those contractors who do not have robust safety management systems in place will be penalised by higher premiums. This approach will automatically set risky contractors aside, and will motivate them to invest on safety in their organisations to ensure business continuity. The proposed strategy also advocates the partnering arrangement in WCI for construction whereby a post-project discount system will be introduced to encourage the involvement of both contractors and clients in reducing workers' compensation claims through improved safety during the course of construction. Hence, the implementation of the proposed strategy in the general insurance industry will facilitate accident control in the construction industry, loss minimisation for insurers, and thereby safeguard the interests of workers, clients, design and project management consultants, and contractors.

Table 1.2. Shortcomings of EMR

Author(s)	Criticism
1. Everett and Thomson (1995)	• EMR is a complex approach • EMR cannot fairly compare the safety records of different contractors • New contractors are forced to pay more premiums since they are not experience-rated • The premium is more biased towards the ownership of the company
2. Hinze *et al.* (1995)	EMR is misleading because: • The EMR value is decreased as the project size increased • Highly paying contractors will have lower EMR values
3. Coble and Sims (1996)	EMR can be vulnerable to fraud by contractors to obtain low premiums in three ways: • Manipulating the payroll of workers • Misrepresenting work classification • Manipulating company ownership
4. Hoonakker *et al.* (2005)	• EMR is a lagging indicator • EMR is based on worker classifications and not on jobs, which impedes the interpretation of the results

Source: Imriyas *et al.*, 2007c & 2008.

Because WCI has a strong footing internationally, there are established premium rating models and practices in the international arena. Experience modification rating (EMR) is an established technique wherein the premium charged to a contractor is based on the contractor's claims experience (Clough *et al.*, 2005; Hoonakker, *et al.*, 2005). The general notion is that a contractor has control over the loss ratio and is entitled to a credit for a good loss-prevention record, or, on the other hand, should pay a higher rate if the loss record is poor. This technique is widely used in many states of the US. The Australian insurance industry utilises an adapted version of EMR. Nevertheless, many researchers have criticised that EMR is ineffective for construction applications as summarised in Table 1.2. Without having to remain confined to EMR, a combination of benchmark and heuristics is applied for premium computation in the Singapore insurance industry. WCI premiums are traditionally computed by applying a rate on wage rolls of construction projects. There has been a collective agreement among the insurers that the preferable WCI premium rate for construction projects is 1% of the wage roll. This rate, however, is merely a yardstick. Individual insurers set competitive rates heuristically around the yardstick. However, no strong theory or analysis supports this benchmark norm. In the face of keen competition in the Singapore insurance market, underwriters tend to compromise the technical factors such as the risk profile of projects, and contractors' safety management systems, owing to the lack of a well-balanced framework. This brings about risky projects being insured at lower premiums, causing adverse loss ratios. Most of the general insurance companies in Singapore have been encountering undesirable loss ratios in construction WCI because of inadequate premiums; some have given up issuing WCI altogether and a few other companies have bankrupted. Further drawbacks are also noted in the current WCI system that impede accident control in construction projects. Lingard and Rowlinson (1994) quoted that contractors may not provide proper site safety with an increased reliance on WCI, which shifts their compensation liabilities to insurance companies. In the current WCI system, contractors, whose workers are injured because of contractors' poor safety management systems, are in safe standing. There is no significant financial burden on contractors in worksite accidents because WCI premiums are paid by project owners, while compensations to accident victims are paid by insurers. Because of this arrangement, contractors' enthusiasm and rigour towards minimising worksite accidents seem to be insufficient. This scenario also worsens insurers' risk exposure. In view of these issues, there is an intense need for developing a new methodology for WCI premium rating of construction projects to integrate accident control strategies into insurance as described in the preceding paragraph. Such a methodology should also be able to eliminate the shortcomings of both EMR and other approaches practiced by insurance industries, whilst placing the onus on each party to the policy to minimise accidents.

Leveraging by IT

Knowledge based systems (KBSs) are a class of computer program that can advise, analyse, categorise, communicate, consult, design, diagnose, explain, explore, forecast, form concepts, identify, interpret, justify, learn, manage, monitor, plan, present, retrieve, schedule, test and tutor. They address problems that normally require human specialists for their solutions (Brown and O'Leary, 1995). They mimic human experts' ability of heuristic reasoning from the knowledge and experience gained from years of practice in solving problems. Since KBSs are developed by acquiring the knowledge and experience of many experts in the industry, they provide effective and efficient solutions for problems in a specific domain and produce benefit/cost results well above a human expert. Owing to this high quality, KBSs have had a great commercial acceptance throughout the world; for example, in Great Britain, the Department of Commerce and Industry reported 2,000 commercial KBSs in operation, without considering KBSs working in universities and academic environments (Guardati, 1998). It is therefore convinced that developing a KBS for WCI premium rating would enhance the potential benefits of the new model and strategies proposed in this book. It can also facilitate the implementation of the model in the practical sense.

Negnevitsky (2002) and Durkin (2002) categorised KBSs into seven types, viz.: (1) Rule-based systems; (2) Frame-based systems; (3) Case-based reasoning systems; (4) Fuzzy systems; (5) Evolutionary computation systems; (6) Neural network systems; and (7) Hybrid systems, which combine more than one of the above systems. The selection of an appropriate type of KBS depends on the problem domain and its characteristics. Shapiro (2005) quoted that fuzzy logic applications in insurance and related areas should be a fruitful area for exploration for the foreseeable future. There are many insurance problems that could be resolved by using fuzzy systems. These include classification, underwriting, project liabilities, future and present values estimation, asset allocations and cash flows, and investments. Young (1997) claimed that: (1) fuzzy logic provides a uniform way to handle factors that influence insurance pricing decisions; and (2) it allows one to combine conflicting goals and constraints. Bell and Badiru (1996) noted that the development of predictive models for occupational injuries is often hampered by the variability associated with human abilities and performance; fuzzy set theory provides a tool to address this variability. Moreover, WCI premium rating involves subjective assessments of numerous hazard and safety factors in construction projects, and rating them using an objective scale like the Likert-scale. However, the ratings given by experts may not be precise as they are quantitative expressions of qualitative assessments. Thus, there is a need for accommodating this imprecision in premium rating. Si *et al.* (2001) reported that fuzzy logic gives a more flexible structure for combining qualitative and quantitative information over conventional or other subjective methods.

Many research works have been reported on fuzzy application for the underwriting function of insurance; however, most of them addressed life and health insurance spectrums. DeWit (1982) used a fuzzy expert system to analyse the underwriting practice of a life insurance company. Lemaire (1990) developed a fuzzy system to provide a flexible definition of a preferred policyholder in life insurance. Carreno and Jani (1993) developed a fuzzy KBS to provide an improved decision aid for evaluating life insurance risks. Young (1996) described how fuzzy logic can be used to make pricing decisions in group health insurance. Chen and He (1997) presented a methodology for deriving an Overall Disability Index (ODI) for measuring an individual's disability. Apart from that, Boissonnade (1984) developed a fuzzy model to estimate earthquake insurance premium rates. Lemaire (1990) discussed the computation of the fuzzy premium for a pure endowment policy. Carretero and Viejo (2000) investigated the use of fuzzy mathematical programming in automobile insurance pricing decisions. Additionally, two fuzzy applications related to WCI were also found. Bell and Badiru (1996) discussed a fuzzy expert system for quantifying and predicting the risk of occupational injury of the forearm and hand. Young (1997) described how an actuary could use fuzzy logic to adjust WCI premium rates at given intervals to reflect market changes. Nevertheless, these research works are limited in scope and do not explore the construction risk, which is unique in nature. Hence, leveraging by a fuzzy KBS on construction WCI premium rating function is still a very new area for exploration.

Focus of the Book

In line with the insurance drive mooted above as a strategic direction towards improving safety in the construction industry, this book aims to achieve the following objectives:

1. Exploring the principles of workers' compensation system, and WCI in relation to construction;
2. Critically analysing the variables pertinent to WCI premium rating in construction;
3. Developing a new effective WCI premium rating model that:
   a. Encompasses effective hazard assessment and safety evaluation frameworks
   b. Facilitates effective risk control during the course of insurance coverage
   c. Addresses the drawbacks of existing methods and practices; and
4. Forming the conceptual framework of a fuzzy KBS that automates the premium model above, implementing the KBS, and verifying it.

As the construction industry spans over a wide spectrum of construction activities such as buildings and civil engineering structures, it is believed that, any feasible re-engineering effort to improve WCI and safety in construction should start with the most significant sector that attracts the highest demand. In most countries, buildings take up a significant portion of the total annual demand for construction. The Construction Outlook in the US forecasted the demand for non-residential and transportation construction in the US through to 2011. Non-residential building construction, including healthcare facilities construction, public safety facilities construction, and education facilities construction will amount to $205.6 billion whereas transportation construction will amount to $41.2 billion (Jones, 2008). The percentage calculation of these demand figures reveals that non-residential construction will assume 83% of the total works in the US through to 2011. The Construction Forecasting Council of Australia reported the pattern of demand for construction projects from 2005 to 2007 as illustrated in Table 1.3. The table summarises that 66% of the total demand for construction was taken up by building works in 2005/2006 whilst it was 62% in 2006/2007. Likewise, the annual reports of the Building and Construction Authority of Singapore (BCA) for year 2004 and 2005 highlighted the demand for various types of construction projects as shown in Figure 1.1. It is discernible from this analysis that demand for building projects ranges between 60% and 80% of the total construction demand in most countries. Hence, this book will direct its discussions on hazards and safety towards building projects.

Table 1.3. Construction demand in Australia

Type of construction	Demand (in $bn)	
	2005/2006	**2006/2007**
Residential buildings	61	65
Non-residential buildings	24	27
Engineering construction	44	53
Total	*129*	*145*

Source: Construction Forecasting Council, 2008.

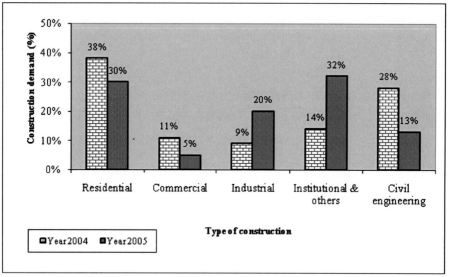

Source: BCA, 2006a&b.

Figure1.1. Construction demand in Singapore

Structure of the Book

The book consists of eight chapters and three appendices describing new strategies and models that will help readers in the insurance and construction industries to re-engineer existing ineffective practices towards minimising accidents, improving profitability, and alleviating liabilities. The contents of each chapter and the appendices are briefly discussed below.

Chapter 1 introduces the book, its context and main themes via arguments covering: (1) the global nature of OHS in construction, and the difficulties facing its stakeholders, (2) the role of workers' compensation insurance in safeguarding the interests of workers, clients and contractors, (3) critical dilemmas facing insurance companies globally, (4) the need and venue for re-engineering the existing insurance practices for improving safety, and (5) the role of IT in facilitating the re-engineering process.

Chapter 2 focuses on the origin and evolvement of workers' compensation system in the international arena. In addition, the chapter explores existing theories, strategies and practices for workers' compensation insurance, as well as their shortcomings in improving safety.

One of the approaches for improving safety in construction is to design a new WCI model such that it encompasses effective risk assessment and accident control strategies. The prime task towards developing a new model is to identify the critical variables that influence WCI premiums for construction projects.

Chapter 3 explores and critically analyses the variables pertinent to WCI premium rating. This chapter identifies all the possible variables that may influence WCI premium rates for construction projects. These variables are then filtered based on industry survey findings, to identify the most critical set that fits into Pareto's 80/20 rule.

The assessments of the intensity of project hazards and the effectiveness of contractor's safety management system are crucial aspects for WCI premium rating. On the other hand, these are generally complex tasks because of the vast variety of work trades, operations, machinery, materials, operatives and subcontractors involved in any one construction project.

Chapter 4 discusses comprehensive construction hazards and safety assessment methods in an easy-to-follow style.

Chapter 5 introduces a new WCI premium rating model for construction. The proposed model will streamline structured analyses of project factors, contractor factors, market conditions, and insurers' internal factors to decide optimal premiums. Moreover, it integrates the partnering notion into construction WCI.

Chapter 6 discusses how fuzzy systems can be practically applied to insurance premium rating. Unlike traditional methods discussed in most books, this chapter discusses efficient and contemporary theories and methods for fuzzy systems development. These are discussed with practical examples from insurance and construction such that readers will be able to grasp the concepts easily and apply them in their vocations.

Chapter 7 describes the conceptual model of a fuzzy knowledge based system (KBS) that automates the new WCI premium rating model, and the developmental process of the KBS. The fuzzy KBS facilitates multi-attribute inference, which usually challenges underwriters' reasoning abilities, and eliminates high reliance on experienced underwriters who job-hop within the insurance industry. It also captures data on workers' compensation claims and contractors' safety performance for future use. Its implementation in the general insurance industry would facilitate accident control in the construction industry, and thereby minimise losses for insurers and safeguard the interests of workers, design and project management consultants, clients and contractors.

Chapter 8 brings together all of the themes and findings in previous chapters into one coherent model, and reports its applications in the construction and insurance industries. The chapter also summarises the contributions to the body of knowledge to benefit the academic community. Finally, it identifies the strong research platform that the book has established, and outlines future directions for research.

Appendix 1 outlines the survey kit used in the research study for the development of the new models discussed in this book. This is enclosed to help readers understand the knowledge acquisition process involved, and to foster a do-it-yourself culture in their vocations if any modifications to the models and the KBS are required to reflect their competitive distinctiveness. Appendix 2 is the user manual for the fuzzy KBS discussed in the book, and Appendix 3 is the fuzzy KBS prototype in CD format. Whilst the user manual describes how to work with the fuzzy KBS, the prototype provides readers with the opportunity to understand cost effective methods for the development of advanced KBSs using general purpose software. These will encourage readers for the self-development of KBSs for other functions in their businesses alike.

The chapters in the book can be read in any sequence. However, it is important that readers appreciate the logical flow that the book adopts in discussing various issues to facilitate readers' understanding.

Chapter II

Workers' Compensation Insurance in Construction

Introduction

This chapter provides a detailed introduction to workers' compensation system and workers' compensation insurance. Firstly, the origin and evolvement of workers' compensation system is discussed. Then a detailed review of existing theories, strategies and practices for workers' compensation insurance is provided. Finally, the shortcomings of, and the impediments posed by these methods in using WCI as a tool to improve safety in the construction industry are explored.

Origin of Workers' Compensation System

During the industrial revolution, injured workers had to prove their employers' negligence to recover medical expenses, lost wages and other damages caused by occupational accidents. Employers had three primary defences for them to avoid liabilities for injuries. The first was the concept of *contributory negligence,* which prevented the employee from recovering any damage if he/she contributed even in a small way to the cause of the accident. Another defence was the *fellow servant doctrine.* If the injury resulted from contributing actions of fellow employees, the employer was not considered liable. The third defence was the *assumption of risk doctrine.* It could limit a worker's recovery of damages if he/she knew of the workplace hazard and assumed those risks by going to work (Clayton, 2004).

Besides overcoming common law defences, injured workers faced other problems in filing lawsuits against the employer, viz. (Newman and Hancher, 1991):

1. Filing lawsuits often resulted in injured workers losing their jobs;
2. The lawsuits were expensive and time-consuming thus workers had difficulty finding lawyers to represent them; and

3. There was no guarantee that the employee would win the lawsuit and collect any damage that is sufficient to recover the loss and the cost of the lawsuit.

Thus, injured workers received no compensation, lost the current job or faced difficulty finding another jobs due to disability. As a result, their families were becoming an increasing burden to the society. To overcome this unfair situation, the workers' compensation system was designed as a trade-off between employers and employees. The underlying principle behind the system is that the cost of on-the-job injuries, regardless of fault, should be borne by employers. In exchange of the guaranteed settlement, the injured workers forfeit the right to sue employers. The basic objectives of workers' compensation are to (Everett and Thompson, 1995):

1. Provide sure, prompt and reasonable benefits to work accident victims or their dependants;
2. Provide a single remedy and eliminate time-consuming and costly trials;
3. Relieve public and private charities of financial drains incidents to uncompensated industrial accidents;
4. Encourage maximum employer interest in safety and rehabilitation; and
5. Promote frank analyses of accident causes and reduce preventable accidents.

Workers' Compensation System

Since its origin in Germany in the 1870s, workers' compensation system has been legislated as an Act in many countries around the world. Each country has its own version of workers' compensation system to suit its context, but they are the same in principle. Understanding the system in one place would be good enough for readers to get a clear understanding as to how the system works. Hence, this chapter focuses on worker's compensation system applicable in Singapore. The motive for using Singapore as a case is that the workers' compensation system is relatively new, which was modified in 2008 to take into account of contemporary issues and challenges.

The Work Injury Compensation Act of Singapore covers all workers in general who are engaged under a contract of service or apprenticeship, regardless of their level of earning. The following types of workers are excluded for work injury compensation under the Act (MOM, 2008):

- Self-employed persons;
- Independent contractors;
- Domestic workers;
- Members of the Singapore armed forces; and
- Officers of the Singapore Police Force, the Singapore Civil Defence Force, the Central Narcotics Bureau and the Singapore Prisons Services.

If in any employment personal injury by accident arising out of and in the course of the employment is caused to a worker, the employer shall be liable to pay compensation in accordance with the provisions of the Act. Compensation is payable when a worker suffers personal injury by accident arising out of and in the course of employment. An accident arising in the course of employment (i.e. during working hours or while on official duties) is regarded as having arisen out of that employment, unless there is evidence to prove otherwise. Compensation is also payable under the following circumstances:

- A worker meets with an accident while travelling as a passenger to and from his place of work in a vehicle operated by or on behalf of the employer and the vehicle is not a public transport; and
- A worker who is residing in Singapore and employed by an employer in Singapore, meets with an accident in a place outside Singapore where he/she is required to work.

On the other hand, an employer shall not be liable to pay compensation in respect of:

- Any injury to a worker resulting from an accident if it is proven that the injury to the worker is directly attributable to the worker having been at the time thereof under the influence of alcohol or a drug not prescribed by a medical practitioner; or
- Any incapacity or death resulting from a deliberate self-injury or the deliberate aggravation of an accidental injury.

Costs Recovered under the Workers' Compensation System

The Work Injury Compensation Act of Singapore enforces the entitlement of five types of benefits to victims of on-the-job accidents, and these are (MOM, 2008):

1. Medical expenses;
2. Temporary incapacity benefits;
3. Permanent incapacity benefits;
4. Dependants death benefits; and
5. Compensation for occupational diseases.

The quantum of benefits provided and the methods of calculation involved for each type of benefit are described below in detail. Apart from these, the Act also allows the worker to sue the employer under the common law rights. In these cases, employer's negligence has to be proven beyond reasonable doubt. Damages granted may be unlimited. An injured worker is limited to choose only one option to claim for benefits; either under the Act or common law rights. Once a worker decides to pursue the claim under the Act, the worker will generally no longer be able to exercise the option to sue the employer under common law, and vice versa.

1. Medical Expenses

When a worker is injured in a work-related accident, the employer will be responsible for all the medical expenses incurred for treatment by any Singapore-registered medical practitioner or in any approved hospital. Medical expenses include the cost of medical consultation fees, medical report fees (for the initial assessment of the extent of injury suffered by the employee), and the costs of medicines, artificial limbs and surgical appliances as certified by the medical practitioner. However, the Act also imposes a ceiling for medical expenses. Any compensation payable by an employer for the medical treatment received by a worker in relation to the injury by accident arising out of and in the course of employment shall be the lower of the following amounts:

- the cost of medical treatment received by the worker within a period of one year after the happening of the accident causing the injury; or
- S$25,000 per accident per worker.

2. Temporary Incapacity

Temporary incapacity, as the name implies, refers to injuries which incapacitate a worker from performing his/her normal duties for a limited duration. Examples of such injuries are sprains, minor cuts or bruises. In such instances, the worker is entitled to a paid medical leave of up to a year. For the first 14 days of the medical leave or 60 days if he/she is hospitalised, the worker is entitled to full wages. Beyond the abovementioned periods, the worker is entitled to a further periodical payment of an amount equal to two-thirds of the earnings during the incapacity or during a period of one year, whichever is shorter. Public holidays, rest days and non-working days should be excluded from the number of days of medical leave granted to the employee. For public holidays, while these are not granted as paid medical leave under the Work Injury Compensation Act, the employee may be paid for the public holidays as his entitlement under the Employment Act.

3. Permanent Incapacity

Permanent incapacity compensation can be for either total or partial incapacity. Total permanent incapacity refers to injuries that incapacitate a worker from doing all work that he/she was capable of doing at the time of the accident and thereby permanently reducing the earning capacity of the worker in every employment. Examples are loss of both arms, either eyes or total paralysis. The amount payable for a total permanent incapacity is given by: *Average monthly earnings x multiplying factor,* subject to a maximum of S$180,000 and a minimum of S$60,000. The multiplying factor for permanent incapacity is determined by the age of the worker (on the next birthday at the time of the accident) as shown in Table 2.1. If a doctor certifies that an injured worker suffering from total permanent incapacity needs the constant help of another person during his/her lifetime, an additional compensation of one-quarter of the amount awarded for total permanent incapacity can be claimed.

On the other hand, partial permanent incapacity reduces the worker's earning capacity in every employment. An example is the loss of one eye. The amount payable for partial permanent incapacity is calculated using the following formula:

Percentage incapacity x average monthly earnings x multiplying factor

or

Percentage incapacity x S$180,000, whichever is lesser

The worker is also entitled to paid medical leave, as in temporary incapacity. The percentage incapacity for an injury is determined according to Table 2.2, and the multiplying factor is determined according to Table 2.1.

Table 2.1. Multiplying factor for permanent incapacity

Age	Multiplying factor
14 and below	181
15	180
16	179
17	178
18	178
19	177
20	176
21	175
22	174
23	173
24	172
25	170
26	169
27	168
28	167
29	165
30	164
31	162
32	160
33	159
34	157
35	155
36	153
37	151
38	149
39	146
40	144
41	142
42	140
43	138
44	136
45	134

Table 2.1. Continued

Age	Multiplying factor
46	132
47	130
48	128
49	126
50	124
51	122
52	120
53	118
54	116
55	114
56	111
57	108
58	105
59	102
60	99
61	96
62	92
63	87
64	82
65	77
66 and above	72

Source: MOM, 2008.

Table 2.2. Percentage incapacity

Item	Injury	Percentage of loss of earning capacity
1	Loss of two limbs	100
2	Loss of both hands or of all fingers and both thumbs	100
3	Loss of both feet	100
4	Total loss of sight, including the loss of sight to such extent as to render the claimant unable to perform any work for which eyesight is essential	100
5	Total paralysis	100
6	Injuries resulting in being permanently bedridden	100
7	Any other injury causing permanent total incapacity	100
8	Loss of an arm at shoulder	75
9	Loss of an arm between elbow and shoulder	75
10	Loss of an arm at elbow	75
11	Loss of arm between wrist and elbow	70
12	Loss of a hand at wrist	70

Item	Injury	Percentage of loss of earning capacity
13	Loss of 4 fingers and thumb of one hand	70
14	Loss of 4 fingers	60
15	Loss of thumb —	
	(a) both phalanges	30
	(b) one phalanx	20
16	Loss of index finger —	
	(a) three phalanges	14
	(b) two phalanges	11
	(c) one phalanx	9
17	Loss of middle finger —	
	(a) three phalanges	12
	(b) two phalanges	9
	(c) one phalanx	7
18	Loss of ring finger —	
	(a) three phalanges	7
	(b) two phalanges	6
	(c) one phalanx	5
19	Loss of little finger —	
	(a) three phalanges	7
	(b) two phalanges	6
	(c) one phalanx	5
20	Loss of metacarpals —	
	(a) first or second (additional)	8
	(b) third, fourth or fifth (additional)	3
21	Loss of leg —	
	(a) at or above knee	75
	(b) below knee	65
22	Loss of foot	55
23	Loss of toes —	
	(a) all of one foot	20
	(b) great, both phalanges	14
	(c) great, one phalanx	3
	(d) other than great, if more than one toe lost, each	3
24	Loss of sight of one eye	50
25	Loss of hearing, one ear	30
26	Total loss of hearing	60

Total permanent loss of the use of a member shall be treated as loss of that member.

Where there is a loss of two or more parts of the hand, the percentage shall not be more than the loss of the whole hand.

Loss of remaining arm, leg or eye if one has already been lost, shall be the difference between the compensation for the total incapacity, and compensation already paid or that which would have been paid for the previous loss of limb or eye.

Source: MOM, 2008.

4. Dependants Death Benefits

When a worker dies in a work-related accident, compensation is payable to the dependants of the deceased. Dependants here would include the spouse, parent, grandparent, step-parent, child, grandchild, step-child, sibling, and half-sibling. The amount payable for a fatal accident is given by: *average monthly earnings x multiplying factor,* subject to a maximum of S$140,000 and a minimum of S$47,000. The multiplying factor for fatal accidents is determined by the age of the deceased worker (on the next birthday at the time of the accident) as shown in Table 2.3.

Table 2.3. Multiplying factor for fatal accident

Age	Multiplying factor
14 and below	136
15	135
16	135
17	134
18	134
19	133
20	132
21	132
22	131
23	130
24	129
25	128
26	127
27	127
28	125
29	124
30	123
31	122
32	121
33	120
34	118
35	117
36	115
37	114
38	112
39	110
40	108
41	107
42	106
43	105
44	104
45	103

Age	Multiplying factor
46	102
47	101
48	100
49	98
50	96
51	94
52	92
53	90
54	88
55	86
56	84
57	82
58	80
59	78
60	75
61	72
62	68
63	63
64	58
65	53
66 and above	48

Source: MOM, 2008.

5. Compensation for Occupational Diseases

If a worker contracts a disease that is related to that occupation or if a worker contracts that disease within 12 months or in the case of silicosis or asbestosis within 36 months, after ceasing to be so employed, and if incapacity or the death of the worker results from that disease, compensation shall be paid as if the disease were a personal injury by accident arising from that employment. Table 2.4 describes the occupational diseases that are related to various natures of occupations in construction projects.

Table 2.4. Occupational diseases in construction

No	Occupational disease	Nature of occupation
1	Asbestosis	Any occupation involving exposure to asbestos dust.
2	Barotrauma	Any occupation involving subjection to compressed air.
3	Cataract produced by exposure to the glare of, or rays from, molten glass or molten or red-hot metal	Any process involving frequent or prolonged exposure to the glare of, or rays from, molten glass or molten or red-hot metal.
4	Chrome ulceration	Any process involving the use or handling of chromic acid, chromates or bi-chromates or any preparation or solution containing any of these substances.

Table 2.4. Continued

No	Occupational disease	Nature of occupation
5	Compressed air illness or its sequelae	Any occupation involving subjection to compressed air.
6	• Epitheliomatous cancer or ulceration of the skin • Localised new growth of the skin, papillomatous or keratotic • Ulceration of the corneal surface of the eye	Any occupation involving the use or handling of, or exposure to tar, pitch, bitumen, mineral oil (including paraffin), soot or any compound, product, or residue of any of these substances.
7	Industrial dermatitis	Any occupation or process involving the exposure to or contact with cutaneous irritants or sensitisers such as alkalis and acids, solvents, mineral oils, synthetic and natural resins, certain woods, formaldehyde, nickel salts, chromates and bichromates, mercury compounds, chlorinated naphthalenes, rubber accelerators, fibre-glass and other chemicals.
8	Repetitive strain disorder of the upper limb	Any process or activity involving frequent or repeated movements of the upper limb.
9	Inflammation, ulceration or malignant disease of the skin or subcutaneous tissues or of the bones, or leukaemia, or anaemia of the aplastic type	Any process involving exposure to x-rays, ionising particles, radium, or other radio-active substances or other forms of radiant energy
10	Leptospirosis or its sequelae	Any occupation involving contact with a source or sources of leptospiral infections e.g. abattoir, drainage and sewerage work, refuse collection, road sweeping and work with animals.
11	Liver angiosarcoma	Any occupation involving the use or handling of, or exposure to vinyl chloride monomer.
12	Mesothelioma	Any occupation involving the use or handling of, or exposure to asbestos.
13	Noise-induced deafness	Any occupation involving prolonged exposure to a high level of noise.
14	Occupational asthma	Any occupation involving the use of or handling of or exposure to a chemical or other agent which may irritate or sensitise the respiratory system, e.g. isocyanates, rosin, formaldehyde, proteolytic enzymes.
15	Poisoning by:	Any occupation or process involving:
	• Arsenic	The use or handling of, or exposure to the fumes, dust or vapour of arsenic or a compound of arsenic, or a substance containing arsenic or exposure to any solution containing

No	Occupational disease	Nature of occupation
		arsenic or compound of arsenic;
	• Benzene or a homologue	The use or handling of, or exposure to the fumes of, or vapour containing benzene or any of its homologues;
	• Cadmium	The use or handling of, or exposure to the fumes, or dust of cadmium or its compounds;
	• Carbamate	The production, use or handling of carbamate;
	• Carbon disulphide	The use or handling of, or exposure to the fumes or vapour of, carbon disulphide or a compound of carbon disulphide, or a substance containing carbon disulphide;
	• Carbon monoxide gas	The exposure to carbon monoxide, e.g. where blast furnaces and internal combustion engines are used;
	• Cyanide	The use or handling of, or exposure to the fumes, dust or vapour of, cyanide or compound of cyanide, or a substance containing cyanide;
	• Halogen derivatives of hydrocarbon compounds	The production, liberation or use of any halogen derivative of hydrocarbon compounds;
	• Hydrogen sulphide	The exposure to hydrogen sulphide, e.g. in oil refining, sewerage work and manholes;
	• Lead	The use or handling of, or exposure to the fumes, dust or vapour of, lead or compound of lead, or a substance containing lead;
	• Manganese	The use or handling of manganese or substance containing manganese;
	• Mercury	The use or handling of, or exposure to the fumes, dust or vapour, mercury or a compound of mercury, or a substance containing mercury;
	• Nitrous fumes	The use or handling of nitric acid or exposure to nitrous fumes;
	• Organophosphates	The production, use or handling of organophosphates;
	• Phosphorus	The use or handling of, or exposure to the fumes, dust or vapour of, phosphorus or a compound of phosphorus, or a substance containing phosphorus.
16	Silicosis	Any occupation involving exposure to silica dust, e.g., in granite quarries and foundries with sand moulds.
17	Toxic hepatitis	Any process involving the use or handling of or exposure to tetrachloroethane, nitro-derivatives or amino-derivatives of benzene, vinyl chloride monomer, or other poisonous substances.

Source: Adapted from MOM, 2008.

Workers' Compensation Insurance (WCI)

Construction projects are highly vulnerable to accident risks, thereby exposing contractors to definite risks. The quantum of these risks is uncertain; i.e. one project can have one or many occupational accidents. In the case of Singapore's Work Injury Compensation Act, the compensation to an accident victim can be as high as S$180,000. If a project has many of such victims, the burden on the contractor will be unbearable. This situation may lead to the contractor's insolvency, resulting in injured workers being uncompensated. Workers' compensation insurance is a technique of shifting or transferring these risks to a professional insurer. In consideration of a specific payment (the premium) by the contractor, the insurer is contracted to indemnify the contractor up to the full extent for the occupational injuries that may occur at unpredictable timing, frequency and severity. The significance of WCI in construction is overwhelming. It is a statutory requirement in most countries for all the construction contractors to obtain WCI for all their workers to eliminate such financial burden in the event of any worksite injuries/fatalities. Failure to do so is an offence punishable with a fine of up to S$10,000, imprisonment for up to 1 year or both, in Singapore. In the insurance industry's perception, WCI is an integral part of the business. It is the third largest insurance class in Singapore (GIA, 2006), having an overall portfolio of 9.9% net for the first quarter of year 2006 (MAS, 2006).

Premium Rating Methods for WCI

Traditionally, there are three basic approaches of premium rating for insurance policies, viz.:

- Exposure rating;
- Experience modification rating; and
- Retrospective rating.

The exposure rating uses the claims experience with a broad group of policyholders to estimate the expected claims of an individual. Insurance companies accumulate data over many years, involving many policy holders, to gain a broad knowledge base. Under the experience modification rating approach, the premium charged to a policyholder is based on the claims experience with that policyholder. The retrospective rating approach is a self-rated program under which the actual losses during the policy period determine the final premium for the coverage, subject to a maximum and a minimum. A deposit premium is charged at the inception of the policy and then adjusted after the policy period has expired, to reflect actual losses incurred (Vaughan and Vaughan, 1996; Booth et al., 1999). Among these three approaches, the experience modification rating (EMR) is an established technique for WCI premium rating whereby the premium charged to a contractor is based on the contractor's claims history (Clough et al., 2005; Hoonakker, et al., 2005). The general notion is that a contractor has control over the loss ratio and is entitled to a credit for a good loss-prevention record, or, on the other hand, should pay a higher rate if the loss record is poor. The exposure rating approach is common in health and motor insurance where the risk exposure is similar across policyholders unlike in construction projects whereby each project is unique. The retrospective rating is less appreciated by contractors and clients as it does not provide a price certainty, which is crucial for tender decisions. EMR is widely used in many states in the US for construction WCI. The Australian insurance industry utilises an adapted version of EMR. However, other ad-hoc methods are also noted in various countries. A detailed account of these techniques and their pitfalls are described in the upcoming sections.

Experience Modification Rating (EMR) Approach for Premium Rating

Under the experience modification rating approach, the WCI standard premium is based on formula (1). To get the final WCI premium, a number of other factors like the discount rate and economies of scale in overhead expenses may be considered for application in the standard premium. These are marketing options adopted by insurers (Everett and Thompson, 1995).

Standard premium = Manual rate x Payroll units x EMR (1)

Each of the three factors in the formula (manual rate, payroll units and EMR) is explained below in detail.

Manual Rate

The manual rate, also known as book rate, is the unit of premium per one hundred dollars of payroll for accident and disease coverage. It gives a rough indication of the risk associated with each work type. Some work types are more likely to result in injuries and fatalities than others. Thus, the manual rate varies among work types. The manual rate is based on the idea that the frequency of losses for a particular type of work is statistically predictable. Typically, each year, a state rating bureau has to determine the manual rate for each work classification based on claims that have been filed in that state for that work classification. Insurance companies are required to provide the state rating bureau with information on payroll and workers' compensation benefits paid for each work classification. The manual rate is calculated by formula (2) (Oglesby *et al.*, 1989).

$$Manual\ rate = \frac{(Benefits\ paid\ for\ a\ work\ type\ +\ overhead\ cost\ for\ administering)}{Straight\ time\ payroll}$$

(2)

Manual rates vary among work classifications within each state. Manual rates also vary from state to state for the same work classification. Table 2.5 is an extract of the manual rates applicable in Massachusetts, US, as of September 2008, which were released by the Workers' Compensation Rating and Inspection Bureau of Massachusetts.

Table 2.5. Manual rates in Massachusetts, US

Work classification	Code	Manual rate
Masonry	5022	11.62
Carpentry, one-and toe-family	5645	7.50
Concrete, residential	5215	5.07
Electrical wiring, interior	5190	3.17

Source: WCRIB, 2008a.

Payroll Unit

The risk exposure associated with performing a certain type of work is a function of the time spent working. Thus, the payroll unit accounts for the number of person-hours involved by a particular type of worker. It is calculated by formula (3).

$$\text{Payroll unit} = \frac{\text{Employer's straight time direct labour cost}}{\$100} \tag{3}$$

Experience Modification Rate (EMR)

EMR, also known as x-mod rate, modifier or experience modification factor, accounts for the loss experience of each contractor and is used to modify the manual rate. It helps predict future losses based on past experience. Contractors with poor safety records will have a higher EMR and pay more for WCI. In other words, EMR tailors the WCI premium for a given contractor. EMR is calculated by formula (4) (Hinze *et al.*, 1995; Hoonakker *et al.*, 2005).

$$EMR = \frac{\text{Actual primary losses} + \text{Weighting value} \times \text{Actual excess losses} + \text{Ballast value} + (1 - \text{Weighting value}) \times \text{Expected excess losses}}{\text{Expected losses} + \text{Ballast value}} \tag{4}$$

Actual primary losses are a measure of the contractor's loss frequency history. There is a maximum primary loss value for each actual loss. For instance, suppose the maximum primary loss value is $5000, for each actual loss less than or equal to $5000, the entire loss amount is used as the primary value; for each loss over $5000, the primary value is $5000. Actual excess losses give an indication of the contractor's loss severity history. For each actual loss, the actual excess loss is the difference between the actual loss and the actual primary loss. In the previous example, if the actual loss of an accident is $7000, the actual excess loss is $2000. For losses less than or equal to $5000, the actual excess loss is deemed as $0.

The calculation of expected loss, expected primary loss and expected excess loss use the following formulas:

$$\text{Expected loss (E)} = \sum_{\text{all types of work}} \text{Expected loss ratio (ELR) x Payroll units} \qquad (5)$$

Where:

ELR = Benefits paid for a work type / Straight time payroll

$$\text{Expected primary loss} = \text{Expected loss x Discount ratio (D-ratio)} \qquad (6)$$

Where:

$$D-ratio = \frac{Primary\ serious\ loss}{Total\ serious\ loss} x\ serious\ D-ratio\ factor$$

$$+ \frac{Primary\ non-serious\ loss}{Total\ non-serious\ loss} x\ non-serious\ D-ratio\ factor \qquad (7)$$

$$+ \frac{Primary\ medical\ loss}{Total\ medical\ loss} x\ medical\ D-ratio\ factor$$

$$\text{Expected excess loss} = \text{expected loss - expected primary loss} \qquad (8)$$

Expected loss ratios and D-ratios are published by a state rating bureau in each state. Table 2.6 is an extract of expected loss ratios and D-ratios applicable in Massachusetts, US.

Table 2.6. ELR and D-ratio in Massachusetts, US

Work classification	Code	ELR	D-ratio
Masonry	5022	5.28	0.14
Carpentry, one-and toe-family	5645	3.41	0.17
Concrete, residential	5215	2.54	0.18
Electrical wiring, interior	5190	1.44	0.18

Source: WCRIB, 2008b.

Ballast value, a function of expected loss (E), helps stabilise EMR against large changes from a single loss. Formula (9) calculates the ballast value.

$$B = E\left[\frac{(0.1E + 2570G)}{(E + 700G)}\right] \qquad (9)$$

Where:
E = expected losses

$$G = \frac{SACC\ (State\ Average\ Cost\ per\ Claim)}{1000}$$

Ballast values are published by a state rating bureau in each state. Table 2.7 shows an extract of ballast values applicable in Massachusetts, US.

Table 2.7. Ballast values in Massachusetts, US

Expected losses	Ballast values
0 - 37,651	17,500
37,652 - 64,802	21,000
64,803 - 95,998	24,500
95,999 - 128,908	28,000
128,909 - 162,618	31,500
162,619 - 196,752	35,000
196,753 - 231,132	38,500
231,133 - 265,669	42,000
265,670 - 300,309	45,500
300,310 - 335,022	49,000

Source: WCRIB, 2008c.

A weighting value W determines the percentage of excess losses used in the EMR calculation. W is calculated by formula (10).

$$W = \frac{E + B}{E + C} \qquad\qquad (10)$$

Where: $C = E\left[\dfrac{\left(0.75E + 203825G\right)}{\left(E + 5100G\right)}\right]$

Table 2.8. Weighting values in Massachusetts, US

Expected losses	Weighting values
81,299 - 100,030	0.10
100,031 - 119,130	0.11
119,131 - 138,766	0.12
138,767 - 159,046	0.13
159,047 - 180,058	0.14
180,059 - 201,878	0.15
201,879 - 224,578	0.16
224,579 - 248,231	0.17
248,232 - 272,911	0.18

Source: WCRIB, 2008d.

Weighting values are also published by a state rating bureau in each state. Table 2.8 shows an extract of weighting values applicable in Massachusetts, US.

A detailed example for EMR calculation and subsequently WCI premium calculation using the EMR method is described in the following section, which was adapted from Everett and Thompson (1995).

Example of WCI Premium Calculation

1. Calculate the EMR for XYZ Construction Company, which is operating in Massachusetts, for the year 2008. The workers' compensation claims filed by XYZ during 2004 - 2006 are shown in Table 2.9.
2. Calculate the WCI premium for XYZ that has the work classification payroll breakdown as depicted in Table 2.10.

Table 2.9. XYZ company's claims

Year	Work classification	Claim amount ($)
2004	Masonry	5,700
2004	Carpentry	15,010
2004	Carpentry	3,700
2004	Carpentry	41,200
2004	Concrete	3,600
2004	Miscellaneous	11,500
2004	Miscellaneous	12,100
2005	Masonry	19,000
2005	Masonry	5,900
2005	Carpentry	3,300
2005	Electrical	8,400
2005	Electrical	31,000
2005	Electrical	4,500
2005	Miscellaneous	2,300
2006	Carpentry	11,500
2006	Carpentry	6,700
2006	Carpentry	17,000
2006	Electrical	3,100
2006	Electrical	6,100
2006	Electrical	30,000

Table 2.10. Payroll breakdown

Work classification	Payroll
Masonry	420,000
Carpentry	700,000
Concrete	345,000
Electrical	210,000

Computing the EMR

The steps involved in the calculation of EMR for XYZ Construction Company for the year 2008 are explained below. Table 2.9 shows the claims filed by XYZ in the years 2004-2006, the three-year rating period to be used for EMR calculation for year 2008. Claims for year 2007 are not used.

- Column [8] in Table 2.11 shows the actual incurred losses, the total of the indemnity, medical and rehabilitation costs, including reserves. These figures are taken from Table 2.9.
- The actual incurred losses are split into primary and excess losses in column [9] and column [10], respectively.
- Column [3] and column [4] show the ELR and the D-ratio applicable to each work classification, and these are taken from Table 2.6.
- Column [5] shows the payroll units for each work classification from 2004 to 2006. These are computed based on the payroll data supplied by XYZ for those years.
- Column [6] shows the expected losses, equal to ELR (column [3]) x Payroll units (column [5]).
- Column [7] shows the expected primary losses, equal to D-ratio (column [4]) x Expected losses (column [6]).
- The total expected loss is shown in box [d] and the total expected primary loss is shown in box [e].
- Box [c] shows the total expected excess loss = box [d] - box [e].
- W-factor and ballast values appear in box [a] and box [b], which are taken from Table 2.7 and Table 2.8, respectively
- By substituting these values in formula (4), the EMR for XYZ for 2008 is calculated, which is 1.29.

Table 2.11. EMR calculation for XYZ

[1]	[2]	[3]	[4]	[5]	[6] = [3]*[5]	[7]=[4]*[6]	[8]	[9]	[10]=[8]-[9]
Year	Work Classification	Expected loss ratio	D-ratio	Payroll units	Expected losses	Expected primary losses	Actual incurred losses	Actual primary losses	Actual excess losses
2004	Masonry	5.28	0.14	4,100	21,648	3,031	5,700	5,000	700
	Electrical	1.44	0.18	1,900	2,736	492	15,010	5,000	10,010
	Concrete	2.54	0.18	3,520	8,941	1,609	3,700	3,700	0

[1]	[2]	[3]	[4]	[5]	[6] = [3]*[5]	[7]=[4]*[6]	[8]	[9]	[10]=[8]-[9]
Year	Work Classification	Expected loss ratio	D-ratio	Payroll units	Expected losses	Expected primary losses	Actual incurred losses	Actual primary losses	Actual excess losses
	Carpentry	3.41	0.17	7,250	24,723	4,203	41,200	5,000	36,200
							3,600	3,600	0
							11,500	5,000	6,500
							12,100	5,000	7,100
	Total for 2004			16,770	58,047	9,335	92,810	32,300	60,510
2005	Masonry	5.28	0.14	4,350	22,968	3,216	19,000	5,000	14,000
	Electrical	1.44	0.18	1,950	2,808	505	5,900	5,000	900
	Concrete	2.54	0.18	3,590	9,119	1,641	3,300	3,300	0
	Carpentry	3.41	0.17	7,100	24,211	4,116	8,400	5,000	3,400
							31,000	5,000	26,000
							4,500	4,500	0
							2,300	2,300	0
	Total for 2005			16,990	59,106	9,478	74,400	30,100	44,300
2006	Masonry	5.28	0.14	4,290	22,651	3,171	11,500	5,000	6,500
	Electrical	1.44	0.18	1,990	2,866	516	6,700	5,000	1,700
	Concrete	2.54	0.18	3,210	8,153	1,468	17,000	5,000	12,000
	Carpentry	3.41	0.17	7,750	26,428	4,493	3,100	3,100	0
							6,100	5,000	1,100
							30,000	5,000	25,000
	Total for 2006			17,240	60,098	9,647	74,400	28,100	46,300
[a]		[b]	[c] =[d]-[e]		[d]	[e]	[f]	[g]	[h]
	W	Ballast value	Total expected excess		Total expected loss	Total expected primary	Total actual incurred	Total actual primary	Total actual excess
	0.14	35,000	148,790		177,251	28,461	241,610	90,500	151,110

Computing the WCI Premium

Table 2.12 illustrates the computation of the standard premium for XYZ.

- Column 1 shows the work classifications. Massachusetts' manual rates for these work classifications form column 2, which are taken from Table 2.5.
- Column 3 presents the payroll units, which are calculated based on the payroll data supplied by XYZ for the new WCI policy.
- Column 4 shows the EMR (1.29) for XYZ that was previously calculated. XYZ has a single EMR that is applied to all work classifications.
- The WCI standard premium for each work classification is computed separately by using formula (1), and totalled to get the premium amount for XYZ. The total WCI standard premium for the new policy is $161,834.

Table 2.12. XYZ's predicted 2008 WCI standard premium

Work classification	Manual rate	Payroll unit	EMR	Standard premium($)
Masonry	11.62	4,200	1.29	62,957
Carpentry	7.5	7,000	1.29	67,725
Concrete	5.07	3,450	1.29	22,564
Electrical	3.17	2,100	1.29	8,588
Total standard premium				**161,834**

Shortcomings of the EMR Approach

Although the EMR approach is widely used in the insurance industry to date, many limitations and shortcomings are noted in its application that impede the usage of WCI as a tool to improve safety in the construction industry.

EMR is essentially an incentive for firms to strive for good safety records, as firms with poor safety records will pay higher premiums. However, Hinze *et al.* (1995) empirically proved the following shortcomings and concluded that EMR is clearly not an appropriate sole measurement of safety performance:

1. EMR value is decreased as the project size increases. When a contractor employs more workers the EMR value is decreased for the same previous safety records;
2. The contractor paying the higher hourly wage will have a lower EMR value when the injury frequency is held constant; and
3. Injury frequency has more impact on EMR over injury severity. When the frequency is more, the EMR value is increased. Supposing company "A" has a claim of $30,000 and company "B" has five claims for the total of $20,000. The EMR of company "B" may be higher than that of company "A" although the injury severity is lesser.

Everett and Thompson (1995) quoted the following problems with the EMR method:

1. The experience period used in the EMR calculation process is the three-year period ending one year prior to the date that the modification becomes effective. The most recent year is not used though there may have been improvements in safety records. It is omitted for the next two years;
2. EMR is a function of many factors that are independent of actual losses or safety records. EMR cannot fairly compare the safety records of different contractors. Two contractors, who perform identical work and person-hours of work and having identical actual losses, can have two different EMR values merely because of wage rate differences;
3. New businesses are not experience-rated until they meet the minimum premium requirements. New entrants to the market are forced to pay more for premium since they do not possess previous records although their safety management systems may be robust enough to combat any accident outbreaks;

4. Using payroll units is not a good measure of risk exposure. An hour of work exposes the worker to the same risk, whether he/she earns $12, S$18 or $24 in that hour;

5. The premium is more biased towards the ownership of the company. If a company's ownership is changed while all other employees, operational methods, records etc. remain the same, the EMR is considered as 1.00 for the company and this is solely because of the ownership; and

6. Very complex formulas and processes.

Coble and Sims (1996) explored the history of fraud in workers' compensation. They noted that the EMR method of premium calculation can be vulnerable to fraud by contractors in three ways so as to obtain a low premium. These are:

1. Manipulating the payroll of workers;
2. Misrepresenting the work classification; and
3. Manipulating the ownership of the company.

Hoonakker *et al*. (2005) noticed the following negative characteristics of EMR:

1. EMR is a lagging indicator that uses data from the last full three years, and it does not consider the prevailing safety and risk management system;

2. EMR is based on worker classification and not on jobs, which makes it harder to interpret the result: for example, both a carpenter and a concreter can be involved in the same construction activity at the same location, but the job of the carpenter is perceived as a lower risk job;

3. It gives greater weight to loss frequency than loss severity. EMR is designed such that a major accident will not severely alter it. On the contrary, it is designed to be severely altered by many minor injuries;

4. EMR is designed to protect small contractors from large losses; and

5. EMR is partly dependent on payroll units, which can mean that high-wage-paying contractors pay more premium than low-wage-paying contractors for the same work classifications.

Lee and Halpin (2003) commented that EMR does not consider the safety condition on site at the time of insurance application to predict the potential loss/claim that could be posed by the insured during the course of construction. Previous safety record is not a clear guarantee for safety performance in the current project because safety management is subjective and unique to every site. Furthermore, the lack of accidents does not mean there is no risk of accidents.

Ad-hoc Methods for Premium Rating

Without having to remain confined to the EMR approach, the insurance industries in many countries use ad-hoc methods. However, these methods seem to be ineffective in one way or another. For instance, the technique used in the Singapore insurance industry is analysed as a case example to reinforce this argument.

A combination of a benchmark and heuristics is applied for premium rating in the Singapore insurance industry. WCI premiums are traditionally computed by applying a rate on the wage rolls of construction projects. There has been a collective agreement among the insurers that the preferable WCI premium rate for construction projects is 1% of the wage roll. This rate, however, is merely a benchmark. Individual insurers set competitive rates heuristically around the benchmark, mainly considering three variables: project type/scope, market competition and previous claims history of the contractor. However, no strong theory or analysis supports this benchmark norm. In the face of keen competition in the Singapore insurance market, underwriters tend to compromise the technical factors such as risk profile of the project and contractor's safety management systems, owing to the lack of a well-balanced framework that performs structured analyses on project risk profiles, safety preparedness of the contractor, and market factors. This results in risky projects being insured at lower premiums, causing adverse loss ratios for insurers. Many general insurance companies in Singapore have been encountering undesirable loss ratios in construction WCI because of inadequate premiums; some have given up issuing WCI altogether and a few other companies have even bankrupted (Imriyas *et al*, 2007a). The industry statistics for the year 2006 of the General Insurance Association of Singapore reinforced that WCI is the third largest class of insurance in Singapore. It continued to struggle in 2005 with an underwriting loss of S$7 million in the first half of 2005 compared to the same period in 2004, when it lost S$1 million. The incurred loss ratio has climbed from 72% to 80%. WCI business has sustained poor underwriting results over the years. This is mainly due to unrealistic pricing, under declaration of wages by some companies as well as aggravated and fraudulent injury claims by some foreign workers (GIA, 2006).

Drawbacks of the System

The key drawbacks of this system may be noted as follows:

1. The 1% benchmark is static, obsolete and not kept updated to accommodate the changes in workers' compensation costs over the years;
2. No appropriate framework for risk assessment is present;
3. The safety preparedness of the contractor is deduced based on previous claim records. However, no clear protocol is evident as to how it is analysed;
4. No proper market analysis model is evident in the system; and
5. The premium decision is highly variable as the perceptions of individuals about potential risks, safety preparedness, and competition are inconsistent.

Conclusion

Many countries around the world have legislated workers' compensation system to safeguard the interests of industrial accident victims and their families. Under the system, victims of on-the-job accidents are entitled to five types of benefits, including medical benefits, temporary incapacity benefits, permanent incapacity benefits, dependant death benefits, and compensation for occupational diseases. Because the accident risk in construction is relatively high, the financial burden of compensating on contractors is heavy. Workers' compensation insurance is thus procured to transfer this risk to an insurance company for a fee called the premium. Experience modification rating technique has been used extensively to compute the WCI premium in construction. Nevertheless, it possesses many significant drawbacks that impede accident minimisation in construction because of the ineffective steps involved in the technique for computing the premium. Other ad-hoc methods used by the industry pose pitfalls alike. Hence, there is an intense need for re-designing the WCI premium model such that it: (1) integrates effective safety assessment and accident control strategies into insurance; (2) eliminates the shortcomings of both EMR and other ad-hoc approaches in the industry; and (3) places the onus on each party to the policy to minimise accidents. The next chapter will focus on the critical factors to be considered for such re-engineering efforts.

Critical Factors for Premium Rating of Workers' Compensation Insurance in Construction

Introduction

One of the approaches for improving safety in construction projects is to design a new WCI model such that it encompasses effective risk assessment and accident control strategies. The prime task towards developing a new model is to identify the critical variables that influence WCI premiums for construction projects. The aim of this chapter is to explore and critically analyse the variables pertinent to WCI premium rating. The chapter identifies all the possible variables that may influence WCI premium rates for construction projects. These variables are then filtered, based on industry survey findings, to discover the most critical set that fits into Pareto's 80/20 rule. Insurance claim control strategies that are adopted in other classes of insurance are also explored to get insights there out for revamping construction WCI.

Premium Rating Variables for Construction WCI

In insurance, unlike in other industries, the cost of production is unknown when the contract is sold, and it will remain unknown until the policy has expired. Therefore, the pricing for insurance must be based on predictions of losses, expenses, and incomes in the future. Under WCI, the commitment of an insurer is extremely broad; there are no exclusions, and there is no maximum limit on the insurer's liability (Vaughan and Vaughan, 1996). Setting an appropriate cost for some future contingency of unpredictable timing, frequency, and size requires the estimates of future claims, investment income, administrative expenses, profit, and tax. In addition, the price can profoundly influence the volume of the business attracted (Booth *et al.*, 1999). Hence, WCI premium rating is a critical management function for any insurance company that should decide on premiums that are high enough to cover all the future costs, yet low enough to meet the market competition. The premium rating is regarded as a two-stage process (Booth *et al.*, 1999):

1. The costing exercise – this is a scientific method that calculates the cost of future claims from the insured risks and all associated expenses; and
2. The pricing exercise – this is a commercial adjustment to technical costs that considers broader corporate and market factors.

Predicting Future Claims in Construction WCI

The scientific approach to determine the cost of future claims of a WCI policy entails an assessment of project and contractor-related variables. Under the project-related variables, the following were identified by various authors:

1. Worrall and Buttler (1988) noted that the wage roll, project duration, and the expected workers' compensation liability per wage roll unit need to be accounted for when predicting potential claims;
2. The Canadian Wood Council (2005) reported that base rates are influenced by the: (1) location of the project; (2) type of construction; and (3) general industry experience on loss history for projects of similar type and location; and
3. Lott (2005) added that an assessment of the workers' risk management program will lead to an effective prediction of the costs to be incurred. This assessment should scrutinise the following aspects:
   a. Management commitment and employees participation in workers' risk control;
   b. Workplace hazards, population demographics, and previous incident rates;
   c. Implementation of pertinent risk/safety programs; and
   d. Training of supervisors and workers.

As for the contractor-related variables, Groth (1996) commented that WCI premium rating must consider contractors' past claims history. Coble *et al.* (1998) noticed that a contractor's size has a bearing on premium rates. The Canadian Wood Council (2005) suggested that insurers must consider the following variables:

1. Contractors' knowledge, experience and safety consciousness;
2. Compliance with loss control and underwriting recommendations by the insurer;
3. Acceptance of deductible, that is, a retention of part of the claims cost by the contractor;
4. Potential future business; and
5. Placement of multiple policies with the same insurer.

Determining the Mark-up for Construction WCI

The adjustment of the technical costs of risks for commercial interests necessitates the consideration of insurers' corporate factors, and market factors. The variables pertinent to insurers were recognised by many authors in the literature, viz.:

1. Vaughan and Vaughan (1996) identified three variables that influence the mark-up:
   a. The expenses of acquiring and administering the business (overhead costs);
   b. The profit required by the insurer; and
   c. The return from the investment of premiums by the insurer;
2. Young (1997) quoted that premium rates are adjusted on account of the profit/loss experience of the insurer in the past, and the outstanding claims to the insurer from all projects at a particular time. The competition and the volume of business in the market also influence the mark-up;
3. Booth *et al.* (1999) reported that corporate objectives of insurers will have a significant bearing on the mark-up; and
4. Phifer (1996) observed that the reinsurance premium, which insurance companies pay for risk sharing with reinsurers, does influence the pricing.

Research Methodology

In 1906, an Italian economist Vilfredo Pareto created a mathematical formula known as the 80/20 rule, which states that a small number of causes (20%) is responsible for a large percentage of (80%) the effect. This principle can be a very effective tool for optimisation and effective management (Reh, 2006). Hence, it was aimed to discover the most critical variables for WCI premium rating, according to Pareto's 80/20 rule, for developing an effective premium rating model. Opinion research methodology was used for an industry-wide field study. This methodology was most suitable because the study sought to obtain factual information about the local market and its business tactics, and views, judgements and opinions of insurance practitioners. The general insurance industry of Singapore was used as a case for this field study. Interview questionnaire survey technique was used for data collection because having a questionnaire administered face to face by an interviewer has the following advantages over mail out surveys (Babbie, 1992):

- Interview surveys attain higher response rates than mail out surveys;
- If the respondent misunderstands questions or indicates that he/she does not understand, the interviewer can clarify matters, thereby obtaining relevant and accurate responses;
- The presence of an interviewer generally reduces unanswered questions; and
- The interviewer can observe and ask questions for additional explanations.

The small population size of 23 companies targeted for the survey in the Singapore general insurance industry also made the chosen data collection technique most appropriate for the study.

From the preceding section, 17 variables pertinent to WCI premium rating of construction projects were identified and classified into four categories as shown in Table 3.1. Subsequently, a questionnaire was designed with the objective of determining the most significant variables. The questions in the questionnaire assessed the significance of the 17 variables for deriving the optimal premium rate on a ten-point Likert scale, whereby 1= "low importance" and 10= "high importance". Appendix 1.1 shows the interview questionnaire survey form used for the study.

Table 3.1. Premium rating variables

Variable category	Pertinent variable
Project factor	• Wage roll • Project duration • Project hazard level • Effectiveness of the safety management system on site
Contractor factor	• Contractor's claims history • Placement of multiple policies by the contractor • Expectation of potential business from the contractor • Co-operation by the contractor • Contractor's size
Insurer factor	• Corporate objectives of the insurer • Investment income from underwritten premiums • Overhead costs of insurance • Amount of outstanding claims to the insurer • Profit/loss experience in WCI business • Reinsurance cost
Market factor	• Competition • Volume of business in the market

After pilot testing, a set of interview questionnaire survey forms was first emailed to relevant respondents in the targeted insurance companies so the respondents would be well prepared for the interview. This was then followed up with personal interviews with the relevant professionals of those companies. All 23 companies were covered in the survey. At every interview session, the interviewer went through the questions in the questionnaire with the interviewee to obtain pertinent responses to the questions from the interviewees. Additional explanations were also rendered when needed. Moreover, interviewees were invited to elaborate on the rationale for their answers.

Profile of Respondents

As shown in Figure 3.1, the designations of the interviewees were top management (48%) and middle management (52%). The top management interviewees comprised of managing directors, general managers, senior managers, and managers. The middle management interviewees were deputy managers, assistant managers and assistant general managers. The mean working experience of the interviewees was 21 years. The minimum and maximum working experiences were 8 and 35 years, respectively. Also, more than 75% of the interviewees had experience of above 10 years. From the interviewees' profile, it is understood that all of them are well-qualified and well-experienced in the subject matter. Hence, the data collection is perceived to be reliable.

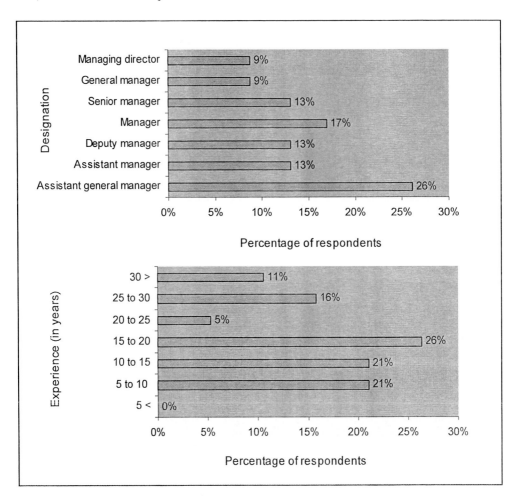

Figure 3.1. Profile of the respondents

Data Analysis and Discussion

In the past, Ekanayake and Ofori (2004), Teo *et al.* (2005), and Ocal *et al.* (2006) utilised descriptive statistics such as mean and standard deviation of the ratings by respondents in their research when categorising variables as "not significant", "less significant" and "significant" for developing their theoretical models. These past studies suggest that descriptive statistics are reasonable measures for filtering variables. This study also used descriptive statistics to identify the most important variables for developing an effective premium rating model. Hence, descriptive statistics were computed for each category of variables as shown in Table 3.2. The meanings of the descriptive statistical terms are explained below.

- Mean is the average of relative importance scores for a variable on the ten-point Likert scale.
- Median is the midpoint of the orderly arranged relative importance scores for a variable.
- Mode is the most frequently occurred score for a variable.
- Standard deviation is the measure of dispersion – the average distance of a set of scores from the mean.
- Xmax is the highest score rated in the survey on the ten-point Likert scale for the variables.
- Xmin is the lowest score rated in the survey on the Likert scale. For some of the variables Xmin=0 although the least score on the ten-point Likert scale is 1. It is because some respondents perceived that those variables are irrelevant for premium-rating.
- Skewness is the measure of the degree of asymmetry of the distribution, and kurtosis is the degree of peakedness of the distribution. Since the analysis is done on population data and inferential statistics are not used, the skewness and kurtosis properties of the data set can be negligible.

Table 3.2. Descriptive statistics of industry survey findings

Variables	Descriptive statistics							
	Mean	Standard deviation	Median	Mode	Kurtosis	Skewness	X_{Min}	X_{Max}
Project factor								
Wage roll	8.33	1.32	9	9	0.41	-0.81	5	10
Project duration	5.10	3.10	6	3	-1.30	-0.12	0	10
Project hazard level	9.33	0.71	9	10	-0.76	-0.63	8	10
Effectiveness of the safety management system on site	7.67	2.17	8	8	3.67	-1.74	1	10
Contractor factor								

Variables	Descriptive statistics							
	Mean	Standard deviation	Median	Mode	Kurtosis	Skewness	X_{Min}	X_{Max}
Contractor's claims history	8.33	1.21	9	9	-1.18	-0.19	6	10
Placement of multiple policies by the contractor	5.00	2.56	5	8	-0.66	-0.66	0	8
Expectation of potential business from the contractor	3.76	2.60	4	0	-1.09	0.00	0	8
Co-operation by the contractor	4.90	3.15	5	2	-1.34	0.01	0	10
Contractor's size	3.38	2.92	3	0	-1.26	0.37	0	9
Insurer factor								
Corporate objectives of the insurer	8.05	1.13	8	7	-0.80	0.32	6	10
Investment income from underwritten premiums	7.24	1.23	7	8	-0.34	0.33	5	10
Overhead costs of insurance	7.10	1.34	7	8	-1.22	-0.06	5	9
Amount of outstanding claims to the insurer	6.62	2.15	7	7	0.14	-0.92	2	9
Profit/loss experience in WCI business	6.76	2.51	7	10	-1.10	-0.34	2	10
Reinsurance cost	6.71	1.91	7	9	0.05	-0.67	2	9
Market factor								
Competition	7.38	1.68	7	7	-1.23	-0.14	5	10
Volume of business in the market	4.52	2.52	5	6	-0.72	0.09	0	9

The 17 variables were reorganised, as illustrated in Table 3.3, into three groups, namely: important variables, less important variables, and unimportant variables, based on their mean importance ratings, which are further underpinned by their respective medians and standard deviations. Unimportant variables have mean importance ratings < 4.00, important variables possess mean importance ratings > 7.00, and the rest are less important variables. The above grouping notion was adapted from the medical industry of Singapore where Goh (2004) proposed a pain scale, as shown in Figure 3.2a, to measure cancer pain intensity in patients. Based on that scale, the nine equal intervals in the ten-point Likert scale were rearranged into three equal intervals as illustrated in Figure 3.2b.

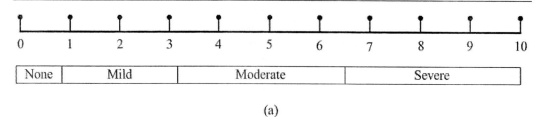

(a)

(b)

Figure 3.2. (a) Pain scale (Goh, 2004); (b) Intervals of rating

Table 3.3. Reorganisation of variables

Variables group	Pertinent variable
Important variables	• Wage roll • Project hazard level • Effectiveness of the safety management system on site • Contractor's claims history • Competition • Corporate objectives of the insurer • Overhead costs of insurance • Investment income from underwritten premiums
Less important variables	• Profit/loss experience in WCI business • Reinsurance cost • Amount of outstanding claims to the insurer • Project duration • Placement of multiple policies by the contractor • Co-operation by the contractor • Volume of business in the market
Unimportant variables	• Expectation of potential business from the contractor • Contractor's size

Important Variables for Premium Rating

Eight important variables for premium rating were identified out of the 17 variables (see Table 3.3). A brief discussion on each variable is provided below, based on the qualitative explanations rendered by the interviewees.

Wage Roll

In the Singapore insurance industry, WCI premiums are traditionally computed by applying a rate on wage rolls of construction projects. There has been a collective agreement among the insurers that the preferable WCI premium rate for construction projects is 1% of the wage roll. This rate, however, is merely a benchmark. Individual insurers set competitive rates around the benchmark heuristically considering other important variables. The wage roll is also considered as a representation of the project duration since both are positively correlated.

On another perspective, when the wage roll is high, the premium amount is high though the premium rate is low. But, claims and administrative costs will be proportionately less, making it possible for insurers to earn more money by insuring bigger projects. Thus, projects with large wage rolls drive keen competition.

Hence, a project's wage roll is a key variable for insurers to infer the workforce size, project duration, and competition. The risk exposure of insurers is correlated with the workforce size and project duration.

Project Hazard Level

The project hazard is directly correlated with the frequency and severity of accidents and thereby the amount of compensation to be paid by the insurer. Therefore, the higher the project hazard, the higher the premium rate. The project hazard has to be assessed in line with the project's scope. The assessment should peruse if the project involves demolition works, explosive works, excavation works, works at heights, works involving lifting and cranes, and/or works in confined spaces. The hazard in each type of work has to be assessed via a rigorous analysis of relevant attributes. For example, the hazards present in works at heights can be deduced by the total height of the building. Moreover, the characteristics of the project location/vicinity should also be assessed. Among the attributes to be scrutinized for project locality are: soil condition, site congestion level, and/or the presence of any chemical/manufacturing factory or combustible source.

Most insurers use a protocol, which was developed in-house, to assess the hazard level. However, these protocols are fairly simple and do not consider all the risk attributes in a construction project.

Effectiveness of the Safety Management System on Site

The presence of an effective safety management system on site is significant in reducing claims; thus, the better the safety management system, the lower the premium rate. All the insurers recognized that inspecting the safety management system of the project is essential in inferring potential claims. However, they encounter difficulties because of the lack of guidelines to assess the effectiveness of the safety management system.

Contractor's Claims History

Insurers examine a contractor's claims records for the past five years to deduce the contractor's safety performance as an alternative to assessing the safety management system. From the survey, it would appear that records with low severity and high frequency infuse higher premiums than records with high severity and low frequency. However, it may be ineffective because the lack of accidents does not imply an absence of accident risks. Moreover, undesirable loss ratios can be a result of both frequency and severity of claims.

Although contractor's claims history is not the perfect measurement for the effectiveness of the safety management system on site, it could be used as a passive indicator. The analysis of past WCI claims of a contractor can give an indication of the loss ratio for insurers with the contractor. This information can be utilised to determine the mark up for a new policy.

Competition

Triumphing competition is crucial in any business. A well-thought strategy is necessary to assess the competition level by considering the number of competitors, regional economic condition, prestige in the project, and the project size. This can subsequently be used to adjust the mark-up that the higher the competition, the lower the mark-up.

Corporate Objectives of the Insurer

The mark-up in a premium coheres with an insurer's corporate objective(s). The corporate objective of an insurer at any given time can be one or more of the following:

1. Ensuring the survival of the company;
2. To write a given premium volume;
3. Achieving an overall operating ratio across the whole portfolio;
4. Achieving an adequate level of profitability or return on equity; and
5. Achieving a target premium growth rate.

For objectives 1-3, an insurer may intentionally quote a low premium while for objectives 4 and 5, the same insurer may wish to quote an average premium.

Overhead Costs of Insurance

Overhead costs are key components of a mark-up; the higher the overhead costs, the higher the mark-up. Overhead costs for WCI include brokerage fees and administrative costs for underwriting and claims management. The brokerage fee is a fixed percentage in the Singapore market, which is 10% of the underwritten premium. Administrative costs vary from company to company, which are estimated to be in the range of 15-35% of the underwritten premium. In total, overhead costs for insurance companies amount to 25-45% of the underwritten premium in Singapore.

Investment Income from Underwritten Premiums

The underwritten premium can be invested by the insurer on shares, subsidiary companies, real estate, etc. The rate of return on these investments influences the premium rate significantly. If the investment returns are high, the insurer can quote attractive premiums as the insurer's reserve is stable. In other words, the higher the investment returns, the lower the mark-ups for WCI policies.

Less Important Variables for Premium Rating

Seven variables seem less important for WCI premium rating of construction projects.

Profit/loss Experience in WCI Business

When an insurer experiences a remarkable profit/loss over a period of time, it is acceptable to adjust the premium rate for new undertakings. If there is a profit growth, the insurer may wish to reduce the premium so as to win more projects, as there is a buffer to assume the risk and to develop the business. To the contrary, if the experience is bad, premiums for new projects could be increased with consideration of market trends because losing business is preferred to suffering from losses. However, such adjustments in WCI's context are not encouraged by most of the Singapore insurers because profitable years will have to be balanced with less profitable years.

Reinsurance Cost

Reinsurance is the principal mechanism that insurance companies use to transfer part or all of the risks assumed through their own underwriting activities. The reasons for reinsuring are as follows:

- For balance sheet protection – reinsurance is purchased to protect the solvency of the insurance company; and
- To increase the capacity – the risk exposure that an insurer can reasonably accept is restricted by the size of its capital base. Reinsurance allows taking larger risks, which makes the company more attractive to insurance brokers and their clients.

Risk of an insurer can be ceded to a reinsurer via facultative reinsurance and treaty reinsurance arrangements. Under the facultative arrangement, each risk is underwritten by the reinsurer on its own merits with a separate reinsurance contract. Under the treaty system, reinsurance is underwritten for a class of insurance, annually. The treaty reinsurance is further categorised into proportionate treaty and non-proportionate treaty. The subsets of the proportionate treaty are quota share reinsurance and surplus reinsurance while the subsets of the non-proportionate treaty are excess-of-loss (XOL) reinsurance and stop-loss reinsurance. The Singapore insurance industry adopts the XOL treaty reinsurance for WCI.

A reinsurer decides the XOL treaty premium for an insurer based on the estimated premium income, loss ratio, risk profile of the business covered, and the excess point of the treaty. Insurers can decide upon attractive premiums for their policies, depending on their treaty premiums. However, reinsurance cost is usually less than 10% of the underwritten premium. Hence, it is not a major concern for premium rating. Most of the companies incorporate the reinsurance cost into overhead costs.

Amount of Outstanding Claims to the Insurer

When a particular class of insurance, like WCI, experiences too many claims, the insurer may prefer to increase the premium for new projects so as to recover losses from the existing projects. Nevertheless, market competition restrains such adjustments. On the other hand, decreasing the premium rate to attract more business for cash flow purposes is also unfeasible because WCI has been the riskiest insurance class in Singapore.

Project Duration

When the project duration is longer, the risk exposure of an insurer is longer and the earned premium, along with the net profit for the year, is reduced. Project duration is therefore a moderate consideration for some insurance companies in Singapore. However, the other set of insurance companies perceive that the duration is built into the wage roll; thus, it can be negligible for premium rating.

Placement of Multiple Policies by the Contractor

When contractors take multiple policies for projects, discounts may be considered as the risks can be spread among policies. Contractor's all risk (CAR) insurance and WCI are the main construction insurances. WCI is ranked as the worst policy by insurers, which earns small premiums but large claims. Meanwhile, CAR insurance has been contrary in this aspect. Mostly, the loss in WCI is covered by the total premium from both policies. Most of the insurers prefer selling insurance packages rather than individual policies. Hence, the placement of multiple policies is more of a prerequisite than a discounting factor in the Singapore insurance market.

Cooperation by the Contractor

The Singapore construction industry is heavily reliant on foreign workers from neighbouring developing countries such as India, China, Bangladesh, Thailand, Indonesia and the Philippines. The objective of these workers is to earn enough money as fast as possible to return to their home countries for a comfortable life. There were incidents in Singapore whereby: (1) some of the injured workers chose to claim under common law rights to reap greater compensation; and (2) some workers injured themselves or acted recklessly to get injured in order for claiming compensation (Kyodo, 1991). It is therefore important for insurers to scrutinise the root cause(s) of accident(s), the negligence of contractors to provide safe workplaces, and any fraudulent action(s) of workers, to reduce insurers' risk. Contractors' support is paramount in such situations, which could be a consideration in premium rating. Nonetheless, it is a weak factor because there could still be claims although the contractor is supportive.

Volume of Business in the Market

It would be acceptable to increase WCI premium rates when the construction industry undergoes an economic boom. Nonetheless, new insurance companies tend to enter the market when the demand is high; if not the existing insurance companies expand their business to provide WCI for construction projects. This makes the Singapore insurance market constantly competitive.

Unimportant Variables for Premium Rating

Two insignificant variables for premium rating are identified below.

Expectation of Potential Business from the Contractor

The expectation of potential business from contractors are irrelevant for premium rating because construction projects are secured through competitive bidding, thus the prediction of potential projects for contractors is difficult.

Contractor's Size

Large contractors with good safety records demonstrate their capacity to use sophisticated and less hazardous construction methods. It would be therefore beneficial for insurance companies to favour large contractors. However, multilayered subcontracting is commonly observed in construction whereby a chain of subcontractors work in a single project under a main contractor. Thus, subcontractors' experiences, operational methods, and safety consciousness would be more pertinent concerns in this regard. As per insurers' experience, most reported accidents involved subcontractors' workers whereby the main contractor had provided the WCI cover.

Summary of Survey Findings

The survey findings reveal that:

- Three variables are critical for predicting potential WCI claims in construction projects. These variables include wage roll, project hazard level, and the effectiveness of the safety management system on site;
- Five variables are crucial for determining an appropriate mark-up for a WCI policy in concern. Among the crucial variables are: overhead costs of insurance, contractor's claims history, competition, corporate objectives of the insurer, and investment income from underwritten premiums; and
- The assessments of project hazards and safety in construction are cumbersome tasks. The incorporation of comprehensive guidelines for these purposes is indispensable for a new WCI model to be effective and value adding.

Risk Control Strategies for Insurance Companies

Procuring workers' compensation insurance is a risk transfer mechanism exploited by contractors to indemnify them from any financial burden. This, on the other hand, explicitly advises that insurance companies are at obvious risk. It is therefore vitally important for insurance companies to implement proper risk control strategies during the course of coverage for minimising their risk exposure. Consequently, the study was extended to analyse the risk control strategies exploited by other classes of insurance so valuable insights for construction WCI may be realised. The insurance industry of Singapore was again used as the case for this exploratory work. Because health and motor insurance classes seem to enjoy well-established risk control systems, the study directed its focus on them.

Health insurance

Risks in health insurance are controlled by a co-payment scheme in Singapore. The co-payment is the portion of a covered expense (medical expenditure) that must be paid by the insured. The co-payment encourages the insured to be responsible in the use of healthcare benefits. Policyholders are encouraged to use healthcare services only when necessary. For instance, the co-payment system applied by an insurance company in Singapore is described in Table 3.4. Policyholders are required to co-pay in varying quanta depending on the type of medical service used.

Table 3.4. Health insurance co-payment scheme

Medical service type	Co-payment limit
Primary care doctor	S$5
Accident and emergency visit	S$10
24-hour clinics	S$10
Specialist visit	S$15
Specialised investigations (e.g. CT scan)	10% of the bill
Hospitalisation and surgery	10% of total hospital bill

Source: NTUC income, 2006.

Motor Insurance

Risks in motor insurance are controlled via two strategies in Singapore, and these are:

1. Excess (also known as deductible); and
2. Discounting system.

An excess is the portion of any claim that is not covered by the insurance provider. It is normally quoted as a fixed amount or percentage. The excess must be paid by the insured, before the benefits of the policy can apply. For example, a vehicle owner might have a motor insurance policy with a $500 excess on collision coverage. If the vehicle owner were in an accident that did $800 worth of damage to the vehicle, then the insurance company would pay him/her $300. The insured is responsible for the first $500 of damage (the excess), and the insurance company pays the balance. Typically, a general rule is: the higher the deductible, the lower the premium, and vice versa.

In spite of excess, a well-structured discounting scheme is noticed in motor insurance in Singapore to minimise insurers' risks. Vehicle owners are entitled to three kinds of discounts as described below.

No Claims Discount (NCD)

If a vehicle owner is under a comprehensive motor policy for a continuous 12-month period and there is no claim made on the policy, the insured will be entitled to a No Claims Discount (NCD) on renewal of the policy. The percentage of the NCD increases with the number of claims-free years. The insured will lose the NCD entitlement if he/she makes a claim.

Incentive for Clean Driving Records

If a vehicle owner has not been fined during previous years, the traffic police in Singapore will issue a commendation letter with zero demerit points. Insurers incentivize vehicle owners for clean driving records.

Loyalty Rebate

A rebate of 5% is entitled to a given insured if he/she has been insured by the same insurance company for three consecutive years.

While the excess is a direct risk minimisation measure in motor insurance, the NCD and the clean driving incentive are indirect measures that make policy holders conscious drivers.

Insights for Construction WCI

Many insurance companies appear to have some sort of discount for contractors for keeping their workers' compensation claims to a minimum. However, the method used to compute the discount amount is not well-defined. The risk control strategies used in motor and health insurance may be adapted to develop an effective risk control mechanism for construction WCI. Most of the risk control strategies in health and motor insurance are modelled on the perception that the insured is the key risk control source and has control over loss/risk, and thus they should be leveraged. When this notion is applied to construction WCI, the main contractor of a project would be the control source. Yet, Huang and Hinze (2006) empirically proved that clients' involvement in safety management during the course of construction significantly improves safety performance on sites. It is therefore equally important to recognise and encourage the involvement of both contractors and clients through bona fide incentives. In view of the WCI philosophy, the concept of neither excess nor co-payment is applicable as a risk control measure in WCI. Nevertheless, it is believed that the introduction of a post-project discount system for both contractors and clients, inferring from the NCD concept, to urge their involvement in reducing claims or improving safety during the course of construction would be a feasible risk control strategy for construction WCI.

Conclusion

This chapter established three key sub processes for an effective WCI model for construction projects, including claims prediction, mark-up determination, and risk control. The process of claims prediction needs to assess three variables such as wage roll, project hazard level, and the effectiveness of the safety management system on site. Five variables need to be analysed for determining an appropriate mark-up for a WCI policy, including overhead costs of insurance, contractor's claims history with the insurer, competition, corporate objectives of the insurer, and investment income from underwritten premiums. The risk control process may utilise a post-project discount system that incentivize contractors and clients for their involvement in improving safety in the project that minimised losses for the insurer. The assessments of construction hazards and safety for predicting WCI claims are complex tasks, which need comprehensive protocols. The next chapter is therefore dedicated to developing these protocols.

Chapter IV

Assessing Hazards and Safety in Building Construction Projects

Introduction

The assessments of the intensity of project hazards and the effectiveness of contractor's safety management system are crucial aspects for WCI premium rating. On the other hand, these are generally complex tasks because of the vast variety of work trades, operations, machinery, materials, operatives and subcontractors involved in any one construction project. This chapter discusses comprehensive construction hazards and safety assessment methods in an easy-to-follow style. Firstly, the nature of occupational injuries in construction is described, followed by the identification of attributes for assessing hazards in various work trades in building construction projects. Finally, the factors pertinent to safety rating of construction projects are explored.

Nature of Occupational Injuries in Construction

Occupational injuries from construction activities in general are defined by Davies and Tomasin (1996) as:

- Danger of physical injuries and fatalities; and
- Health problems.

Construction accidents resulting in physical injuries and fatalities can be broadly categorised into the following eight basic groups (Hinze, 2005; Haslam *et al.*, 2005):

1. Falling from heights – involves workers falling from higher floors to lower floors/ground level, and falling from ground level to excavation level;

2. Struck by falling objects/moving vehicles – primarily involves workers being struck by equipment, private vehicles, falling objects, vertically hoisted materials and horizontally transported materials;

3. Excavation-related accidents – encompass cave-in, contact with underground utilities, subsidence of nearby structures, falling of materials/vehicles/objects onto people working in the excavation, fumes, and inrushes of water at the bottom of excavations;

4. Accidents by the operation of machinery/tools – caused by toppling of machinery, collapse of the parts of machinery, and unsuitable or unsafe hand-held tools;

5. Electrocution – caused by contact with electric current from machines, appliances, light fixtures, faulty electrical equipment and tools, and contact with overhead/underground power lines;

6. Fire/explosion – resulting from the explosion of pressure vessels or gasoline pipes, and fire due to welding/hot works;

7. Failure of temporary structures – involves the failure of formworks and scaffoldings; and

8. Others - e.g. slipping on the same level, oxygen deficiency in confined spaces, lightning strike, etc.

Health problems affecting construction workers are shown in Table 4.1.

Table 4.1. Health problems in construction

Health hazard	Cause
1. Skin diseases	Contact with cement, slaked lime, paint, varnish thinner, solvents, strong chemicals, grouts, seals & adhesives
2. Hardness of hearing	Noise
3. Respiratory diseases	Inhalation of toxic dusts, vapour & ashes
4. Muscular and bone diseases	High static stress and unnatural working postures
5. Cancer	Carcinogenic materials
6. Mental illness	Stress, and inhalation of toxic materials affecting brain & central nervous system
7. Diseases caused by vibration	Vibration

Source: Imriyas *et al.,* 2007.

Estimating Accident Risks in Construction

Abdelhamid and Everett (2000), and Haslam *et al.* (2005) intensely analysed the root causes of occupational accidents in construction. The root causes can be summarised by four clusters, including working condition, management failure, unsafe act of workers, and non-human related events. Table 4.2 shows the factors under each cluster. The working condition is an inherent hazard, owing to the scope and location of the project. The inherent hazard is managed through a safety management system, which can cause occupational accidents when flaws exist. The negligent attitude of workers to forego safety standards also causes accidents, although it is less quantifiable. Non-human related events are beyond control and prediction. Hence, the estimation of occupational injury risks in construction projects would assess two factors: (1) project's inherent hazard intensity; and (2) effectiveness of the safety management system. Figure 4.1 schematically explains how these two factors counteract each other. As portrayed in the figure, hazard force inclines the project towards the accident zone while safety force pulls it towards the safe zone. When the safety force is at least equal in magnitude to the hazard imposed, the project stays in the neutral zone. Safety below hazard level moves the project towards the accident zone. Hence, the prediction of occupational accidents in a construction project entails the assessment and collation of the magnitudes of project hazard intensity and safety preparedness.

Table 4.2. Root causes of construction accidents

Cluster	Factor
• Working condition	• Type of work • Work location • Status of tools, equipment & temporary structures • Physical layout of the workplace
• Management failure	• Poor housekeeping • Violation of workplace safety standards • Poor supervision & inspection of work progress, tools, equipment & temporary structures
• Unsafe acts of workers	• Disregarding safety rules • Horseplay • Shortage of skills & training
• Non-human related events	• Unexpected ground conditions/terrain • Adverse weather/earthquake/tsunami, etc. on site

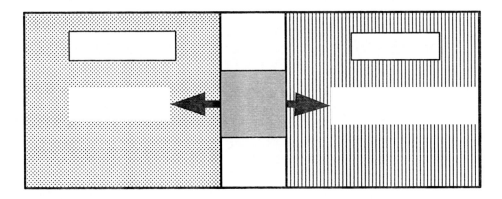

Figure 4.1. Hazard versus Safety trade-off (Imriyas *et al.*, 2007b)

Hazards in Building Construction Projects

The combination of work by Davies and Tomasin (1996), and Jannadi and Assaf (1998) produced a list of high hazardous trades in building construction projects. The hazardous trades are as follows:

1. Demolition works;
2. Excavation works;
3. Scaffolding and ladder works;
4. False works (temporary structures);
5. Roof works;
6. Erection of structural frameworks;
7. Crane use;
8. Construction machinery and tools usage;
9. Works on contaminated sites;
10. Welding and cutting works; and
11. Works in confined spaces.

A particular project may have all of these or a few of these trades, and the intensity of hazard inherent in each trade is determined by its respective risk attributes. The ensuing sections identify the significant attributes that contribute to the intensity of hazard in each of the hazardous trades above.

Demolition Hazards

Demolition is one of the high-risk activities of the construction industry with a fatal and major injury incidence rate of about 17 times of that for the whole of the construction industry. Approximately 10% of all fatal accidents each year in the construction field occur in the demolition sector (Davies and Tomasin, 1996). Demolition workers face a variety of hazards (King and Hudson, 1985), viz.:

- Falling from heights;
- Being hit or trapped by falling objects;
- Excessive noise from hand-held tools, demolition balls, pneumatic drills, explosives and falling parts;
- Vibration from hand-held pneumatic tools;
- Respiratory hazards from dust which may contain toxic constituents such as asbestos and silica;
- Flying particles causing eye and skin injuries; and
- Fires and explosives, especially when demolishing tanks that contained oils or flammable chemicals.

Davies and Tomasin (1996) described that the risk in demolition works is influenced by four variables, and these are:

- Volume/size of demolition;
- Type of structure;
- Method of demolition; and
- Level of site supervision.

Excavation Hazards

Davies and Tomasin (1996) categorised excavations into three types: trenches, basements and wide excavations, and pits/shafts (for pad and pile foundations). They expose workers to similar hazards and accidents. Workers in the underground construction industry, especially water, sewer and utility line companies, have traditionally had a higher accident and injury rate than other workers in the heavy construction industry (Arboleda and Abraham, 2004). According to OSHA (2002), the fatality rate for excavation works is 112% higher than the rate for general construction. Accidents in excavation works occur in one of the following ways (HSE, 2005):

- Collapse of sides/cave-in: Cave-in is perhaps the most feared and chief cause of accidents in excavation works. It buries workers and/or cause crushing injuries to survivors;
- Contact with underground utilities: Works in excavations often encounter obstructions from intersecting utility lines that may cause injuries and/or fatalities to workers by: (1) electrocution and/or explosion when electrical cables and/or gasoline pipes are damaged; (2) collapse of excavation due to flooding led by damage to water lines and/or sewer lines; and/or (3) drowning in floods from damaged water/sewer lines;
- Dangerous atmospheres: Dangerous atmospheres in excavations may result from oxygen deficiency as well as the presence of carbon dioxide, carbon monoxide, nitrous fumes and methane gas, which suffocate workers, kill or cause respiratory problems;
- Workers being struck by falling materials/objects from top; and
- Workers falling into excavations.

Hinze (2005), and Lee and Halpin (2003) analysed excavation-related accidents and identified five hazard rating variables for excavation works, viz.:

- Excavation configuration (depth, width and length);
- Geological condition (soil type and water table);
- Presence of underground utilities (electrical, water and sewer lines);
- Nearby vehicular traffic (vibration and surcharge load); and
- Nearby structures.

Scaffolding and Ladder Hazards

Scaffolding is the most common way of providing platforms to works at heights. The following hazards are associated with scaffold use (Davies and Tomasin, 1996):

- Workers falling from the working platform;
- Workers below the working platform being struck by materials falling from it; and
- The scaffold or part of it collapsing and throwing workers off the collapsed structure, and crushing workers under it or nearby.

Access to scaffolds is provided by ladders. Also, ladders themselves are often used as working platforms for light works. Many serious accidents result from the use of ladders: (1) ladders slip when users are climbing or working from them; (2) users slip or miss their footing while climbing; (3) users overbalance when carrying materials or tools; and (4) when defective ladders are used, they fracture under the weight of the user.

Bentley *et al.* (2006) investigated the scaffolding and ladder-related accidents and reported two key risk factors:

- Design factors - height of the scaffold/ladder, suitability of the type for the task and height, and the adequacy of design (member size, bracing, guardrails, platform size, and toe board); and
- Work environment and conditions – defects in the members of the scaffold/ladder, slippery condition on the platform, loading of materials and workers on the platform, and the nature of the platform the scaffold/ladder is rested on.

False Work Hazards

A false work is defined as a temporary structure used to support a permanent structure during its construction and until it becomes self-supporting. False works may be required to support in-situ and pre-cast concrete construction, masonry arches as well as timber and steel frameworks. Accidents in false works occur by two means:

- Total or partial collapse of false works leading to workers being thrown off or falling off their place of work; and
- Workers slip and fall from false works through unprotected edges and holes of decking, and access ladders.

Davies and Tomasin (1996) identified two causes for false works collapses:

- Inadequate design – poor quality false work designs are caused by: (1) failure to correctly estimate the type and extent of loading; (2) inadequate foundation; (3) incorrect choice or use of materials; and/or (4) lack of provision for lateral stability; and

- Poor assembly – caused by: failure to inspect the materials (such as struts, planks, etc.), poor soil condition at the foundation, and improper false work erection.

Roof Work Hazards

The occupation of roofers has been rated as one of the most dangerous occupations, with a fatality rate of 29 per 100,000 workers (Toscano, 1997). Roofers are at about six-time higher risk for fatal occupational injuries than the average worker, with falls being fatal events in 75% of cases (Ruser, 1995). Falls from roofs constitute the leading cause for work-related fall fatalities and they represent more than one-fifth of all occupational fatal falls (BLS, 1997b). Analyses of occupational fatality data between 1994 and 1996 indicate an increasing trend in the number of fatal falls from roofs during construction (BLS 1996 & 1997a). Additionally, falls from roofs are a serious cause of non-fatal injuries in the construction industry. In 1996, an estimated 2,550 serious injuries in the USA were as a consequence of construction-related falls from roofs (BLS, 1998). Injuries caused by falls from roofs are typically extremely severe, requiring long periods of treatment and recovery, and resulting in substantial medical costs (Parsons and Pizatella, 1985; Gillen *et al.*, 1997). King and Hudson (1985) observed a higher proportion of roofing accidents during maintenance period/activities too. These include roof edge falls, falls through fragile roofing materials, and falls from the internal structure of roofs. Hsiao and Simeonov (2001) analysed the fall-initiation factors in roofing works and categorised them under three groups as shown in Table 4.3.

Table 4.3. Roofing hazard attributes

Factor category	Fall-initiation factor
1. Design factors	• Height of the roof • Roofing material property such as slipperiness, brittleness, asbestos, etc. • Inclination of the roof
2. Task factors	• Load handling on the roof top • Complexity of the task • Working environment, which causes fatigue and loss of balance
3. Worker factors	• Age and safety consciousness • Experience and training in roofing works • Under use/misuse of personal protective equipment

Hazards in Erecting Structural Frameworks

The most serious accidents that occur during the erection and assembly of structural steel or pre-cast frameworks are (Davies and Tomasin, 1996):

- Erectors falling from heights when at their places of work, and going to or returning from them;
- The collapse of the whole or part of the framework causing workers to fall or striking those at lower levels; and
- Workers at lower levels being struck by tools or materials falling or being thrown down.

Hazard intensity in erection works is dictated by the following variables:

- Height and size of the structure/erection;
- Design and erection method; and
- Provision of a safe workplace such as safe access/egress, safe working platform at heights, safe tool containers and safety equipment (safety belt, harness, net, etc.).

Crane Hazards

Cranes are remarkable and invaluable tools for hoisting and carrying, but they are heavily represented in the industrial injury and fatality statistics. Most of them occur in the construction industry (Shepherd *et al.*, 2001). In the US, approximately 30-50 crane fatalities occur in the construction industry per year, with there being a total of approximately 70 crane fatalities across all industries per year (OSHA, 1996). MacCollum (1993) estimated that crane hazards are the source of 25-33% of casualties in construction and maintenance activities. With regards to fatalities only, Ontario recorded an average of 10% of construction fatalities related to cranes (CSAO, 1994), and the New South Wales construction industry, Australia indicated that approximately 12% of fatalities were crane-related (AFCC, 1987). Davies and Tomasin (1996) identified five crane-related hazards: (1) overturning of a crane or the structural failure of its parts; (2) dropping of the suspended load; (3) electrocution; (4) trapping of people; and (5) accidents during erection and dismantling as well as loading and unloading.

The causes of different crane failures are shown in Figure 4.2. Davies and Tomasin (1996) quoted that the overturning of a crane or parts of it occurs because of overloading, differential settlement of the crane support or foundation, operating on a slope (for mobile cranes) and/or operational methods. Ederer (2006) reported that basic causes of dropping the load are overloading and improper maintenance of the crane and its parts. Neitzel *et al.* (2001) criticised that electrocution and trapping are caused due to the lack of communications between the operator, slingers and flagman/supervisor whereas erection and dismantling injuries are caused by the unsafe work practice of erectors and the lack of supervision.

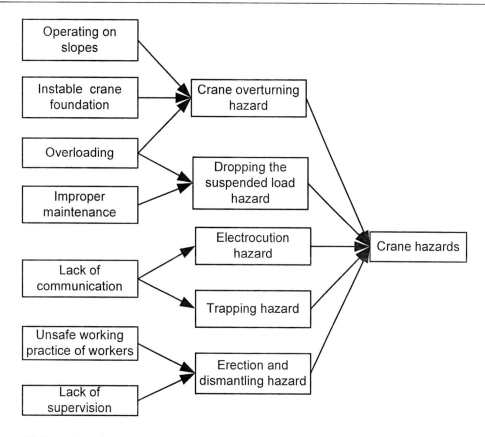

Figure 4.2. Crane hazards

Construction Machinery and Tools Hazards

Of all the construction industry fatalities, 18% occurs with construction machinery (Helander, 1991). The types of machinery involved in accidents include excavators and shovels, earthmoving equipment (i.e. crawler tractors and bulldozers, scrapers and graders), dumpers and dump trucks, forklift trucks, road rollers, and lorries. Accidents in construction machinery usage occur in one of the following modes (Helander, 1991; Davies and Tomasin, 1996):

- Workers being run-over or struck by machinery moving forward or reversing;
- Collision between machinery or with fixed objects such as false works or scaffoldings;
- Overturning of machinery while in operation; and
- Workers falling from machinery.

These accidents are caused by the following major factors:

- Failure of machinery- inoperative back-up alarms, brake failures, etc.;

- Inadequate site planning resulting in poor visibility, inadequate manoeuvre space, inadequate signboards, and poor site traffic control;
- Lack of supervision and training to workers and operators; and
- Construction noise that masks the sound of back-up alarms and the sound of plant.

Axelsson and Fang (1985) observed that for 18% of the accidents, the primary external factor was hand-held tools. Helander (1991) sorted construction tools in the descending order of hazard, viz.: (1) Knife; (2) Hammer, sledge hammer, etc.; (3) Grinding/cutting machine; (4) Jackhammer; (5) Drill; (6) Manual saw; (7) Crowbar, spit, etc.; (8) Tools for screwing; (9) Welding equipment – gas; (10) Axe; (11) Spade/excavation tools; (12) Gripping, holding, pinching, pulling tools; (13) Chain saw; (14) Nail gun; (15) Compass saw, hole saw, etc.; (16) Welding equipment – electrical; (17) Circular saw; (18) Cutting tools; and (19) Other tools. The use of construction tools cause injuries and fatalities to workers by the following ways (Helander, 1991; Fredericks, *et al.*, 2002; Pontes, 2005):

- Eye injuries caused by foreign objects getting into eyes by operations such as grinding, welding, cutting, drilling and breaking;
- Finger/hand injuries by cuts and burns;
- Injuries caused by moving/broken machine parts;
- Electrocution; and
- Vibration from powered hand-held tools, causing a group of diseases. One of them is blood circulation disturbance known as "vibration white finger".

Fredericks *et al.* (2002) noted that workers of mechanical contractors have contacted with considerable tool-related accidents, notably those who are involved in: (1) heating, ventilation and air conditioning (HVAC) systems; (2) site utilities such as water supply, storm water drainage system, sanitary disposal system and gas supply systems; (3) plumbing works - water distribution, water treatment and sanitary facilities; (4) fire protection; and (5) specialty systems. Most of the accidents are the result of faulty tools and/or unsafe handling of tools. Moreover, the type of tools and the duration of use also caused the accidents.

Hazards on Contaminated Sites

A contaminated site can have one or many of the following substances, which are harmful to workers' health (Worksafe Victoria, 2005):

- Metals (e.g. lead);
- Inorganic compounds (e.g. cyanide compounds);
- Oils and tars;
- Pesticides;
- Other organic compounds (e.g. benzene, toluene and polychlorinated biphenyls);
- Toxic, explosive or asphyxiant gases (e.g. methane);
- Combustible substances (e.g. petrol);

- Fibres (e.g. asbestos and synthetic mineral fibres);
- Putrescible or infectious materials (e.g. medical/biological wastes);
- Radioactive wastes; and
- Other harmful wastes (e.g. unexploded ordinance and syringes).

Contamination may have been the result of: (1) industrial processes carried out on the site previously; (2) materials stored or dumped on the site; (3) some agricultural processes on the site such as a sheep dip or farm chemicals were mixed for application; (4) contaminants in imported fill; and/or (5) demolition. Davies and Tomasin (1996) quoted that sites where contamination might be expected include: (1) asbestos producers; (2) chemical plants and depots; (3) dockland areas; (4) explosive factories and depots; (5) landfill sites of domestic and industrial wastes; (6) metal smelting and refining plants; (7) metal treatment and finishing works; (8) mines and quarries; (9) oil production and storage depots; (10) paint and graphite factories and depots; (11) railway yards; (12) scrap yards; (13) sewage works; (14) steel works; and (15) tanning and associated trades.

Short or long term health damages to people exposed to contaminants depend on the following variables (Worksafe Victoria, 2005):

- The type of contaminants on site;
- The quantum of contaminants present; and
- The duration that the workers are exposed on site.

Welding and Cutting Work Hazards

Welding and cutting works on construction sites expose workers to both accidents and health problems. Injuries and fatalities in welding and cutting works are caused by:

- Fire or explosion due to extreme temperatures (up to 10,000° F) from welding sparks coming into contact with flammable materials (e.g. coatings of metals, gasoline, oil, paint, thinner, wood, cardboard, paper, acetylene, hydrogen, etc.);
- Electric shock from excessive moisture (e.g. perspiration or wet conditions) and contact with metal parts which are "electrically hot";
- Flying sparks, particles of hot metals, molten metals, liquid chemicals, acids or caustic liquids, or chemical gases or vapours; and
- Falls during work on ladders, above ground and in confined spaces for welding and cutting operations.

Health problems and their causes in welding works are:
- Exposure to high noise levels from welding equipment, power sources and processes may result in hearing problems;
- Exposure to ultraviolet (UV) radiation resulting in skin burns and skin cancer. "Welder's flash" (brief exposure to UV radiation) may result in temporary swelling and fluid excretion of the eyes or temporary blindness;

- Irritation of lungs due to heat and UV radiation; and
- Exposure to fumes and chemical substances may cause respiratory diseases.

The intensity of hazard in welding and cutting works depends on the following variables (Welder, arc, 2005):

- The volume of work;
- The location of welding and cutting works (confined spaces, underground, ladders, etc.);
- The use of safety protective equipment; and
- Housekeeping.

Hazards in Confined Spaces

The term "confined space" refers to a space, which by design has limited openings for entry and exit, unfavourable natural ventilation that could contain or produce dangerous air contaminants, and is not intended for continuous employee occupancy. Confined spaces include tanks, process vessels, pits, silos, vats, degreasers, boilers, utility vaults, pipelines, manholes, box girders, and columns. Workers are required to enter confined spaces for tasks such as repair, inspection and maintenance, and are often exposed to multiple hazards. Suruda *et al.* (1994) reported that death certificate data identified 803 deaths in 681 incidents in confined spaces for the nine-year-period, for an average of 89 deaths per year, and 1.2 deaths per fatal incident. Of the 803 deaths, 499 (62%) were caused by atmospheric hazards and 223 (28%) were caused by mechanical suffocation. Eightyone victims (10%) died from other causes of injury. Fatal injuries that occur in confined spaces are most likely to be from atmospheric hazards. The types of atmospheric hazards in confined spaces can be quite varied – some examples are shown in Table 4.4. Rescue attempts in confined spaces can expose the unprepared rescuer to the risk of asphyxiation in an atmosphere that is unable to support respiration.

The main characteristics that recognise the intensity of hazard in a confined space are as follows (EH&S, 2006):

- Space configuration (i.e. size of the space and size of the ingress/egress);
- The current use of the confined space (i.e. if it is currently being used);
- Activity to be involved inside the space (i.e. welding, application of solvents/adhesives, etc.); and
- The level of ventilation inside the space.

Table 4.4. Atmospheric hazards in confined spaces

Type of atmospheric hazard	Example
• Toxic gas	• Hydrogen sulphide • Carbon monoxide • Hydrogen cyanide
• Inert gas	• Argon • Helium • Nitrogen
• Simple asphyxiant	• Nitrogen • Methane • Carbon dioxide
• Oxygen deficiency	• Oxygen in air consumed or displaced
• Solvents	• Freon • Chlorinated hydrocarbons • Gasoline
• Explosive mixtures	• Methane • Toluene vapour

Source: Suruda *et al.*, 1994.

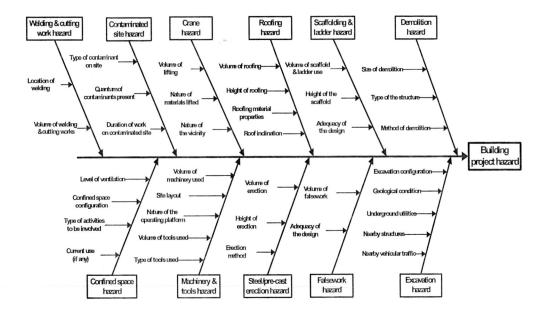

Figure 4.3. Fishbone model for hazard intensity assessment

Assessing Hazard Intensity in Building Projects

Figure 4.3 summarises the discussions on hazards in a fishbone model that facilitates the assessment of hazard intensity in building projects. The model incorporates all the 11 hazardous trades and their respective risk attributes. Hazard evaluation in each trade needs to be performed by considering the context of the project and the trade assessed. However, not every trade may be applicable to every project, but relevant hazardous trades for a particular project need to be identified and hazard rated carefully. The exploitation of the model in WCI is discussed in the next chapter.

Safety Performance Measurement Method for WCI

There are three key approaches for measuring the performance of safety systems in construction projects, including accident statistics, workplace inspection, and the evaluation of documented safety system (Hislop, 2000; Jannadi and Al-Sudairi, 1995; Kavianian and Wentz, 1990).

1. Accident statistics:

    Accident statistics are the most commonly used measures of safety performance. Occupational injury rates in terms of frequency and severity over a specific period of man-hours worked provide a relative measure of the effectiveness of the safety program in place. Nevertheless, injury statistics only provide a retrospective analysis of injury experience and it is an indicator of how effectively a safety program was managed.

2. Workplace inspection:

    Workplace inspection is a more effective means of evaluating the safety program than relying only on statistics. Through inspections, the assessor can determine the degree of influence being exercised over site conditions, the control of hazards, the enforcement of safety standards, the use of required personal protective equipment, and the degree to which safe work practices are being applied. This approach is also referred to as safety auditing.

3. Evaluation of documented safety system:

    The new Workplace Safety and Health Act (WSHA) 2006 of Singapore, which repeals the Factories Act enforces two regulations, viz.:

    •   The contractor shall submit together with the tender document for approval by the client, the contractor's proposed safety management system for the project, which complies in all aspects with the WSHA 2006 and the Singapore's Code of Practice for Safety Management Systems for Construction Sites (SPSB, 1999); and

    •   Unlike the previous Factories Act whereby the contractor is accountable for any accidents on a construction site, the new WSHA 2006 will hold responsibility on the client, consultants and the contractor for any accidents on construction sites, as the case may be.

    A contractor's proposed safety management system is therefore expected to be evaluated meticulously by the client and the consultants at the tendering stage, and to be monitored during the construction stage. Hence, an external safety assessor for a construction project may evaluate the proposed/documented safety system and may assess its effectiveness.

WCI is underwritten at the bidding stage when the contractor has yet to set up the necessary safety system on site. Thus, it is hard to adopt the workplace inspection approach (safety audit) for the project to be insured. However, the insurer may inspect a similar project of the contractor and infer a project safety index for the new project. Alternatively, the insurer may evaluate the documented safety system for the project and derive a project safety index. It is also applicable to use a combination of safety auditing of a current project and the evaluation of the documented safety system for the new project. In any scenario, a methodical approach for performing the audit or evaluation must be set forth (Hess-Kosa, 2006).

Essentials of Project Safety Systems

The new WSHA 2006 lists six key obligations of contractors with regards to construction safety, viz. (MOM, 2006):

1. Providing and maintaining a workplace that is safe, without risk to health, and adequate as regards to facilities and arrangements for workers' welfare at work;
2. Ensuring that adequate safety measures are taken in respect of any machinery, equipment, plant, article or process used by workers;
3. Ensuring that workers are not exposed to hazards arising out of the arrangement, disposal, manipulation, organisation, processing, storage, transport, working or use of things in their workplace or near their workplace under the control of the contractor;
4. Developing and implementing procedures for dealing with emergencies that may arise while workers are at work;
5. Ensuring that every work person has adequate instructions, information, training and supervision as is necessary for that person to perform the work; and
6. Giving workers all necessary information about the way the activities and operations on site are conducted as might affect their safety or health while they are on site.

The key elements of a construction safety management system to meet contractors' obligations under WSHA 2006 were identified from WSHA 2006, SSCP 79:1999, Rowlinson (1997), and Teo *et al.* (2005), and described below.

1. Project safety organisation:
   The contractor shall appoint the following persons to ensure safety, health and welfare of all persons on site:
   - A workplace safety and health officer or co-ordinator approved by the commissioner for workplace safety and health;
   - A workplace safety and health auditor approved by the commissioner, whose duties shall be to audit:
     i. The safety and health management system on the site;
     ii. The risk assessment of all works undertaken on the site; and

      iii. Any of the work processes carried out and the site itself.

- A workplace safety and health committee comprising representative of workers, subcontractors and the main contractor of the site to:
  - i. Keep under review circumstances at the workplace, which affect or may affect the safety or health of persons at the workplace;
  - ii. Promote co-operation between the management and workers in achieving and maintaining safe and healthy working conditions;
  - iii. Carry out from time to time inspections of the scene of any accident or dangerous occurrence in the interests of the safety and health of the workers; and
  - iv. Exercise such other functions and duties as may be prescribed or conferred on the committee.

2. Risk assessment and management:

   The contractor shall establish procedures to identify and analyse all existing and potential risks to workers. The risk assessment method shall include: (1) identification and recording of existing and potential risks; (2) identification of persons exposed to the risks; and (3) development and implementation of preventive or control measures.

3. Safe work practices:

   The contractor shall establish and maintain procedures for the safe execution of works based on the codes of practice. These practices will encompass: (1) safe procedures; (2) permit-to-work systems; and (3) personal protective equipment use systems.

4. Safety training and the competency of people involved:

   The contractor shall establish procedures to identify training needs and provide adequate safety training to management personnel, supervisors and workers.
   - i. All management personnel shall be trained in safety policy, safety management system, safety organisation, statutory requirements on safety, and their duties and responsibilities in safety;
   - ii. All supervisors shall be trained so as to achieve a better understanding of the safety aspects of the work operations and to ensure that the operations are carried out safely; and
   - iii. All workers shall be trained in-house, before they commence works, in safe work practices.

5. Safety inspection system:

   The contractor shall establish and maintain a documented procedure for safety inspection to ensure that unsafe conditions and practices at the worksite are identified, and corrective measures are implemented promptly and effectively. Regular and thorough site inspections shall deal with: (1) construction operations; and (2) site conditions (housekeeping).

6. Machinery and tools use and maintenance regime:

   The contractor shall inspect that all machinery and tools brought to the site are tested and certified, and they are in good condition for use. The contractor shall also implement an effective inspection and maintenance program to ensure a safe and efficient operation of machinery and tools on site.

7. Subcontractors' safety systems:

The contractor shall perform an evaluation of subcontractors' safety performance before selecting them. The evaluation shall encompass: (1) company's safety management system; (2) safe work practices; (3) training records of managers, supervisors and workers; (4) status of construction machinery and tools; and (5) safety track records.

The contractor shall also: (1) establish an effective on-going program to evaluate the safety performance of subcontractors; (2) carry out periodic inspections to ensure subcontractors comply with safety requirements; (3) review safety training records of subcontractors; and (4) evaluate the status of construction machinery and tools.

8. Emergency management system:

The contractor shall establish an emergency plan and an emergency committee, and conduct drills for any emergency situations that may arise on site. The emergency plan shall include: (1) procedure for the notification and raising of alarms and communication to relevant authorities such as police, civil defence force, etc.; (2) initial response procedures and site layout plans for various emergency situations; (3) an effective evacuation plan; and (4) procedures and means of loss control such as first aid and emergency equipment, etc.

Safety Performance Assessment Protocol

In order to analyse and assess the adequacy and effectiveness of safety management systems in construction projects, a safety auditing protocol is developed as shown in Table 4.5. The protocol covers all the key safety factors and their respective sub-factors, which were discussed above. The attributes that need to be scrutinised under each safety factor/sub-factor were identified from SSCP 79:1999, Teo *et al.* (2004), and Hess-Kosa (2006). These are listed under relevant headings and subheadings in the protocol.

Table 4.5. Safety performance assessment protocol

Safety Performance Assessment Protocol for Construction Projects
A) Project safety organisation   *Competency and duties of:*
1. Workplace safety and health coordinator
2. Workplace safety and health auditor
3. Workplace safety and health committee
B) Risk assessments and management   *Risk management system with:*
1. Risk assessment team and responsibilities
2. Risk assessment procedures
3. Reporting procedures to workers of identified risks
4. Control measures for risks identified

Table 4.5. Continued

Safety Performance Assessment Protocol for Construction Projects

C) Safe work practices

Safe work procedures for:

1. Concrete works
2. Structural steel and pre-cast assembly
3. Erection and dismantling of scaffolds and false works
4. Works at heights
5. Demolition works Excavation works
6. Piling operations
7. Welding and cutting works
8. Works in confined spaces
9. Works in toxic/contaminated environments
10. Use of construction plant such as excavators, trucks, etc.
11. Use of cranes
12. Electrical installation and use

Permit-to-work(PTW) system for:

1. Works at heights
2. Excavation works
3. Works in confined spaces
4. Welding and cutting works
5. Demolition works
6. Works in toxic/contaminated environments

Personal protective equipment (PPE) for:

1. Concrete works
2. Structural steel and pre-cast assembly
3. Erection and dismantling of scaffolds and false works
4. Works at heights
5. Demolition works
6. Excavation works
7. Piling operations
8. Welding and cutting works
9. Works in confined spaces
10. Works in toxic/contaminated environments
11. Use of construction plant such as excavators, trucks, etc.
12. Use of cranes
13. Electrical installation and use

D) Safety training and competency of people involved

Certification of and safety training to:

1. Crane erector(s)
2. Crane operator(s)
3. Riggers(s)
4. Signal men
5. Scaffold erector(s) and/or suspended scaffold rigger(s)
6. Erectors of hoists and lifts
7. Operators of hoists and lifts
8. Operators of plant such as excavators, bull dozer, etc.

9.	Construction vehicle drivers

Safety training to:

1. Demolition works supervisor(s)
2. Excavation works supervisors(s)
3. Piling works supervisor(s)
4. Lifting operations supervisor(s)
5. Scaffold and/or suspended scaffold supervisor(s)
6. False works supervisor(s)
7. Welding and cutting works supervisor(s)
8. Confined space works supervisor(s)
9. Toxic/contaminated environment works supervisor(s)
10. Project management team members

In-house safety training to workers on:

1. Site rules & regulations and proper use of PPE
2. Emergency responses for various possible incidents
3. First aid procedures
4. Safe handling of tools and equipment

E) Safety inspection system

Inspection of:

1. Excavations by a competent person on a daily basis and after hazardous events (e.g. inclement weather)
2. Scaffoldings by a scaffold supervisor on a weekly basis and after inclement weather
3. False works by a PE or other competent person before, during and after casting and after inclement weather
4. Demolition by a competent person on a daily basis and after inclement weather
5. Material loading platforms by a competent person on a regular basis and after inclement weather
6. Temporary structures such as site office, canteen, site hoardings and concrete batching plant on a regular basis
7. Specialised structures or operations like the use of customised shoring system by a competent person
8. General site by a safety personnel or site manager

Housekeeping of:

1. Construction worksite
2. Workers' quarters
3. Toilets and washing facilities
4. Canteen or eating places
5. Site offices
6. Storages for materials, tools & wastes

F) Machinery and tools use and maintenance regime

Test certificates for:

1. Lifting gears (12 monthly)
2. Lifting appliances (12 monthly)
3. Lifting machines (12 monthly)
4. Hoists and lifts (6 monthly)
5. Air receivers (24 monthly)
6. Explosive power tools (36 monthly)

Table 4.5. Continued

Safety Performance Assessment Protocol for Construction Projects
Inspection of:
1. Cranes by crane operators on a daily basis
2. Electrical distribution board by a competent person on a daily basis
3. Electrical equipment and tools by operators or a competent person on a regular basis (weekly/more frequent)
4. Construction vehicles such as trucks, forklifts, bull dozers, etc. by drivers or a designated person on a daily basis
5. Temporary electrical installation by a licensed electrical worker
6. Specialised equipment by a competent person
Maintenance of:
1. Tower crane(s)
2. Mobile crane(s)
3. Gondola(s)
4. Piling machine(s)
5. Passenger hoist(s)
6. Mobile working platform(s)
7. Construction vehicles such as trucks, forklifts, bulldozers, etc.
G) Subcontractors' safety systems
Subcontractors':
1. Safe work procedures
2. Safe use of plant, machinery and tools
3. Safety inspection systems
4. Trained operatives and supervisors
5. Adherence to safety requirements during construction
H) Emergency management system
Emergency response plan for:
1. Fire & explosion
2. Failure & collapse of structures/temporary supports
3. Failure & collapse of heavy machinery & equipment
4. Leakage of hazardous substances
5. Adverse weather & flooding
Emergency response team with:
1. Emergency coordinator(s)
2. Site safety personnel
3. Designated rescuer(s)
4. First-aider(s)
5. Specialist operator(s)
Emergency equipment for:
1. Fire & explosion
2. Failure & collapse of structure/temporary support
3. Failure & collapse of heavy machinery & equipment
4. Leakage of hazardous substances
5. Adverse weather & flooding

Conclusion

Assessing the degree of potential accident risk in a project is crucial for insurers to decide on an adequate premium for a WCI cover. However, this is relatively hard in construction projects because of their inherent complexities, as opposed to risk assessment exercises in other work environments. This chapter streamlined this process with new perspectives to hazards and safety assessments. A fishbone model that includes eleven hazardous factors and their respective attributes for assessing the intensity of inherent hazards in building projects was derived. Likewise, a detailed safety auditing protocol was introduced to help assess the safety preparedness of contractors. The following chapter exploits these findings to develop a detailed new risk assessment sub-model that is integrated into the new WCI premium rating model proposed in the next chapter.

Chapter V

New Premium Rating Model for Workers' Compensation Insurance in Building Construction

Introduction

This chapter introduces a new WCI premium rating model for building construction projects exploiting the research findings discussed in the previous chapters. Discussions in the chapter cover the new WCI model and its three sub modules, which include claims prediction module, mark-up determination module, and risk control module. The details of the processes involved in each sub module are described clearly. Finally, the effectiveness of the new model is analysed in comparison to the existing techniques for premium rating.

Proposed Model for WCI Premium Rating of Building Construction Projects

A new model for WCI premium rating of building construction projects is proposed based on the research findings that were discussed in the previous chapters. The model is illustrated in Figure 5.1. As per the new model, it is proposed that:

1. The net optimal WCI premium for a construction project would have three components as shown in formula (1).

$$WCI\ net\ premium = Risk\ fee - CCI_{Contractor} - SMD_{Client} \tag{1}$$

Where:

$Risk\ fee$ The gross price of the risk covered by the insurer and it has to be paid by the contractor at the underwriting stage and subsequently reimbursed by the client via interim payments;

$CCI_{Contractor}$ A claim control incentive for the contractor, which is to be furnished by the insurer to the contractor at the policy expiration stage for controlling the actual claims below the predicted amount; and

SMD_{Client} A safety monitoring discount for the client, which is to be furnished by the insurer to the contractor at the policy expiration stage for monitoring the contractor's safety management on site, which minimised claims in the project.

2. The computation of the net premium would be performed in two stages, viz.:
    - The computation of the *risk fee* would be carried out at the underwriting stage (construction bidding stage); and
    - The computation of the $CCI_{Contractor}$, SMD_{Client} and the net premium would be carried out at the policy expiration stage.

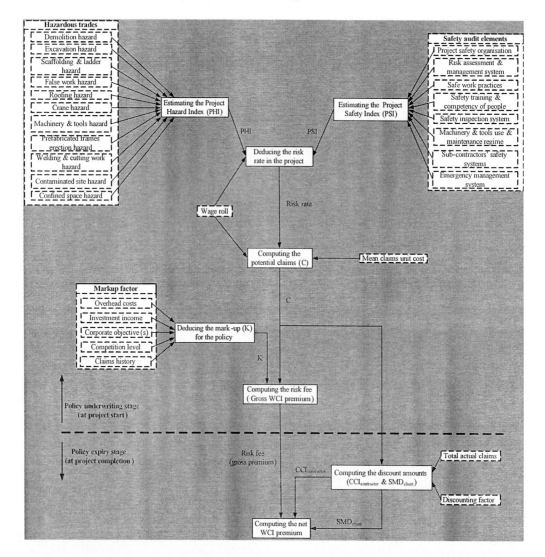

Figure 5.1. Proposed model for WCI premium rating

Computing the Risk Fee

As described above, the *risk fee* is the gross price for the accident risks that an insurer will have to assume in the project. This is estimated at the bidding stage of a project, according to formula (2).

$$Risk\ fee = (1+K)\ x\ C \tag{2}$$

Where:
C = The potential claims in the project; and
K = The mark-up for the policy.

The prediction of the potential claims (C) in a project would adopt formula (3).

$$C = Wage\ roll\ x\ Mean\ claims\ unit\ cost\ x\ Risk\ rate \tag{3}$$

Where:
    Wage roll =   The total wages of the workers in the project;
    Mean claims unit cost =   The average break-even point of workers' compensation claims for building construction projects for the insurer; and
    Risk rate =   The degree of risk that would deviate the actual claims unit cost in the project from the mean claims unit cost.

The *risk rate* for a given project is deduced heuristically taking into account the wage roll, project hazards, and project safety. A fuzzy algorithm is used to compute the risk rate in the knowledge based system that automates the proposed model, which is discussed in detail in Chapter seven. Nevertheless, the relationship between these variables is illustrated plainly in formula (4) below. The rationale for utilising these three variables in the formula is described below.

$$Risk\ rate = f_a\left(Wage\ roll, PHI, PSI\right) \tag{4}$$

1. Wage Roll
As per insurers' experience, the claims rate is not linearly correlated with the project size. Thus, an appropriate rate that may not be linearly distributed should be matched with the project size, which is represented by the wage roll size.

2. Project Hazard Index (PHI)
PHI portrays the intensity of hazard in a project ($0 \leq PHI \leq 1.0$); PHI = 0 is no hazard and PHI = 1.0 is extreme hazard. The hazard intensity in a project is scrutinised by assessing the project scope and the vicinity/location. Eleven hazardous trades in building projects and their respective attributes for assessing each trade's hazard intensity were identified in Chapter 4 using a fishbone model. Based on that, a framework for estimating the PHI for

building projects is proposed as shown in Table 5.1. As per the framework, the estimation of PHI espouses the steps described below.

- Identifying the project-pertinent hazardous trades which are agents for the occurrence of accidents;
- Identifying the principal trade hazard attributes in a trade, and rating the hazard posed by each attribute in that trade;
- Estimating the trade hazard index by analysing and assessing the effect that the rated attributes have on the trade's hazard intensity;
- Reiterating the process for all the hazardous trades in the project;
- Analysing and aggregating the estimated trade hazard indices based on a predetermined trade hazard weighting; and
- Deriving the PHI.

Table 5.1. Framework for estimating PHI

Estimating project hazard index					
1. Demolition works					
Rate the level of hazard posed by the following parameters in demolition works in this project.					
	Low				High
• Volume/size of demolition	1	2	3	4	5
• Type of structure	1	2	3	4	5
• Method of demolition	1	2	3	4	5
Trade score					
2. Excavation works					
Rate the level of hazard posed by the following parameters in excavation works in this project.					
• Excavation configuration (depth, width and length)	1	2	3	4	5
• Geological condition (soil type, water table, etc.)	1	2	3	4	5
• Underground utilities (electrical, water and sewer lines)	1	2	3	4	5
• Nearby vehicular traffic (vibration and surcharge)	1	2	3	4	5
• Nearby structures	1	2	3	4	5
Trade score					
3. Scaffolding & ladder usage					
Rate the level of hazard posed by the following parameters in scaffolding and ladder usage in this project.					
• Volume of scaffolding & ladder usage	1	2	3	4	5

Table 5.1. Continued

Estimating project hazard index					
• Height of the scaffold/ladder to be used	1	2	3	4	5
• Adequacy of design (type of material, member size, bracing, guardrails, platform size, and toe board)	1	2	3	4	5
Trade score					
4. False works (temporary structures)					
Rate the level of hazard posed by the following parameters in false works in this project.					
• Volume of false work involved in the project	1	2	3	4	5
• Adequacy of design (type of material, member size, bracing, guardrails, platform size, and toe board)	1	2	3	4	5
Trade score					
5. Roof works					
Rate the level of hazard posed by the following parameters in roof works in this project.					
• Volume of roofing involved	1	2	3	4	5
• Height of the roof	1	2	3	4	5
• Roofing material property such as slipperiness, brittleness, asbestos etc.	1	2	3	4	5
• Inclination of the roof	1	2	3	4	5
Trade score					
6. Erection of steel/pre-cast concrete structures					
Rate the level of hazard posed by the following parameters in the erection of steel/pre-cast concrete structures in this project.					
• Volume of erection work	1	2	3	4	5
• Height of erection work	1	2	3	4	5
• Erection method (partial/full erection at height, and labour involvement level)	1	2	3	4	5
Trade score					
7. Crane use					
Rate the level of hazard posed by the following parameters in lifting and crane use in this project.					
• Volume of lifting involved	1	2	3	4	5
• Nature of materials lifted	1	2	3	4	5
• Operating platform	1	2	3	4	5
• Nature of site vicinity (nearby structures, overhead cables, etc.)	1	2	3	4	5
Trade score					
8. Construction tools & machinery use					
Rate the level of hazard posed by the following parameters in plant and tools use in this project.					

Table 5.1. Continued

Estimating project hazard index					
• Volume of plant and machinery used	1	2	3	4	5
• Operating platform of plant and machinery (i.e.; slope etc.)	1	2	3	4	5
• Site layout	1	2	3	4	5
• Volume of tools used	1	2	3	4	5
• Type of tools used	1	2	3	4	5
Trade score					
9. Works on contaminated sites					
Rate the level of hazard posed by the following parameters in working on contaminated site in this project.					
• Type of contaminants on the site	1	2	3	4	5
• Quantum of contaminants present	1	2	3	4	5
• Duration of work on contaminated site	1	2	3	4	5
Trade score					
10. Welding & hot works					
Rate the level of hazard posed by the following parameters in welding and hot works in this project.					
• Volume of welding & hot works	1	2	3	4	5
• Location of welding (confined spaces, underground, ladders, etc.)	1	2	3	4	5
Trade score					
11. Works in confined spaces					
Rate the level of hazard posed by the following parameters in confined space works in this project.					
• Confined space configuration	1	2	3	4	5
• Type of activity to be involved (e.g. welding, waterproofing etc.)	1	2	3	4	5
• Level of ventilation	1	2	3	4	5
• Current usage of the confined space (if any)	1	2	3	4	5
Trade score					
Total project score (PHI)					

3. Project Safety Index (PSI)

PSI portrays the effectiveness of the site safety management system ($0 \leq PSI \leq 1.00$). If the safety management system is sufficiently robust, the PSI will yield a score of 1.00. Otherwise, it will yield a score of between 0 and 1.00, depending on the degree of safety preparedness of the contractor. The PSI estimation requires an exhaustive safety audit. Eight safety factors and their sub-factors of a construction safety auditing framework were identified in Chapter 4. Based on that, a framework for PSI estimation is proposed as depicted in Table 5.2. It guides in the auditing of each safety factor in detail by scrutinising the sub-factors and their respective safety attributes via the following steps:

- Identifying project safety factors and safety sub-factors from the framework;
- Identifying safety attributes belonging to each safety sub-factor and rating their adequacy in the project assessed;
- Estimating the factorial safety index by analysing and assessing the effect that the rated attributes have on the safety sub-factor and thereby on the safety factor;
- Reiterating the process for all the safety factors in the project; and
- Analysing and aggregating the estimated safety factor indices based on a predetermined safety factor weighting, and deriving the PSI for the project.

Table 5.2. Framework for estimating PSI

Estimating project safety index						
A) Project safety organisation						
Please rate the adequacy of the duties and responsibilities of the following personnel/team in the project safety organisation.	Low				High	
1. Workplace safety and health coordinator	1	2	3	4	5	
2. Workplace safety and health auditor	1	2	3	4	5	
3. Workplace safety and health committee	1	2	3	4	5	
Section score						
B) Risk assessments and management system						
Please rate the adequacy of the following aspects of the risk assessment and management system in the project.	Low				High	
1. Risk assessment team and responsibilities	1	2	3	4	5	
2. Risk assessment procedures	1	2	3	4	5	
3. Reporting procedures to workers of identified risks	1	2	3	4	5	
4. Control measures for risks identified	1	2	3	4	5	
Section score						
C) Safe work practices						
C.1) Work procedures: Please rate the effectiveness of the work methods and procedures for the following trades.	Low			High		
1. Concrete works	1	2	3	4	5	NA
2. Structural steel and pre-cast assembly	1	2	3	4	5	NA
3. Erection and dismantling of scaffolds and false works	1	2	3	4	5	NA
4. Works at heights	1	2	3	4	5	NA

Table 5.2. Continued

Estimating project safety index						
5. Demolition works	1	2	3	4	5	NA
6. Excavation works	1	2	3	4	5	NA
7. Piling operations	1	2	3	4	5	NA
8. Welding and cutting works	1	2	3	4	5	NA
9. Works in confined spaces	1	2	3	4	5	NA
10. Works in toxic/contaminated environments	1	2	3	4	5	NA
11. Use of construction plant such as excavators and trucks	1	2	3	4	5	NA
12. Use of cranes	1	2	3	4	5	NA
13. Electrical installation and use	1	2	3	4	5	NA
Subsection score						
C.2) Permit-to-work (PTW) system: Please rate the effectiveness of the PTW systems for the following trades.	Low				High	
1. Works at heights	1	2	3	4	5	NA
2. Excavation works	1	2	3	4	5	NA
3. Works in confined spaces	1	2	3	4	5	NA
4. Welding and cutting works	1	2	3	4	5	NA
5. Demolition works	1	2	3	4	5	NA
6. Works in toxic/contaminated environments	1	2	3	4	5	NA
Subsection score						
C.3) Personal protective equipment(PPE) use: Please rate the adequacy of the PPE use for the following trades.	Low				High	
1. Concrete works	1	2	3	4	5	NA
2. Structural steel and pre-cast assembly	1	2	3	4	5	NA
3. Erection and dismantling of scaffolds and false works	1	2	3	4	5	NA
4. Works at heights	1	2	3	4	5	NA
5. Demolition works	1	2	3	4	5	NA
6. Excavation works	1	2	3	4	5	NA
7. Piling operations	1	2	3	4	5	NA
8. Welding and cutting works	1	2	3	4	5	NA
9. Works in confined spaces	1	2	3	4	5	NA
10. Works in toxic/contaminated environments	1	2	3	4	5	NA
11. Use of construction plant such as excavators and trucks	1	2	3	4	5	NA
12. Use of cranes	1	2	3	4	5	NA
13. Electrical installation and use	1	2	3	4	5	NA
Subsection score						
Section score						

D) Safety training and competency of people involved						
D.1) Safety training to management team: Please rate the adequacy of the safety training to the following personnel in the project.	Low				High	
1. Demolition works supervisor(s)	1	2	3	4	5	NA
2. Excavation works supervisor(s)	1	2	3	4	5	NA
3. Piling works supervisor(s)	1	2	3	4	5	NA
4. Lifting operations supervisor(s)	1	2	3	4	5	NA
5. Scaffold and/or suspended scaffold supervisor(s)	1	2	3	4	5	NA
6. False works supervisor(s)	1	2	3	4	5	NA
7. Welding and cutting works supervisor(s)	1	2	3	4	5	NA
8. Confined space works supervisor(s)	1	2	3	4	5	NA
9. Toxic/contaminated environment works supervisor(s)	1	2	3	4	5	NA
10. Project management team members	1	2	3	4	5	NA
Subsection score						
D.2) Certification of & safety training to operators: Please rate the adequacy of the certification & safety training of the following operators in the project.	Low				High	
1. Crane erector(s)	1	2	3	4	5	NA
2. Crane operator(s)	1	2	3	4	5	NA
3. Riggers(s)	1	2	3	4	5	NA
4. Signal men	1	2	3	4	5	NA
5. Scaffold erector(s) and/or suspended scaffold rigger(s)	1	2	3	4	5	NA
6. Erectors of hoists and lifts	1	2	3	4	5	NA
7. Operators of hoists and lifts	1	2	3	4	5	NA
8. Operators of plant like excavators, bull dozer, etc.	1	2	3	4	5	NA
9. Construction vehicle drivers	1	2	3	4	5	NA
Subsection score						
D.3) In-house safety training to workers: Please rate the adequacy of the following modules of the in-house safety training to workers in the project.	Low High					
1. Site rules and regulations, and proper use of PPE	1	2	3	4	5	
2. Emergency response for various possible incidents	1	2	3	4	5	
3. First aid procedures	1	2	3	4	5	
4. Safe handling of tools and equipment	1	2	3	4	5	
Subsection score						
Section score						

Table 5.2. Continued

Estimating project safety index						
E) Safety inspection system						
E.1) Inspection of worksite: Please rate the adequacy of the inspection system for the following items in the project.	Low				High	
1. Excavation inspection by a competent person on a daily basis and after hazardous events (e.g. inclement weather)	1	2	3	4	5	NA
2. Scaffolding inspection by a scaffold supervisor on a weekly basis and after inclement weather	1	2	3	4	5	NA
3. False works inspection by a PE or other competent person before, during and after casting and after inclement weather	1	2	3	4	5	NA
4. Demolition inspection by a competent person on a daily basis and after inclement weather	1	2	3	4	5	NA
5. Material loading platform inspection by a competent person on a regular basis and after inclement weather	1	2	3	4	5	NA
6. Inspection of temporary structures such as site office, canteen, site hoardings and concrete batching plant on a regular basis	1	2	3	4	5	NA
7. Inspection of specialised structures or operations like use of customized shoring systems by a competent person	1	2	3	4	5	NA
8. General site inspection by a safety personnel or the site manager	1	2	3	4	5	NA
Sub-section score						
E.2) Housekeeping: Please rate the adequacy of the housekeeping for the following locations/items in the project.	Low				High	
1. Construction worksite	1	2	3	4	5	NA
2. Workers' quarters	1	2	3	4	5	NA
3. Toilets and washing facilities	1	2	3	4	5	NA
4. Canteen or eating places	1	2	3	4	5	NA
5. Site offices	1	2	3	4	5	NA
6. Storages for materials, tools & wastes	1	2	3	4	5	NA
Sub-section score						
Section score						
F) Machinery and tools use and maintenance regime						
F.1) Testing & certification of machinery: Please rate the adequacy of the testing & certification of the following machinery in the project.	Low				High	
1. Lifting gears (12 monthly)	1	2	3	4	5	NA

2.	Lifting appliances (12 monthly)	1	2	3	4	5	NA
3.	Lifting machines (12 monthly)	1	2	3	4	5	NA
4.	Hoists and lifts (6 monthly)	1	2	3	4	5	NA
5.	Air receivers (24 monthly)	1	2	3	4	5	NA
6.	Explosive power tools (36 monthly)	1	2	3	4	5	NA
	Sub-section score						

F.2) Inspection of machinery & tools: Please rate the adequacy of the inspection system for the following machinery in the project.	Low				High	
1. Cranes by crane operators on a daily basis	1	2	3	4	5	NA
2. Electrical distribution board by a competent person on a daily basis	1	2	3	4	5	NA
3. Electrical equipment and tools by a competent person on a regular basis (weekly/more frequent)	1	2	3	4	5	NA
4. Construction vehicles like trucks, forklift, bull dozer, etc. by drivers or a designated person on a daily basis	1	2	3	4	5	NA
5. Temporary electrical installation by a licensed electrical worker	1	2	3	4	5	NA
6. Specialized equipment by a competent person	1	2	3	4	5	NA
Sub-section score						

F.3) Maintenance of machinery: Please rate the adequacy of the maintenance regime for the following machinery in the project.	Low				High	
1. Tower crane(s)	1	2	3	4	5	NA
2. Mobile crane(s)	1	2	3	4	5	NA
3. Gondola(s)	1	2	3	4	5	NA
4. Piling machine(s)	1	2	3	4	5	NA
5. Passenger hoist(s)	1	2	3	4	5	NA
6. Mobile working platform(s)	1	2	3	4	5	NA
7. Construction vehicles like truck, forklift, bulldozer, etc.	1	2	3	4	5	NA
Sub-section score						
Section score						

G) Sub-contractors' safety systems Please rate the adequacy of the following items of sub-contractors in the project.	Low High				
1. Safe work procedures	1	2	3	4	5
2. Safe use of plant, machinery and tools	1	2	3	4	5
3. Safety inspection system	1	2	3	4	5
4. Trained operatives and supervisors	1	2	3	4	5
5. Adherence to safety requirements during construction	1	2	3	4	5
Section score					

Table 5.2. Continued

Estimating project safety index					
H) Emergency management system					
H.1) Emergency response plan: Please rate the adequacy of the emergency response plan for the following emergency scenarios in the project.	Low				High
1. Fire and explosion	1	2	3	4	5
2. Failure and collapse of structures/temporary supports	1	2	3	4	5
3. Failure and collapse of heavy machinery and equipment	1	2	3	4	5
4. Leakage of hazardous substances	1	2	3	4	5
5. Adverse weather and flooding	1	2	3	4	5
Sub-section score					
H.2) Emergency response team: Please rate the adequacy, competency and set-responsibilities of the following emergency response team members for various emergency scenarios in the project.	Low High				
1. Emergency coordinator(s)	1	2	3	4	5
2. Site safety personnel	1	2	3	4	5
3. Designated rescuer(s)	1	2	3	4	5
4. First-aider(s)	1	2	3	4	5
5. Specialist operators(s)	1	2	3	4	5
Sub-section score					
H.3) Emergency equipment: Please rate the adequacy of the emergency response equipment and facilities for the following emergency scenarios in the project.	Low High				
1. Fire and explosion	1	2	3	4	5
2. Failure and collapse of structures/temporary supports	1	2	3	4	5
3. Failure and collapse of heavy machinery and equipment	1	2	3	4	5
4. Leakage of hazardous substances	1	2	3	4	5
5. Adverse weather and flooding	1	2	3	4	5
Sub-section score					
Section score					

Computing the Mark-up

The derivation of the mark-up *(K)* is performed by assessing five variables: (1) overhead costs of the policy; (2) investment income from the underwritten premium; (3) corporate objective(s); (4) competition; and (5) contractor's claims history. The formula for K is written as:

$$K = f_b \begin{pmatrix} Overhead\ costs, Investment\ income, \\ Corporate\ objectives, Competition, Claims\ history \end{pmatrix} \qquad (5)$$

Akin to the risk rate formula, this formula is also translated into a fuzzy algorithm, which is discussed in detail in Chapter seven.

Computing the $CCI_{Contractor}$ and the SMD_{Client}

The $CCI_{Contractor}$ and the SMD_{Client} are claims experiential incentives proposed for the contractor and the client, respectively. These are introduced in the model as a strategy to control accidents on site and thereby workers' compensation claims for the insurer. As described in the preceding part, the $CCI_{contractor}$ is presented to the contractor at policy expiry for controlling the claims so that the actual claims amount is less than the predicted claims in the project. The SMD_{client} is likewise presented to the client at policy expiry for monitoring the contractor's safety management on site, which minimised accidents. Both the $CCI_{Contractor}$ and the SMD_{Client} are preferred to be equal amounts, and the following algorithm produces the respective amounts.

If "$TAC < C$" Then
$CCI_{Contractor} = SMD_{Client} = \left[0.5 \times \alpha \times (C - TAC) \right]$ Else
$CCI_{Contractor} = SMD_{Client} = 0$

Where:
TAC =   Total of actual claims incurred in the project; and
α =   The discounting factor; the α value is at the discretion of the insurer and it may equate to 2/3, 1/2 or as the case may be. If an insurer chooses 2/3 for α, for example, this implies that the insurer is willing to share the savings equally among the insurer, the client and the contractor.

The insurer, the contractor or the client will not know the amounts for the $CCI_{Contractor}$ and the SMD_{Client} at the policy underwriting stage. However, the contractor and the client must be informed about the discount/incentive scheme so that they will be motivated to execute the implemented safety management system effectively on site.

Advantages of the Proposed New Model

The proposed new model advocates the partnering arrangement in WCI for construction projects. According to the proposed model, the WCI premium has three components: (1) risk fee; (2) claim control incentive ($CCI_{contractor}$); and (3) safety monitoring discount (SMD_{client}).

The risk fee is the price for assuming the risks inherent in the project, which is to be paid at the underwriting stage. The $CCI_{contractor}$ is an incentive for the contractor and the SMD_{client} is a discount for the client for their efforts to minimise accidents, which are to be paid to them by the insurer at the policy expiration stage. By adopting this strategy, the proposed model pulls all the parties to WCI with a monetary steer to ensure a safe workplace. This will eventually pave the way to reduce construction accidents and thereby insurers' losses.

The proposed model is more advanced than the EMR approach in the following aspects:

1. It assesses the real-time status of hazards and safety in a project whereas EMR is a lagging indicator;
2. Unlike EMR, the risk indicator (risk rate) in this model is not misled by the project size, wage roll or the experience of the contractor;
3. The utilisation of EMR needs such published data as manual rates, ballast values and weighting factors whereas the proposed model is independent of any external data;
4. Unlike the EMR approach, the proposed model establishes an effective risk control strategy via a structured incentive scheme; and
5. The EMR approach is silent with respect to the determination of the mark-up, but the proposed model incorporates a structured method.

Unlike the static benchmark approach exploited in the Singapore insurance market, the proposed model proves to have a strong scientific basis, and takes into account the dynamic factors in the marketplace. As opposed to the 1% of wage roll benchmark, the mean claims unit cost used in the proposed model allows insurance companies to determine their own benchmarks and break-even points independently based on their experiences. This also provides insurance companies with the flexibility to make adjustments to the break-even rate continually from time to time or from project to project. The existence of PHI and PSI estimation frameworks in the model set clearly defined protocols for assessing the risk in a given project. Additionally, the model functions in line with the philosophy of the new Workplace Safety and Health Act 2006 in Singapore whereby everyone in the supply chain must involve in ensuring safety on construction sites. The model demonstrates to have the capacity to move the Singapore insurance market from the current gray practices to a crystal clear arena. With the model in place in the general insurance industry, insurance companies would be able to make informed business decisions.

Conclusion

This chapter proposed a new premium rating model for building construction projects. As per the new model, the WCI premium for a construction project has three components: (1) *risk fee* - paid by the contractor at the underwriting stage, and subsequently reimbursed by the project owner, for the risk inherent in the project; (2) $CCI_{contractor}$ – to be rewarded to the contractor by the insurer at policy expiration if the claims were below the predicted amount; and (3) SMD_{client} – to be rewarded to the project client by the insurer at policy expiration if the client had monitored the contractor's safety level so as to minimise accidents during the course of construction. The *risk fee* is computed by: (1) predicting the potential claims in the project by assessing the wage roll, project hazard level and the project safety level; and (2) marking-up the predicted claims value to account for insurer's overhead costs, corporate objectives, investment income, competition, and contractors' claims history. The amounts for $CCI_{contractor}$ and SMD_{client} are founded on the total amount of actual claims in the project. If the total actual claims are lesser than the predicted claims at the underwriting stage, the saving will be shared by the insurer with the contractor and the client. This way, the proposed model: (1) advocates the partnering arrangement in construction WCI; (2) promotes accident control through monetary incentives; and (3) functions in line with the philosophy of the new Workplace Safety and Health Act 2006 of Singapore. Moreover, the proposed new model eliminates the drawbacks of the EMR approach for WCI premium rating.

In order to practically implement the proposed model in the insurance industry, it needs to be presented to the audience in a tangible format. The model is therefore translated into a fuzzy KBS. While the next chapter discusses how fuzzy systems can be practically applied to insurance premium rating, Chapter 7 elaborates the process involved in automating the proposed model into a fuzzy KBS.

Chapter VI

Fuzzy Inference System
Development Methodologies

Introduction

The first chapter of this book unveiled that automating the new WCI model into a fuzzy inference system would address the cumbersomeness associated with risks assessment and premium rating. Presumably most readers in insurance and construction domains have limited understanding of fuzzy inference systems, and therefore this chapter aims to enrich their understanding. Firstly, an introduction to fuzzy sets and fuzzy logic is given wherein the concepts of fuzzy sets, membership functions, linguistics variables, fuzzy rules and fuzzy inference systems are described. Subsequently, the development steps of fuzzy inference systems are explored in detail with examples from insurance. This chapter provides a non-technical introduction to fuzzy set mathematics, fuzzy logic and fuzzy inference systems. Rather than focusing on mathematical details, the chapter concentrates on making the concept as clear as possible for readers.

Classical Set Theory

The notion of set occurs frequently in our life as we tend to organise, summarise and generalise knowledge about objects in the environment. It would be fair to say that the fundamental nature of human beings is to organise, arrange, and systematically classify information about the diversity of objects in any environment. The encapsulation of objects into a collection whose members all share some general properties naturally implies the notion of a set. Sets are used often and almost unconsciously in our everyday life; for example, *Year 1 students* in Construction Management Program at UNSW. In this expression the part *"Year 1 students"* implies a set. The universe (also known as the universe of discourse) for this set is *"all students in construction management program at UNSW"*.

Sets are conventionally denoted with capital letters. For the example above we can name the set, *Year 1 students* in Construction Management Program at UNSW, as *A*. The universe may be named as *X*. If John is a year 1 student of construction management program at UNSW, he is an element/member of set A; so, John $\in$ *A*. Likewise, if Mary is a year 2 student, she is not a member of set A; so, Mary $\notin$ *A*. This classification can be expressed in a characteristic (membership) function as illustrated in Figure 6.1. In Figure 6.1, the horizontal axis represents the universe of discourse of "students in construction management program at UNSW", which John and Mary belong to. The part shown by a parallel arrow line represents the set "year 1 students", which John belongs to. Since John is a member of the set "year 1 students", the membership grade for John is equal to 1. Likewise, Mary is not a member of "year 1 students" and her membership grade is 0. In other words: consider the question "*is Alfred a year 1 student?*" There can be only one of two possible answers; either *yes* or *no*. If the answer is *yes* then the membership grade for Alfred is 1, and if otherwise, the membership grade is 0. Intuitively, sets introduce a fundamental notion of *dichotomy*. The membership function for this set can be defined as follows:

$$\mu_A(x) = \begin{cases} 1 & \text{if } x \in A \\ 0 & \text{otherwise} \end{cases}$$

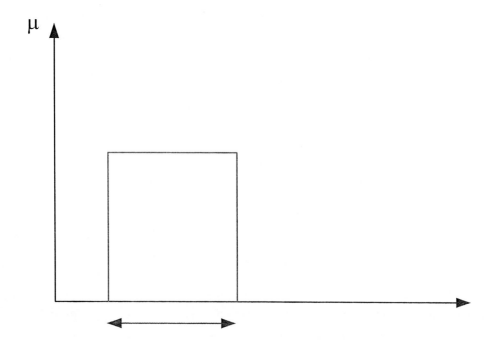

Figure 6.1. Example of a membership function

In the classical set theory $\mu_A(x)$ has only the values 0 (``false") and 1 (``true"), thus the two values of truth. Such sets are also called *crisp sets*. The function induces a constraint, with a well-defined boundary, on the objects of a universe *X* that may be assigned to a set *A*.

Limitations of Classical Set Theory

There are a great number of situations in real life in which we have to choose between mutually exclusive alternatives (binary values). For example, *does contractor X undertake piling works?* The answer to this question will be either "*yes*" or "*no*" depending on contractor X's association/membership to the category of contractors (a "set" of contractors) in the national registry of contractors (the "universal set" of contractors). There are also situations whereby we make decisions using binary logic. For example, *if it is a sunny day, go to the beach.* This concept of Boolean answers and Boolean reasoning is well-handled by classical set and probability theories. However, in everyday life we encounter scenarios that cannot be dealt with satisfactorily on a simple "*yes*" or "*no*" basis. Consider the example of categorising people as *tall* and *not tall*. Let us fix that anybody who exceeds 2.0m height is considered *tall*. According to the dichotomy principle for this set, others will be considered *not tall*. If Alex is 1.9m, is he tall or not tall? According to the crisp set categorisation above, Alex will be classified as *not tall*. However, in real life this argument may not be realistic. Therefore, it can be best indicated by a shade of gray, rather than by the black or white of a simple dichotomy. Classical set theory is incapable of handling this kind of vagueness. In 1965, Zadeh suggested an extension to set theory namely "fuzzy set" to best deal with vagueness in data (Zadeh, 1965). Fuzzy set theory provides a mathematical toolbox for analysing situations like this with precision, not via a definite cut-off, but by defining a degree of membership between the qualitatively different states of definitely *tall* and definitely *not tall*. In fuzzy set theory, an individual member could have a degree of membership to a set which ranges over a continuum of values, rather than being either 0 or 1. That is: in a crisp set the degree of membership of a member is either 1 or 0, but in a fuzzy set it is expressed as $0 \leq$ degree of membership ≤ 1.0. For the example above, the membership functions for *tall* and *not tall* in both crisp set and fuzzy set are depicted in Figure 6.2. In the crisp set, Alex definitely belongs to *not tall* set whereas in the fuzzy set Alex belongs to *not tall* set with a membership degree of 0.2 and to *tall* set with a membership degree of 0.8. The underlying concept of fuzzy sets is to relax the membership requirement and admit intermediate values of class members.

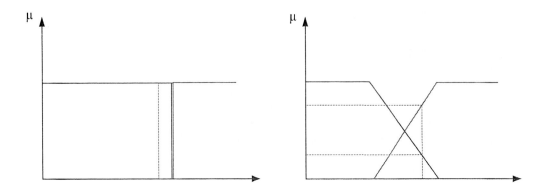

Figure 6.2. (a) Crisp set for Tall; (b) Fuzzy set for Tall

The human reasoning scheme inherits two important characteristics. Firstly, the human mind tends to use a series of ambiguous, imprecise and qualitative terms and logics. For example, *if the weather is bad and the speed of the car is high then apply the brake hard.* The human mind can correctly interpret this kind of terms and logics using its context without any problems. The second characteristic is the human ability to extract correct conclusions from this imprecise information by means of approximate reasoning. Zadeh extended fuzzy set theory and developed an inference technique, namely "fuzzy logic", for modelling the vagueness present in natural language, and for emulating the approximate reasoning mechanism used by the human brain.

Fuzzy Sets

A fuzzy set is defined as a collection of objects with membership values between 0 (complete exclusion) and 1 (complete membership). The membership values express the degree to which each object is *compatible* with the properties or features distinctive to the collection. For instance, consider the concept of *high* temperature in an environmental context with temperatures distributed in the interval [0, 50] defined in °C. Clearly 0°C is not understood as a high temperature value, and we may assign a null value to express its degree of compatibility with the *high* temperature concept. In other words: the membership degree of 0°C in the class of high temperature is zero. We may consider 10°C and below are not *high* temperatures, and we may assign a value of 0 to express its degree of compatibility with the concept. Likewise, 30°C and over are certainly *high* temperatures, and we may assign a value of 1 to express a full degree of compatibility with the *high* temperature concept. Therefore, temperature values in the range [30, 50] have a membership value of 1 in the class of high temperatures. The partial quantification of belongingness for the remaining temperature values through their membership values can be pursued as exemplified in Figure 6.3, which actually is a membership function $H: T{\rightarrow}[0,1]$ characterising the fuzzy set H of high temperatures in the universe $T = [0,50]$.

In mathematical terms, a fuzzy set is characterised by a mapping from its universe of discourse into the interval [0, 1]. This mapping is the *membership function* of the set. The notation for the membership function of a fuzzy set A of a given universal base set X is:

$$\mu_A : X \rightarrow [0,1]$$

A fuzzy set A in X is usually represented as a set of ordered pairs of elements and their grade of membership values:

$$A = \left\{ \left(x_i, \mu_A(x_i) \right) / x_i \in X \right\}$$

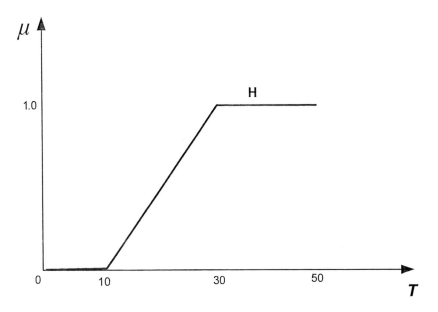

Figure 6.3. Membership function of *"High temperature"*

When X is continuous, a fuzzy set A can be written concisely as:

$$A = \int x_i \, \mu_A(x_i)/x_i$$

When X is discrete, a fuzzy set A is represented as:

$$A = \sum \mu_A(x_i)/x_i$$

or

$$A = \mu_A(x_1)/x_1 + \mu_A(x_2)/x_2 + \ldots\ldots\ldots + \mu_A(x_i)/x_i + \ldots\ldots + \mu_A(x_n)/x_n$$

Where: x_i is an element/member in the fuzzy set A and $\mu_A(x_i)$ is the membership grade for element x_i in the fuzzy set.

In the above, "+", "Σ" and "$\int$" refer to a set union rather than to arithmetic summation and integration, and "/" is simply used to connect an element and its membership value, and has no connection with arithmetic division.

Let us relate this to the above high temperature example for easy understanding. Temperatures 30 and over have membership grades of 1, and temperatures 10 and below have membership grades of 0. As we can deduce from the membership function illustrated in Figure 6.3, temperature values 15, 20 and 25 have membership grades of 0.25, 0.50 and 0.75, respectively. That is,

$\mu(0) = 0$, $\mu(10) = 0$, $\mu(15) = 0.25$, $\mu(20) = 0.50$, $\mu(25) = 0.75$, $\mu(30) = 1$, $\mu(50) = 1$.

This can be represented as follows mathematically:

$$H = 0/0 + 0/10 + 0.25/15 + 0.50/20 + 0.75/25 + 1/30 + 1/50$$

Fuzzy Membership Functions

The membership function $\mu_A(x)$ describes the membership of element x of the base set X in fuzzy set A, whereby for $\mu_A(x)$, a large class of functions can be taken. A case is shown in Figure 6.4. The grade of membership $\mu_A(x_o)$ of membership function $\mu_A(x)$ describes the special element $x = x_o$, to what grade it belongs to fuzzy set A. This value is in the unit interval [0, 1]. The element x_0 can simultaneously belong to another fuzzy set B, such that $\mu_B(x_o)$ characterises the grade of membership of x_o to B.

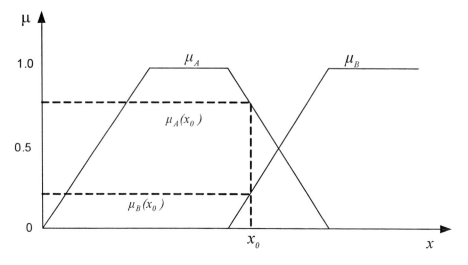

Figure 6.4. Membership grades of x_0 in the sets A and B: $\mu_A(x_o) = 0.75$ and $\mu_B(x_o) = 0.25$.

A set of important properties of fuzzy sets are described below.

- Having two fuzzy sets A and B based on X then both are *equal* if their membership functions are equal, i.e.

$$A = B \Leftrightarrow \mu_A(x) = \mu_B(x), \quad x \in X$$

- The *universal set* U is defined as

$$\mu_u(x) = 1, \quad x \in X$$

- The *height* of a fuzzy set A is the largest membership grade obtained by any element in that set, i.e.

$$hgt(A) = \sup_{x \in X} \mu_A(x)$$

- A fuzzy set A is called *normal* when $hgt(A)=1$, and it is *subnormal* when $hgt(A)<1$.
- An illustration is shown in Figure 6.5, wherein the *support* of a fuzzy set A is the crisp set that contains all the elements of X that have non-zero membership grades in A, i.e.

$$supp(A) = \{x \in X \,/\, \mu_A(x) > 0\}$$

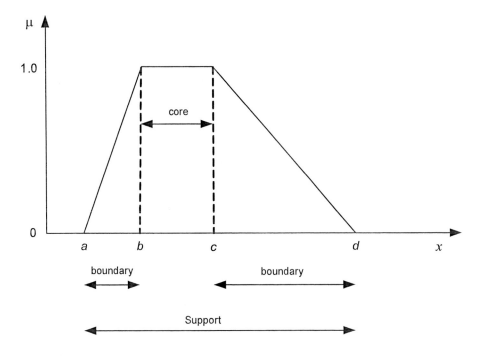

Figure 6.5. Characteristics of a membership function.

- The *core* of a normal fuzzy set A is the crisp set that contains all the elements of X that have the membership grades of 1 in A, i.e.

$$core(A) = \{x \in X \,/\, \mu_A(x) = 1\}$$

- The *boundary* is the crisp set that contains all the elements of X that have the membership grades of $0 < \mu_A(x) < 1$ in A, i.e.

$$bnd(A) = \{x \in X \,/\, 0 < \mu_A(x) < 1\}$$

- Having two fuzzy sets A and B based on X, then both are *similar* if

  core (A) = core (B) and supp (A) = supp (B)
- If the support of a normal fuzzy set consists of a single element x_0 of X, which has the property

  supp (A) = core (A) = $\{x_0\}$

  This set is called a *singleton*.

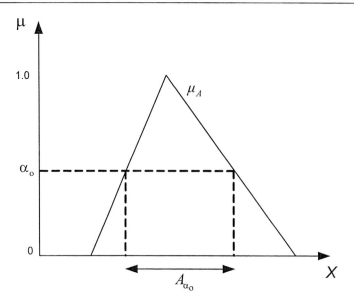

Figure 6.6. α -cut of a fuzzy set.

- α- cut (also called α- level) of a fuzzy set A at α_0, denoted as $A\alpha_0$, is the set of elements whose degree of membership in A is no less than α_0. Mathematically, the α - cut of a fuzzy set A in X is defined as:

$$A\alpha_0 = \{x \in X / \mu_A(x) \geq \alpha_0\}$$

Figure 6.6 graphically illustrates the α -cut.

- The cardinality of a set is the total number of elements in the set. Since an element can partially belong to a fuzzy set, a natural generalisation of the classical notion of cardinality is to weigh each element by its membership degree as given by the following formula:

$$Card\ (A) = \sum_{x_i} \mu_A(x_i)$$

Types of Membership Functions

Five types of membership functions are most often used in practical applications: (1) triangular function; (2) trapezoidal function; (3) Z-function; (4) Gaussian function; and (5) S-function. Whether a particular type is suitable can be determined only in the application context.

1. Triangular membership function:

A triangular membership function (see Figure 6.7) is specified by three parameters {a, b, c} as follows:

$$triangle \quad (x : a, b, c) = \begin{cases} 0 & x < a \\ (x - a)/(b - a) & a \leq x \leq b \\ (c - x)/(c - b) & b \leq x \leq c \\ 0 & x > c \end{cases}$$

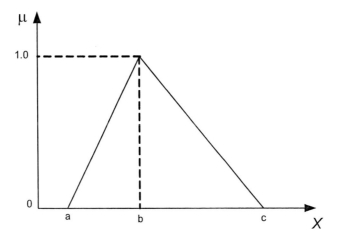

Figure 6.7. Triangular membership function

2. Trapezoidal membership function:

A trapezoidal membership function (see Figure 6.8) is specified by four parameters {a, b, c, d} as follows:

$$trapezoid \quad (x : a, b, c, d) = \begin{cases} 0 & x < a \\ (x - a)/(b - a) & a \leq x \leq b \\ 1 & b \leq x \leq c \\ (d - x)/(d - c) & c \leq x \leq d \\ 0 & x \geq d \end{cases}$$

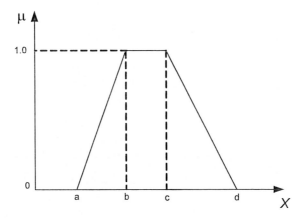

Figure 6.8. Trapezoidal membership function

3. S-membership function:

An S-membership function (see Figure 6.9) is specified with two parameters $\{a, b\}$ as follows:

$$S(x : a, b) = \begin{cases} 0 & x < a \\[2mm] 2\left(\dfrac{x-a}{b-a}\right)^2 & a \le x \le \dfrac{a+b}{2} \\[3mm] 1 - 2\left(\dfrac{x-a}{b-a}\right)^2 & \dfrac{a+b}{2} \le x < b \\[3mm] 1 & x \ge b \end{cases}$$

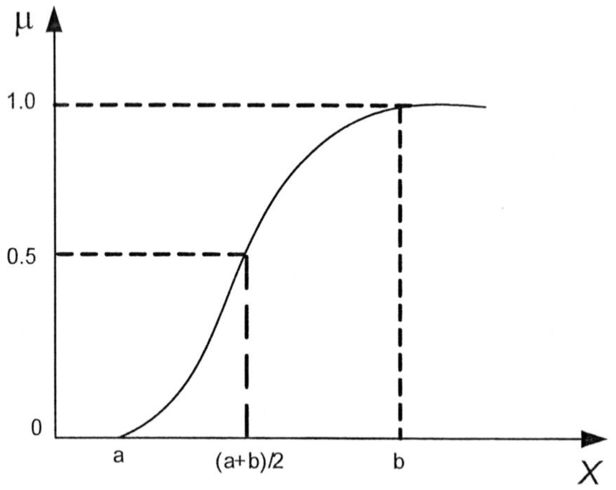

Figure 6.9. S-membership function

4. Gaussian membership function:

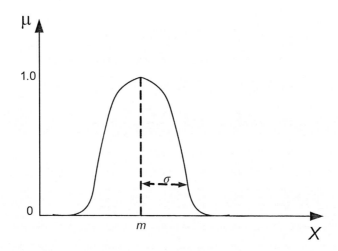

Figure 6.10. Gaussian membership function

A Gaussian membership function (see Figure 6.10) is specified with two parameters $\{m,\sigma\}$ as follows:

$$gaussian(x : m, \sigma) = exp\left(-\frac{(x-m)^2}{\sigma^2}\right)$$

Where: m and σ denote the centre and width of the function, respectively.

5. Z-membership function:

A Z-membership function (see Figure 6.11) is specified with two parameters $\{a, b\}$ as follows:

$$S(x : a, b) = \begin{cases} 1 & x < a \\ 1 - 2\left(\dfrac{x-a}{b-a}\right)^2 & a \le x \le \dfrac{a+b}{2} \\ 2\left(b - \dfrac{x}{b-a}\right)^2 & \dfrac{a+b}{2} \le x < b \\ 0 & x \ge b \end{cases}$$

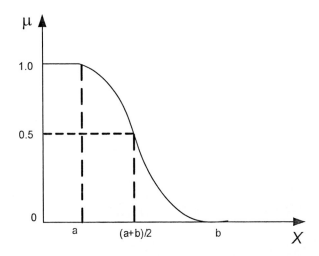

Figure 6.11. Z-membership function

Basic Operations of Fuzzy Sets

The basic connective operations in classical set theory are those of intersection, union and complement. These operations on characteristic functions can be generalised into fuzzy sets in more than one way.

- The *fuzzy intersection* operator ∩ (fuzzy AND connective) applied to two fuzzy sets A and B with the membership functions $\mu_A(x)$ and $\mu_B(x)$ is

$$\mu_{A \cap B}(x) = min\{\mu_A(x), \mu_B(x)\}, \qquad x \in X$$

- The *fuzzy union* operator ∪ (fuzzy OR connective) applied to two fuzzy sets A and B with the membership functions $\mu_A(x)$ and $\mu_B(x)$ is

$$\mu_{A \cup B}(x) = max\{\mu_A(x), \mu_B(x)\}, \qquad x \in X$$

- The *fuzzy complement* (fuzzy NOT operation) applied to the fuzzy set A with the membership function $\mu_A(x)$ is

$$\mu_{\bar{A}}(x) = 1 - \mu_A(x), \qquad x \in X$$

- The *fuzzy intersection* operator ∩ (fuzzy AND connective) can be represented as the *algebraic product* of two fuzzy sets A and B, which is defined as the multiplication of their membership functions:

$$\mu_{A \cap B}(x) = \mu_A(x)\mu_B(x), \qquad x \in X$$

- The *fuzzy union* operator ∪ (fuzzy OR connective) can be represented as the *algebraic sum* of two fuzzy sets A and B, which is defined as:

$$\mu_{A \cup B}(x) = \mu_A(x) + \mu_B(x) - \mu_A(x)\mu_B(x), \qquad x \in X$$

Linguistic Variables

Linguistic variables are variables whose values are words or sentences rather than numbers. For instance, when we refer to environmental conditions, we may express our observations by statements like *cold, warm* or *hot*. These terms translate the various states of temperature in the interval 0-50 °C. Alternatively, *temperature* could be quantified (coded) using labels such as *cold, warm* and *hot,* and therefore is a linguistic variable. Linguistic characterisations are less specific than numerical, but it would certainly be much safer unless one actually knew the exact temperature.

The concept of linguistic variables is fundamental within fuzzy set theory. Intuitively, each linguistic variable represents a universal set and the different linguistic terms are fuzzy sets in the universal set. The different terms or linguistic values are represented with fuzzy sets, characterised by membership functions defined on the universe of discourse (Baturone *et al.*, 2000). Hence, a linguistic variable is characterised by four elements: (1) name; (2) set of linguistic labels or values the variable can take; (3) universe of discourse where the variable is defined; and (4) semantic rules associating each linguistic label with a fuzzy set defined on the universe of discourse. For instance, the four characteristics of the linguistic variable *temperature* are as follows:

- Name: *Temperature*;
- Set of linguistic values: *Cold, Warm, Hot*;
- Universe of discourse: *range 0 –50 °C*; and
- Fuzzy sets for linguistic values: *corresponding fuzzy sets (membership functions) for the linguistic values are shown in Figure 6.12.*

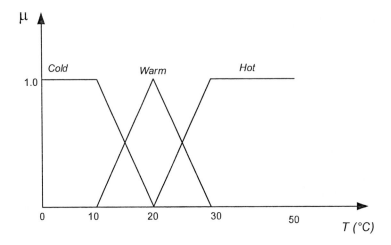

Figure 6.12. Fuzzy sets for a linguistic variable

Another example for a linguistic variable might be *speed*, whose members are *slow, medium* and *fast*, and whose membership functions (fuzzy sets) are shown in Figure 6.13.

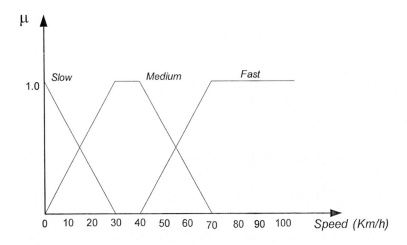

Figure 6.13. Membership functions of linguistic variable speed

Linguistic variables are an essential ingredient in approximate reasoning. The motivations for using linguistic variables in approximate reasoning are:

1. Linguistic variables may be regarded as a form of information compression called granulation (Zadeh, 1994);
2. They serve as a means of approximate characterisation of phenomena that are either too ill-defined, too complex, or both, to permit a description in sharp terms (Zadeh, 1975); and
3. They provide a means for translating linguistic descriptions into numerical and computable ones. Therefore, the duality between symbolic and numerical processing becomes natural instead of antagonistic.

Fuzzy Logic and Approximate Reasoning

Most construction tasks necessitate problem-solving or decision-making capabilities that involve reasoning as an essential part of the effort. Reasoning is the ability to infer information about some unknown facets of a problem based on the available information about domain knowledge. For instance, reasoning is performed when a safety officer attempts to infer the occupational hazards in scaffolding based on the flaws observable in its parts and design. When making decisions, often we perform subjective assessments and qualitative judgments. While we are able to make decisions with linguistic terms of variables, our brain can process these linguistic and subjective descriptions without any difficulty. For example, the sentences *"Take a pinch of salt"* and *"If the wall is not far away and the speed of the car is high then apply the brake hard"* can be understood and reacted on by us without any problem. Conventional computing has limitations to incorporate this pattern of brain processing in decision-making. However, fuzzy logic provides with the tools to handle this successfully. Fuzzy logic is basically a multi-valued logic that allows intermediate values to be defined between conventional evaluations like yes/no, true/false, black/white, etc. Notions like rather warm or pretty cold can be formulated mathematically and algorithmically processed. In this way an attempt is made to apply a more human-like way of thinking in the programming of computers, which is called soft computing. Fuzzy logic involves the manipulation of fuzzy values (linguistic values) defined as fuzzy sets over the interval [0, 1] for drawing conclusions (Yan *et al.*, 1994). Fuzzy sets and fuzzy operators are the subjects and verbs of fuzzy logic, which are represented as fuzzy if-then rules. A fuzzy if-then rule associates a *condition* described using linguistic variables and fuzzy sets to a *conclusion*. An example of a fuzzy rule (fuzzy logic) is as follows:

IF project scope is *large* AND contract duration is *long* THEN risk exposure is *high.*

This particular rule has two antecedent variables (project scope and contract duration) connected by operator "AND" and one consequent variable (risk exposure). A fuzzy if-then rule is a scheme for capturing human knowledge that involves imprecision or vagueness, which also enables inferences to be made. In effect, the use of linguistic variables and fuzzy if-then rules exploits the tolerance for imprecision and uncertainty. In this respect, fuzzy logic mimics the crucial ability of the human mind to summarise data and focus on decision-relevant information. Moreover, the use of fuzzy logic simplifies the development of an inference system with the following features (Yan et al., 1995):

1. Sophisticated knowledge and rich human experiences can be incorporated into the fuzzy knowledge base in an almost natural language;
2. The incorporated knowledge is not necessarily precise and complete;
3. The input facts to be assessed in a fuzzy inference are neither necessarily clear-cut, nor do they have to match the given knowledge exactly; and
4. Partially-matched conclusions can be inferred from fuzzy facts and the established fuzzy knowledge base.

Owing to these advanced qualities, fuzzy inference systems are in wide use in fields such as automatic control, data classification, decision analysis, and computer vision.

Fuzzy Inference Systems

A fuzzy inference system comprises a set of rules that employ linguistic terms similar to those used in natural language, and an inference mechanism that is able to extract correct conclusions from approximate data (Baturone *et al.,* 2000). A fuzzy system essentially includes the blocks shown in Figure 6.14. The kernel of the system is a knowledge base that contains the definition of membership functions for the antecedents and consequents used in rules, and an inference engine that is able to process this information according to a predefined mechanism of inference. Apart from these basic elements, it is necessary to include two interface blocks connecting the inference engine with the inputs and the outputs of the system. These blocks are termed as fuzzifier and defuzzifier, respectively.

In case of an inference:

1. The fuzzifier is in charge of accepting the inputs to the inference system, and evaluating the similarity degree between these inputs and the linguistic labels used in the rule antecedents;
2. The inference engine of the fuzzy system evaluates the different rules in the knowledge base. The activation degree of each rule is calculated from the activation degree of its antecedents and according to the interpretation of the different connectives in use. From this point, the output of each rule is calculated applying the activation degree to the consequent by means of the implication function; and
3. Finally, the conclusions of the different rules are combined by the aggregation operator and the defuzzifier is used to provide the output of the inference system. The output of the inference is a fuzzy set and this is defuzzifed into a crisp value by the defuzzifier.

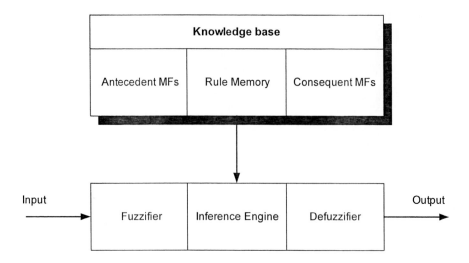

Figure 6.14. Basic structure of a fuzzy inference system (Baturone *et al.,* 2000. p. 40)

Fuzzy Inference Systems Development Cycle

Essentially, there are six fundamental stages in the construction of a fuzzy inference system, as illustrated in Figure 6.15. These steps are elaborated below in detail with a case example for easy understanding.

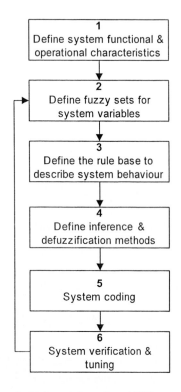

Figure 6.15. Fuzzy system development cycle (Adapted from Cox, 1999)

Defining System Functional and Operational Characteristics

The first step in designing a fuzzy system involves defining three elements, viz.:

- What data will flow into the system (input variables)?
- What transformations are performed on the input data?
- What information elements are eventually output from the system?

These are explained in the case example below.

Case Example

Consider a fuzzy inference system to compute health insurance premiums. Suppose the premium amount is decided based on two variables; age and health status of applicants. If we are to develop a fuzzy system for this function, the functional characteristic of the system can be defined as: *the system will determine an optimal premium by assessing an applicant's age and health status.* Figure 6.16 illustrates a simple model that portrays this function.

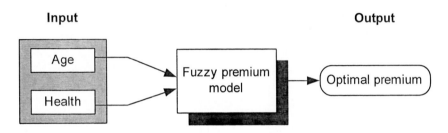

Figure 6.16. Fuzzy premium model - case example

Defining Fuzzy Sets for System Variables

The second step of fuzzy system development involves defining and constructing the fuzzy sets for input and output variables. Three sub-steps are involved in performing this task, viz.:

- Selecting linguistic labels and therefore the number of membership functions to be used for each variable;
- Choosing the type of membership function to be used; and
- Selecting the application range in the universe of discourse for each membership function (distributing different fuzzy sets along the universe of discourse).

The linguistic labels and the numbers will depend on the application context of the fuzzy system. Most of the practical applications reported in the literature used between three and seven labels per linguistic variable. This choice has a double motivation: (1) increasing the number of antecedent labels implies increasing the number of rules, complicating system implementation and slowing down its operation; and (2) when the number of labels and rules exceed a certain threshold, the linguistic significance of the rules is lost.

Five types of membership functions that are most often used in practical fuzzy applications were described in the preceding section. A suitable type of membership function needs to be chosen depending on the application and implementation of the fuzzy system.

Once the number and shape of the membership functions have been decided, the remaining issue is the distribution of the different fuzzy sets along the universe of discourse in which the variable is defined. There are four methods to derive the application range in the universe of discourse for variables. These are:

i.   Probability frequency distribution;
ii. Neural network models;
iii. Mathematical surface sampling; and
iv. Subjective approximation.

Out of these four methods, subjective approximation is the "best guess" theory and corresponds to the way experts and experienced design engineers develop fuzzy systems. Moreover, fuzzy models are very tolerant of approximate fuzzy sets. Hence, this method remains the best in terms of opportunity costs and the easiest way to design and implement fuzzy systems (Cox, 1999).

Each fuzzy set must overlap its neighbouring sets to some degree. However, there is no precise algorithm for determining the minimum or maximum degree of overlap. Experience dictates that the overlap for triangle-to-triangle and trapezoid-to-triangle fuzzy regions averages somewhere between 25% and 50% of the fuzzy set base (Cox, 1999). After analysing several authors, Driankov *et al.* (1993) proposed that the crossing point for two overlapping membership functions must be 50% for control applications and a little lower for classifiers and others.

Case Example (Cont'd)

The health insurance premium example is continued to demonstrate this step as well as the subsequent steps of fuzzy systems development. From experts' experience, it is identified that the input and the output variables can be linguistically termed as follows:

- Age: *youthful, young, middle aged, mature, old*;
- Health status: *excellent, good, average, below average, poor*; and
- Premium: *very low, low, moderately low, moderate, moderately high, high, very high*.

Subsequently, triangular membership functions are chosen for each variable. Figure 6.17 illustrates the arrangement of the fuzzy sets along their respective universes of discourse.

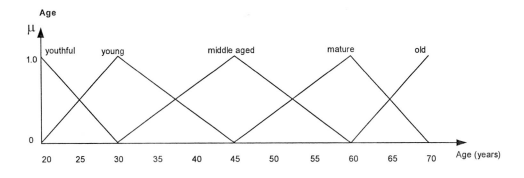

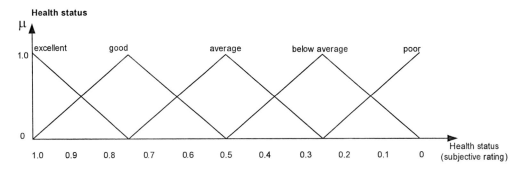

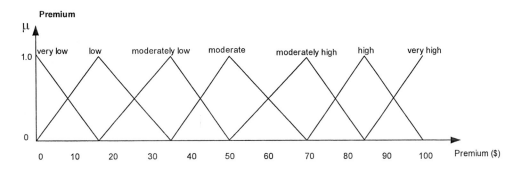

Figure 6.17. Membership functions - case example

Defining the Fuzzy Rule Base

A rule base describes the behaviour of a fuzzy inference system, based on the linguistic terms associated with the input and output variables. The procedures for obtaining the rules of a fuzzy system should be based on either of these mechanisms (Baturone *et al.,* 2000):

- From the knowledge of experts who are trying to express their knowledge about the problem in terms of common sense rules that can be further refined by some tuning procedures; or
- From data corresponding to a correct behaviour, analysing the actions of experts to extract general rules from their responses to particular cases.

Traditionally, rules development for a fuzzy system follows intersection rule configuration (IRC) approach. Under this method, the number of rules in a fuzzy system depends on the number of inputs and on the number of labels. That is, in the health insurance premium example above, there are two input variables and each input variable is described by five labels. Thus, according to the IRC method, the system will need 5^2 rules. When the number of input variables increased, the required number of rules increases exponentially in this approach. For example, if the above fuzzy premium system had four input variables then the rules would have been increased to 5^4, making the system complex and slowing down the inference. This problem is termed as "curse of dimensionality" or "combinatorial rule explosion". Combs and Andrews (1998) introduced an alternative rule configuration methodology, called union rule configuration (URC), which eliminates the combinatorial rule explosion problem. Under this method also the number of rules in a fuzzy system depends on the number of input variables and on the number of labels. However, the total number of rules is reduced considerably. That is, according to the URC method, in the health insurance premium example above, the system will need 5x2 rules. When the number of input variables increased, the required number of rules does not increase exponentially in this approach. For example, if the fuzzy premium system above had four input variables then the rules would have been increased to 5x4.

Case Example (Cont'd)

The development of rules for the premium example is described based on both the IRC and URC approaches.

IRC Approach

The first step is to make a premium matrix of the input variables as depicted in Figure 6.18. The premium matrix places the "health status" along the vertical axis and the "age" along the horizontal axis. The matrix provides one empty cell for each age-health status combination. Each cell contains a fuzzy output value, though not all need to be filled in. Thus, the premium matrix is filled with a suitable linguistic premium value to each age-health status combination.

Age / Health status	Youthful	Young	Middle-aged	Mature	Old
Excellent	(1) Very low	(6) Low	(11) Mod. low	(16) Mod. low	(21) Moderate
Good	(2) Low	(7) Mod. low	(12) Mod. low	(17) Moderate	(22) Mod. high
Average	(3) Mod. low	(8) Mod. low	(13) Moderate	(18) Mod. high	(23) Mod. high
Below average	(4) Mod. low	(9) Moderate	(14) Mod. high	(19) Mod. high	(24) High
Poor	(5) Moderate	(10) Mod. high	(15) Mod. high	(20) High	(25) Very high

Figure 6.18. IRC matrix

Next, use the matrix as the basis to write the actual rules; one rule for each cell. Here is the list of IRC rules; each of which is an *"AND"* rule:

Rule 1: IF the person is *Youthful* AND his/her health is *Excellent* THEN the premium will be *Very low*.

Rule 2: IF the person is *Youthful* AND his/her health is *Good* THEN the premium will be *Low*.

Rule 3: IF the person is *Youthful* AND his/her health is *Average* THEN the premium will be *Moderately low*.

Rule 4: IF the person is *Youthful* AND his/her health is *Below average* THEN the premium will be *Moderately low*.

Rule 5: IF the person is *Youthful* AND his/her health is *Poor* THEN the premium will be *Moderate*.

....

Rule 21: IF the person is *Old* AND his/her health is *Excellent* THEN the premium will be *Moderate*.

Rule 22: IF the person is *Old* AND his/her health is *Good* THEN the premium will be *Moderately High*.

Rule 23: IF the person is *Old* AND his/her health is *Average* THEN the premium will be *Moderately High*.

Rule 24: IF the person is *Old* AND his/her health is *Below average* THEN the premium will be *High*.

Rule 25: IF the person is *Old* AND his/her health is *Poor* THEN the premium will be *Very High*.

URC Approach

In the URC approach, each antecedent element relates directly to its consequent counterpart, the number of output subsets is therefore reduced from seven to five as illustrated in Figure 6.19(a). The union rule matrix can be populated as shown in Figure 6.19(b). Subsequently, use the URC matrix as the basis to write the actual rules; one rule for each cell. Here is the list of URC rules; each one of these fuzzy relations is separated logically by an *"OR"* operator for inference purposes:

Rule: [IF the person is *Youthful* THEN the premium will be *Low*.
OR
IF the person is *Young* THEN the premium will be *Moderately low*.
OR
IF the person is *Middle-aged* THEN the premium will be *Moderate*.
OR
IF the person is *Mature* THEN the premium will be *Moderately high*.
OR
IF the person is *Old* THEN the premium will be *High*].
OR

[IF the person's health is *Excellent* THEN the premium will be *Low*.
OR
IF the person's health is *Good* THEN the premium will be *Moderately low*.
OR
IF the person's health is *Average*, THEN the premium will be *Moderate*.
OR
IF the person's health is *Below Average* THEN the premium will be *Moderately high*.
OR
IF the person's health is *Poor* THEN the premium will be *High*].

Source: Combs and Andrews, 1998

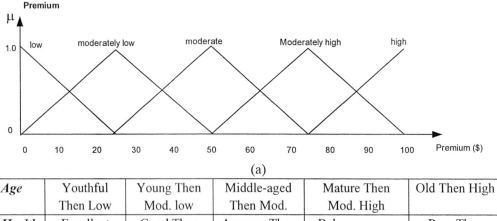

(a)

Age	Youthful Then Low	Young Then Mod. low	Middle-aged Then Mod.	Mature Then Mod. High	Old Then High
Health status	Excellent Then Low	Good Then Mod. low	Average Then Mod.	Below average Then Mod. High	Poor Then High

(b)

Source: Combs and Andrews, 1998.

Figure 6.19. (a) Revised output fuzzy sets; (b) URC matrix

Defining Inference and Defuzzification Methods

An inference method permits obtaining logical deductions of conclusions from premise. Yen and Langari (1999), and Baturone *et al.* (2000) identified three types of inference methods for fuzzy systems, viz.:

1. Mamdani inference method;
2. Tsukamoto inference method; and
3. Takagi-Sugeno inference method.

According to Baturone *et al.* (2000), the Mamdani inference method is the most widely used method for fuzzy systems, which operates on intersection rule configuration. Besides,

Combs and Andrews (1998) empirically proved that the union rule configuration also works better with the Mamdani inference mechanism.

The result of any inference process is a fuzzy set; thus, it is necessary to procure a precise (crisp) value representing this set. Defuzzification process transforms the fuzzy set into a crisp value that is meaningful to the user. There are three most frequently used defuzzification methods for fuzzy systems (Negnevitsky, 2002; Tsoukalas and Uhrig, 1997). These are:

1. Centroid method;
2. Centre of Sums (COS) method; and
3. Mean of Maximum (MOM) method.

Out of these three methods, the centroid defuzzification is the most widely used technique because it has several desirable properties: (1) the defuzzified values tend to move smoothly around the output fuzzy region; (2) it is relatively easy to calculate; and (3) it can be applied to both fuzzy and singleton output set geometries (Cox, 1999). Additionally, Combs and Andrews (1998) proved that the advantages of the centroid defuzzification when used in conjunction with the IRC method are also discernible when used with the URC method.

System Coding

Fuzzy logic employs complex mathematical models aiming to approximate qualitative reasoning, whereby imprecision and uncertainty must be taken into account. Any inference performed by a fuzzy system, no matter how simple it is, implies a greater number of calculations based on a set of parameters. The use of computer-aided design (CAD) techniques and tools is a common practice in many fields of science and engineering. CAD tools ease the conception and further development of complex systems. The user is relieved from repetitive calculations and tuning tasks. The effort can therefore be focused on the more relevant aspects of system design. In the field of fuzzy logic-based systems, the need for a CAD tool is even more justified by the nature of the technology and its application areas (Baturone *et al.*, 2000). There are a number of CAD tools available for fuzzy systems, either commercially or in the public domain. Table 6.1 shows the details of those tools.

System Tuning and Verification

This is the step of checking if (Liu and Ling, 2005):

- The procedures for constructing the fuzzy system (inputs, processing rules, inference method, and defuzzification method) are correct; and
- The reasoning output by the system is reliable.

Fine-tuning of the fuzzy system (input fuzzy sets, fuzzy rules, inference method and defuzzification method) is performed if the verification result does not meet the expected performance.

Table 6.1. CAD tools for fuzzy systems development

Company/Institution	Product	Web address
Aptronix	FIDE	http://www.aptronix.com/fide/fide.htm
Flexible Intelligent Software	FlexTool	http://www.flextool.com/
HyperLogic	CubiCalc	http://www.hyperlogic.com/products.html
Indigo Software	Fuzzy Expert	http://www.indigo.co.uk/fzy.htm
Inform	FuzzyTECH	http://www.fuzzytech.com/
Institute de Microelectronica de Sevilla	Xfuzzy	http://www.imse.cnm.es/Xfuzzy/
Logic Programming Associates	FLINT	http://www.lpa.co.uk/fln.html
Mathworks	MATLAB Fuzzy Logic Toolbox	http://www.mathworks.com/products/fuzzylogic/
SGS-Thomson Microelectronics	Fuzzy Studio	http://eu.st.com/stonline/products/support/fuzzy/
Togai Infralogic	TILShell, TILGen	http://www.ortech-engr.com/fuzzy/TilShell.html
University of Magdeburg	NEFCON, NEFCLASS	http://fuzzy.cs.uni-magdeburg.de/
University of Hannover	VSP Decision Program	http://cld.mst.uni-hannover.de/cldtools/faces/start.jsp
University of Missouri – St. Louis	FID	http://www.cs.umsl.edu/~janikow/fid/
National Research Council Canada	FuzzyCLIPS	http://www.iit.nrc.ca/IR_public/fuzzy/fuzzyClips/fuzzyCLIPSIndex.html
University of Oldenburg	FOOL & FOX	http://www.rhaug.de/fool/
Vienna University of Technology	StarFLIP++	http://www.dbai.tuwien.ac.at/proj/StarFLIP/

Source: Adapted from Baturone *et al.*, 2000.

Conclusion

In decision-making environments, experts process many vague linguistic terms, which are present in natural language, without any problem and derive conclusions based on them. Fuzzy inference systems emulate this approximate reasoning mechanism of the human brain. The development of a fuzzy inference system for decision-making essentially involves six steps, including the identification of system's input and output variables, defining fuzzy sets for the variables, defining fuzzy if-then rules that correlate input and output variables for approximate reasoning, defining reasoning methods, physical coding, and system verification and tuning. Notably effective techniques for these sub-steps include: (1) best guess theory (subjective approximation) for defining fuzzy sets; (2) URC method for rule development; (3) Mamdani method for inference; (4) centroid method for defuzzification; and (5) CAD usage for system coding. The next chapter describes the development of a fuzzy inference system via the six steps along with the notably effective techniques above for automating the WCI premium rating theory that was introduced in Chapter five.

Chapter VII

Fuzzy Knowledge Based System Modelling for WCI Premium Rating

Introduction

This chapter translates the new WCI premium rating model that was proposed in chapter five into a fuzzy knowledge based system (KBS). Discussions in the chapter cover five key aspects, including the system architecture of the proposed fuzzy KBS, knowledge acquisition and representation methods for the KBS, system implementation method, inference mechanism in the KBS, and system verification. Whilst the discussion on system architecture explains the various components and their respective functions in the proposed KBS, the knowledge acquisition and representation part details the scientific approaches exploited to populate the knowledge base with decision-making heuristics. The discussion on inference mechanism details how these heuristics are used for decision-making in the proposed KBS. The system implementation part describes the cost effective methodology used to convert the conceptual model into a physical prototype. The Turing test used to verify the KBS is covered in the system verification part.

Fuzzy KBS Architecture for WCI Premium Rating

The fuzzy KBS architecture that automates the proposed premium rating model in Chapter 5 is depicted in Figure 7.1. The proposed fuzzy KBS consists of five components: (1) Graphical user interface (GUI); (2) System database; (3) Intermediate processing unit (IPU); (4) Fuzzy knowledge base; and (5) Fuzzy inference engine. A detailed description on each component is provided below.

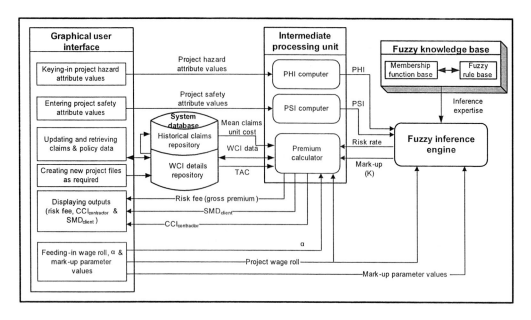

Figure 7.1. Fuzzy KBS architecture

Graphical User Interface (GUI)

The GUI consists of six major interfaces to interact with the user for obtaining inputs and for displaying outputs. The interfaces are as follows:

1. The interface for creating a new project file when a contractor or an insurance agent requests for a WCI quotation;
2. The interface for keying-in values for project hazard attributes for computing the PHI by the IPU;
3. The interface for feeding in values for project safety attributes into the IPU for computing the PSI;
4. The interface for interacting with the system database for:
   - Storing and retrieving WCI policy details of contractors; and
   - Updating claims data and information retrieval from the historical claims repository;
5. The interface for interacting with the fuzzy inference engine for keying in project wage roll and the mark-up parameter values such as overhead costs, corporate objectives, intensity of competition, contractor's claims history, and investment income; and
6. The interface for displaying final outputs; the risk fee (gross premium) at the underwriting stage, and the $CCI_{contractor}$ and the SMD_{client} at the policy expiry stage.

System Database

The system database is partitioned into two components, viz.:

1.   Historical claims repository; and
2.   WCI details repository.

The historical claims repository stores the data such as wage roll and total paid claims in previous projects. The stored data is utilised to compute the real time mean claims unit cost. The mean claims unit cost reveals the average compensation per wage roll that was paid in the past for insuring building construction projects. This can be utilised to predict potential claims from new projects, subject to adjustments for projects' particularity. The factor (risk rate) that adjusts the mean claims unit cost is inferred by the fuzzy inference engine by using the PHI and the PSI from the IPU, and the wage roll from the user. The deployment of the real time mean claims unit cost for predicting the potential claims reaps the following benefits:

- The inflation effect on claims cost is instantly captured. This is important in the Singapore context where safety policies and employment policies are rapidly changing, which indirectly influence the compensation claims for workplace accidents. For example, the Ministry of Manpower, Singapore ceased the medical subsidies for foreign workers in year 2005, which subsequently increased the compensation amount for medical benefits under WCI; and
- If there has been an overall improvement in the safety performance in the construction industry over a period of time because of a stringent enforcement of regulations, it will subsequently reduce the compensation claims for insurers. The deployment of the real time mean claims unit cost will account for such changes constantly.

The WCI details repository stores the policy details that are relevant to building construction projects until the respective WCI policies become obsolete. That is:

1.   At the initial stage, the repository stores the details about the project and the quoted premium for competition. The data stored are the wage roll, PHI, PSI, expected claims (C), mark-up (K), risk fee, and other general details;
2.   If the quotation is successful, the repository is extended to store the claims data for the policy as the project progresses. Prior to policy expiration, these project claims data are summed up to derive the total actual claims (TAC) for the computation of the $CCI_{contractor}$ and the SMD_{client} by the IPU; and
3.   Once the policy has expired, the summary of the claims is appended to the historical claims repository for the future calculation of mean claims unit cost.

Intermediate Processing Unit (IPU)

The IPU contains three sub-components, and their respective functions are described below.

1. *PHI computer*
   Computes the PHI for the project, based on the project hazard attribute values as fed in by the user.
2. *PSI computer*
   Computes the PSI for the project, based on the safety attribute values that are input by the user.
3. *Premium calculator*
   i. Computes the risk fee (gross premium) for the project at the underwriting stage by using:
       a. the intermediate outputs (risk rate and mark-up) from the fuzzy inference sub-system; and
       b. the mean claims unit cost from the historical claims repository and the wage roll from the user.
   ii. Computes the $CCI_{contractor}$ and the SMD_{client} prior to policy expiration, utilising:
       a. the expected claims (C) and the TAC from the WCI details repository; and
       b. the α value from the user.

Fuzzy Inference Engine and Fuzzy Knowledge Base

The fuzzy inference engine, with the support of the fuzzy knowledge base, makes deductions to derive the following intermediate outputs for premium rating:

1. The risk rate that adjusts the mean claims unit cost to accommodate the distinctiveness of a given project in terms of project hazard, project safety and wage roll size; and
2. The appropriate mark-up (K) that adjusts the expected claims (C) in view of overhead costs, corporate objectives, investment income, competition, and contractor's claims history.

Figure 7.2 illustrates the relationship between the input and the output variables in the fuzzy subsystem of the KBS. The Mamdani inference system along with the SUM and PRODUCT inference operators, and the centroid defuzzification method were chosen to develop the fuzzy subsystem because these operators provide a smooth and predictable output that is easily computed (Combs, 1997).

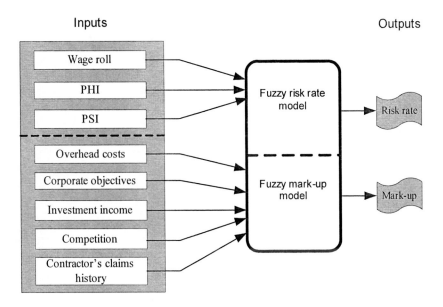

Figure 7.2. Fuzzy subsystem model

Knowledge Acquisition and Representation

The development of the fuzzy sub-models required expert knowledge from industry practitioners to derive the:

- Fuzzy membership functions for the input and the output variables; and
- Fuzzy rules that pattern the input and the output variables for approximate reasoning.

The knowledge acquisition process to develop the knowledge base of the fuzzy sub-models was conducted via a hybrid of past claims data analysis, and structured interviews with experienced domain experts. The general insurance industry of Singapore was again chosen as the case for this field study.

Past Claims Data Analysis

The knowledge elicitation for building the sub-model of the knowledge base for risk rate inference adopted a statistical analysis approach on past workers' compensation claims data. The reason for choosing the quantitative knowledge acquisition has two folds as described below.

- The fuzzy risk rate model utilises quantitative data for its inference; and
- Walker and Wiederhold (1990) quoted that the quantitative knowledge acquisition obtains extra knowledge about relationships among concepts for rules definition in knowledge bases by statistical analysis of a database.

In this exercise, workers' compensation claims data on 44 completed projects were gathered from insurance companies and analysed statistically. The break-even point of claims (claims unit cost) for each project was calculated using the following formula:

$$Claims\ unit\ cost = \frac{Total\ claims}{Wage\ roll}$$

The final values are shown in Table 7.1 where the claims unit cost is expressed as a percentage of the wage roll of a project. The analysis was continued to compute the descriptive statistics for the claims unit costs of all the projects. The outcome is shown in Table 7.2. It was noticed that the mean claims unit cost for the sample was 2.2181% of the wage roll with the median of 1.7757% and the standard deviation of 2.1472%. The minimum and the maximum claims unit costs were 0.0345% and 8.8334%, respectively. The descriptive statistics suggest that it is unrealistic to use the mean claims unit cost directly for the predictions of expected claims in future projects as the standard deviation and the median reveal higher variability. This therefore necessitates the adaptation of the mean claims unit cost on account of a project's context. Hence, the analysis was extended to derive a respective risk rating factor for each of the projects in the sample, based on the computed mean claims unit cost. The risk rate was calculated as:

$$Risk\ rate = \frac{Claims\ unit\ cost\ of\ the\ project}{Mean\ claims\ unit\ cost\ of\ all\ the\ projects}$$

The risk rate portrays how much the actual claims unit cost of a project varies from the mean claims unit cost. It was observed that:

- 20 % of the projects in the sample fall in the risk rate of less than 0.25;
- 23% of the projects fall in the risk rate 0.25 to 0.75;
- 25% of the projects fall in the risk rate 0.75 to 1.00;
- 16% of the projects fall in the risk rate 1.0 to 2.0; and
- 16% of the projects fall in the risk rate of greater than 2.0.

Table 7.1. Break-even point analysis for workers' compensation claims

Project Id	Wage roll (S$)	Contractor's grade	# of claims	Total claims (S$)	Claims unit cost	Risk rate
A	440,000.00	B1	1	38,867.00	8.8334%	3.98
B	473,550.00	C1	2	22,629.93	4.7788%	2.15
C	510,000.00	C3	3	4,023.00	0.7888%	0.36
D	738,000.00	C1	3	27,929.00	3.7844%	1.71
E	770,000.00	B2	1	11,382.00	1.4782%	0.67
F	977,322.00	C3	2	590.84	0.0605%	0.03
G	1,000,000.00	C2	4	20,317.00	2.0317%	0.92

Project Id	Wage roll (S$)	Contractor's grade	# of claims	Total claims (S$)	Claims unit cost	Risk rate
H	1,043,200.00	C3	2	8,978.00	0.8606%	0.39
I	1,280,000.00	B2	2	4,500.00	0.3516%	0.16
J	1,350,000.00	B2	1	6,223.00	0.4610%	0.21
K	1,410,000.00	A2	3	24,090.00	1.7085%	0.77
L	1,410,000.00	C3	1	1,677.00	0.1189%	0.05
M	1,490,000.00	C1	2	71,000.00	4.7651%	2.15
N	1,800,000.00	B2	3	89,820.00	4.9900%	2.25
O	1,875,000.00	A1	4	43,486.79	2.3193%	1.05
P	2,040,000.00	B2	3	167,651.00	8.2182%	3.70
Q	2,210,000.00	A2	1	50,762.00	2.2969%	1.04
R	2,340,000.00	A1	5	29,515.00	1.2613%	0.57
S	2,460,000.00	A1	10	138,631.06	5.6354%	2.54
T	3,150,000.00	A1	3	17,822.00	0.5658%	0.26
U	3,501,135.00	B1	10	62,557.19	1.7868%	0.81
V	4,560,000.00	B1	3	33,400.00	0.7325%	0.33
W	4,720,000.00	B1	1	10,905.00	0.2310%	0.10
X	6,448,640.00	B1	5	46,153.44	0.7157%	0.32
Y	6,498,000.00	A1	6	122,123.86	1.8794%	0.85
Z	7,530,000.00	C3	11	80,489.99	1.0689%	0.48
AA	10,320,306.00	A1	26	182,108.23	1.7646%	0.80
AB	11,130,000.00	A1	11	235,124.47	2.1125%	0.95
AC	11,227,500.00	A1	8	353,024.28	3.1443%	1.42
AD	12,090,000.00	A1	24	279,432.06	2.3113%	1.04
AE	13,772,833.00	B1	72	1,046,334.58	7.5971%	3.42
AF	14,775,000.00	A1	5	41,615.31	0.2817%	0.13
AG	18,720,000.00	A1	11	343,554.92	1.8352%	0.83
AH	20,927,065.00	A1	58	315,620.64	1.5082%	0.68
AI	24,131,700.00	A1	15	322,817.14	1.3377%	0.60
AJ	26,850,000.00	A1	45	779,948.68	2.9048%	1.31
AK	28,124,326.00	A1	9	64,777.48	0.2303%	0.10
AL	29,194,260.00	B1	2	31,519.00	0.1080%	0.05
AM	29,520,000.00	A1	90	518,134.92	1.7552%	0.79
AN	30,005,838.00	A2	1	10,350.00	0.0345%	0.02
AO	30,045,000.00	A1	50	843,318.92	2.8069%	1.27
AP	31,940,370.00	A2	39	577,033.16	1.8066%	0.81
AQ	64,597,923.00	A1	75	1,370,478.98	2.1216%	0.96
AR	80,336,000.00	A1	80	1,779,641.62	2.2152%	1.00

Table 7.2. Descriptive statistics for claims unit costs

Descriptive statistics - Claims unit cost	
Mean	2.2181%
Standard Error	0.3237%
Median	1.7757%
Mode	N/A
Standard Deviation	2.1472%
Sample Variance	0.0461%
Range	8.7989%
Minimum	0.0345%
Maximum	8.8334%
Count	44

Table 7.3. t – Test results for sample means

t-Test results for claims unit cost	
Null Hypothesis μ=	2
Level of Significance	0.05
Sample Size	44
Sample Mean	0.02218143
Sample Standard Deviation	0.021472265
Intermediate Calculations	
Standard Error of the Mean	0.003237066
Degrees of Freedom	43
t-Test Statistic	-610.9911739
Upper-Tail Test	
Upper Critical Value	1.681070704
p-Value	1
Do not reject the null hypothesis	

t-Test results for risk rate	
Null Hypothesis μ=	0.75
Level of Significance	0.05
Sample Size	44
Sample Mean	1.00
Sample Standard Deviation	0.968028858
Intermediate Calculations	
Standard Error of the Mean	0.145935841
Degrees of Freedom	43
t-Test Statistic	1.71308157
Two-Tail Test	
Lower Critical Value	2.016692173
Upper Critical Value	2.016692173
p-Value	0.093900087
Do not reject the null hypothesis	

Additionally, *t*-tests were carried out to infer the respective population statistics for the mean claims unit cost and the risk rate. The test results are shown in Table 7.3. It was noticed during the analysis that the risk rates for projects with high hazard profiles (i.e. high rise buildings and buildings with deep basements) were higher even among the same grade of contractors. It is because high hazard profile projects would yield higher PHI values. However, the details of the specific projects are not disclosed here owing to confidentiality. The projects analysed were constructed by different grades of contractors. The contractor grading system used by the Building and Construction Authority (BCA) of Singapore is shown in Table 7.4. It was observed in the analysis that on average, the claims unit cost and the risk rate yielded smaller values for projects that were constructed by large contractors and vice versa. It could be because large contractors maintain good safety management systems on site, which would yield higher PSI values. This argument is further reinforced by the following quotations:

- Reputable large size contractors tend to be more safety-conscious. It was found that the cost of accident varies from contractor to contractor depending on the amount of their safety investments. An accident cost variation of HK$2.27 was observed per HK$1 of safety investment by contractors. Large size contractors incurred lesser accident cost (Tang *et al.*, 2004); and
- Most of the large size contractors have a safety administration department as part of their organisation, and they apply their own safety codes and practices. Thus, safety performance in projects constructed by large contractors is higher than that of projects constructed by small contractors (Jannadi and Assaf, 1998).

The analysis was also extended to observe the correlation between the project size and the risk rate. Table 7.5 depicts how the risk rate fluctuates for various classes of project size. The project size is represented by the wage roll size. It was concluded that the project size and the risk rate are negatively correlated.

Table 7.4. Grading of contractors

Grading by BCA	Tendering limit (S$)
A1	Unlimited
A2	65 million
B1	30 million
B2	10 million
C1	3 million
C2	1 million
C3	500,000

Table 7.5. Risk rate versus Wage roll

Wage roll (in intervals) S$	Highest risk rate for the interval
< 10 million	3.98
10 – 20 million	3.42
20 – 30 million	1.31
30 – 50 million	1.27
> 50 million	1.00

Extracted from Table 7.1

Designing the Fuzzy Risk Rate Model

The findings of the past workers' compensation claims data analysis were deployed to develop the fuzzy risk rate model in the fuzzy subsystem. Input variables such as PHI, PSI and wage roll, and the output variable (risk rate) were defined by five linguistic terms along the universe of discourse. Membership function types such as Z-function, Gaussian-function and S-function were deployed to describe the fuzzy sets because they allow gradual descent from a complete membership for a number (Bell and Badiru, 1996). The numeric mapping for each fuzzy set along the universe of discourse was derived based on the empirical findings of the past workers' compensation claims data analysis above. Figure 7.3 illustrates the membership functions for all the variables in the risk rate model.

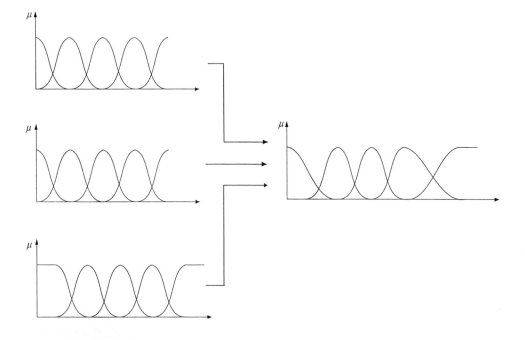

Figure 7.3. Risk rate model – fuzzy membership functions

The union rule configuration method was adopted to develop the inference rules because it eliminates the combinatorial rule explosion problem of the traditional intersection rule configuration technique (Combs and Andrews, 1998). Initially, 15 rules were developed with a rule weightage of 1.00 to model the supposition for risk rate. A sensitivity analysis was performed to fine-tune the rule weightages. That is, for fine-tuning the rule weightage for the input variable PHI in the risk rate model, input values were systematically changed over a suitable range and the effects on the output (risk rate) were observed and plotted for each rule weightage that was changed methodically. Subsequently, an appropriate weightage that best represents the relationship between PHI and risk rate was chosen for the rule. This process was continued for all the input variables in the risk rate model, one by one.

Rules: {[IF PHI is *Very small* THEN risk rate is *Very low*] [1.0]
 OR
 [IF PHI is *Small* THEN risk rate is *Low*] [1.0]
 OR
 [IF PHI is *Moderate* THEN risk rate is *Moderate*] [1.0]
 OR
 [IF PHI is *Large* THEN risk rate is *High*] [1.0]
 OR
 [IF PHI is *Very large* THEN risk rate is *Very high*] [0.05]}
 OR
 {[IF PSI is *Very small* THEN risk rate is *Very high*] [1.0]
 OR
 [IF PSI is *Small* THEN risk rate is *High*] [1.0]
 OR
 [IF PSI is *Moderate* THEN risk rate is *Moderate*] [1.0]
 OR
 [IF PSI is *Large* THEN risk rate is *Low*] [1.0]
 OR
 [IF PSI is *Very large* THEN risk rate is *Very low*] [1.0]}
 OR
 {[IF wage roll is *Very big* THEN risk rate is *Very low*][0.1]
 OR
 [IF wage roll is *Big* THEN risk rate is *Low*] [0.1]
 OR
 [IF wage roll is *Moderate* THEN risk rate is *Moderate*] [0.1]
 OR
 [IF wage roll is *Small* THEN risk rate is *high*] [0.1]
 OR
 [IF wage roll is *Very Small* THEN risk rate is *Very high*] [0.05]}

Interview Survey and Analysis

The knowledge elicitation for building the sub-model of the knowledge base for mark-up inference pursued a structured interview survey because:

- The mark-up determination is a complex process necessitating a critical assessment of various factors simultaneously (Liu and Ling, 2005); and
- A complex knowledge acquisition for fuzzy systems requires common sense reasoning and opinion of experienced experts (Berkan and Trubatch, 1997).

Altogether eight experts from the Singapore general insurance industry were interviewed. Initially, it was intended to interview experts from all the 23 general insurance companies in Singapore (i.e. the population). As the interview survey progressed, similarities between responses were observed. Thus, the interview survey was concluded with eight experts. Moreover, the interview survey with eight experts was considered adequate for knowledge acquisition because:

- Liu and Ling (2005) developed a fuzzy system for construction mark-up estimation based on the knowledge acquired from a single expert; and
- Bell and Badiru (1996) developed a fuzzy expert system to quantify occupational injury risks by interviewing four experts who are from four different areas of expertise, making one expert per domain.

The profile of the interviewees is shown in Table 7.6. The interview guideline used for the survey is available in Appendix 1.2. From the profile of the interviewees, it is perceived that the responses are constructive and reliable in order to build the knowledge base in the Singapore context. The interview survey acquired the experiences and suggestions of the experts with regards to mark-up determination. The acquired knowledge from these experts was then used to develop the fuzzy membership functions and the fuzzy IF-THEN rules for the mark-up model in the knowledge base.

Table 7.6. Profile of the interviewees

Interviewee Id	Designation	Experience in insurance (years)
JB	Senior Manager	25
TL	Manager-underwriting	20
WL	Assistant Manager – Engineering, Liability & WCI	8
CC	Manager- Property & Casualty	20
SL	Manager – Commercial insurance	15
SF	Manager – Commercial underwriting	20
DL	Assistant General Manager- underwriting	20
DT	Executive Vice President	30

It is understood from the interviews that the mark-up for WCI policies in the Singapore insurance industry ranges from 0 through to 30% of the break-even point of the covered risk. The determination of an appropriate percentage within this range pursues a critical analysis of five variables, including overhead costs of insurance, investment income from underwritten premiums, competition, corporate objectives of the insurer, and contractor's claims history. The extent of influence on the mark-up rate by each of these variables is described below.

1. Overhead Costs of Insurance

Each WCI cover will have to incur overhead costs such as brokerage fee, cost of underwriting and claims handling, and miscellaneous expenditures. The brokerage fee is constant for any insurer, which is 10% of the underwritten premium. However, the other components of the overhead costs vary for each company depending on its size. For large organisations it varies from 15% to 25% of the premium whereas for small companies the value varies from 25% to 35% of the premium.

Reinsurance cost is also considered as an overhead cost because insurers are rarely entitled to reinsurance benefits as the reinsurance policy comes into effect only when a claim amount exceeds the predetermined ceiling. However, most of the claims fall below the ceiling, which eliminates the liability of the reinsurer. The cost of reinsurance has a range from 5% to 15% of the premium depending on the company size; large companies incur lower costs than small companies. Hence, small companies have a competitive disadvantage because of these variations. When small companies compete with large companies, they have to consider this difference for mark-up determination.

2. Investment Income from Underwritten Premiums

Insurers in Singapore are open to several investment alternatives for the underwritten premiums such as fixed deposits, bonds, shares, subsidiary companies, and property investments. Most of the insurers prefer to have a spread of investments over a few options because even when an option makes a loss, the rest will help to maintain a constant income. The return on investment varies among options. On average, insurers earn 5% to 7.5% return rate. The minimum rate is obtained from fixed deposits, which is 2.5%, and the maximum is 10% from subsidiary companies and property investments.

3. Competition

The competition level in the market dictates the profit component that is to be added to the mark-up for the policy. Keen competition will inevitably result in a lean profit margin and vice versa. Competition for construction WCI is driven by three parameters among insurance companies in Singapore, viz.:

- *Wage roll size* - when the wage roll is large, the gross premium amount is also large, even with a smaller premium rate. The investment income from the underwritten premium is also high in dollar value. Thus, the break-even point of claims is lower when the wage roll is high;
- *Project hazard nature* – accident claims are highly dependent on the project hazard nature. If the project is less hazardous, insurers would be keener; and

- *Contractor's identity* – accident control is largely dependent on the contractor's safety management on site. Insurers therefore prefer to underwrite established contractors in terms of safety management. For example, it is an established fact among Singapore's general insurers that Japanese contractors are especially meticulous in safety aspects. Thus, when a well-known Japanese contractor wants to purchase a WCI policy, insurers become competitive as they know that the contractor will have fewer claims.

It is understood from the interviews that the profit loading may be up to 15% of the expected claims.

4. Corporate Objectives of the Insurer

Singapore insurers' main corporate objective is to write a given premium volume for the financial year or part of it. It is because, in the small insurance market, there are many suppliers, thereby steering keen competition. Thus, securing projects to meet the targeted premium volume is constantly a challenge for Singapore insurers. Each insurer has a predetermined portfolio ratio for WCI. The ratio varies from 7% to 12.5% of the whole portfolio. The targeted premium volume for WCI depends on the expected turnover of the company, and it is achieved in parts. For example, if an insurer targets to underwrite S$12 million for a year, the company has to write S$1 million/month or S$4 million/quarter. If the company realises that the target may not be met, it has to reduce the premium so as to be highly competitive. The intention behind reducing the premium is that the compromised amount in WCI can be compensated by the contractors' all risk insurance policy since both policies are underwritten as a package. On the contrary, the adjustment to the mark-up should correspond to the outstanding premium target. However, it is not recommended to adjust it below the threshold rate because undertaking risky jobs at cheaper costs will lead to the ultimate loss of the WCI portfolio. Hence, Singapore's insurers adjust premiums for this scenario for up to -15% from the average premium rate.

5. Contractor's Claims History

Insurers explained that customer loyalty is a strong factor in motor and health insurance in which customers stay with the same insurer for many years. This provides an insurer with the opportunity to adjust the premium at policy renewal to reflect the claims history of the policy holder. Nonetheless, this is quite difficult in construction insurance whereby contractors seem to look for the cheapest insurer every time. This disadvantages insurers in that they cannot actively use the claims history of contractors in their pricing. It would be feasible to use an independent indicator that reveals the cumulative claims history of a contractor with different insurers in previous projects. It is therefore proposed to use $CLR_{Contractor}$ (cumulative loss ratio for the contractor) in adjusting the mark-up. The $CLR_{Contractor}$ may be computed by analysing the total amount of workers' compensation claims filed by the contractor from the last few projects, and the total amount of workers' compensation insurance premiums paid for those projects. The following formula may be utilised to compute the $CLR_{Contractor}$ value for a given contractor. The number of past projects analysed for this purpose may be three, four, or five, as the case may be.

$$CLR_{Contractor} = \frac{Total\ claims\ filed}{Total\ premiums\ paid}$$

The indicator gives the flexibility that claims for different insurers from a contractor can be summed up to calculate the total claims filed in previous projects. Likewise, premiums for different insurers from the contractor can be summed up to compute the total premiums paid for the previous projects. The $CLR_{Contractor}$ may be exploited to adjust the profit loading in the mark-up for a new WCI policy for a contractor.

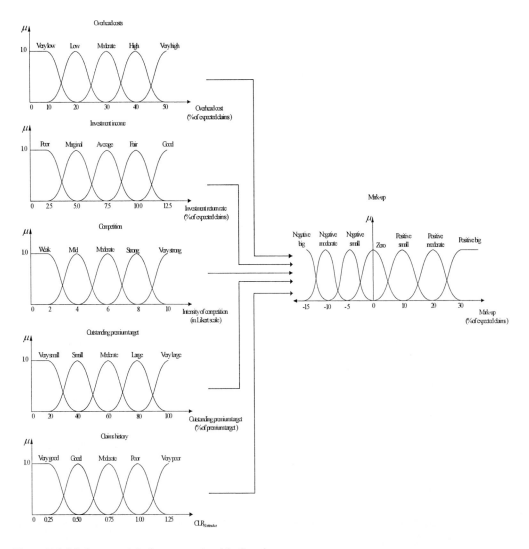

Figure 7.4. Mark-up model –fuzzy membership functions

Designing the Fuzzy Mark-up Model

The knowledge acquired in the interview survey was deployed to develop the mark-up model in the fuzzy subsystem. Input variables such as overhead costs, investment income, competition, outstanding premium target (replacement for corporate objectives), and claims history were defined by five linguistic terms along the universe of discourse while the output variable (mark-up) was defined by seven linguistic terms. Z-functions, Gaussian-functions and S-functions were again deployed to describe the fuzzy sets. The numeric mapping for each fuzzy set along the universe of discourse was derived by subjective assessments of the acquired data in the interview survey. Figure 7.4 illustrates the membership functions for the variables.

Based on the knowledge acquired in the interview survey, 25 fuzzy URC rules were developed and fine-tuned to model mark-up inference as described below.

Rules: {[IF overhead cost is *Very high* THEN mark-up is *Positive big*] [1.0]
   OR
[IF overhead cost is *High* THEN mark-up is *Positive big*] [0.75]
   OR
[IF overhead cost is *Moderate* THEN mark-up is *Positive big*] [0.3]
   OR
[IF overhead cost is *Low* THEN mark-up is *Positive moderate*] [1.0]
   OR
[IF overhead cost is *Very low* THEN mark-up is *Positive small*] [1.0]}
   OR
{[IF investment income is *Good* THEN mark-up is *Negative big*] [0.75]
   OR
[IF investment income is *Fair* THEN mark-up is *Negative moderate*] [0.3]
   OR
[IF investment income is *Average* THEN mark-up is *Negative moderate*][0.05]
   OR
[IF investment income is *Marginal* THEN mark-up is *Negative small*] [0.03]
   OR
[IF investment income is *Poor* THEN mark-up is *Zero*] [0.01]}
   OR
{[IF competition is *Very strong* THEN mark-up is *Negative big*] [1.0]
   OR
[IF competition is *Strong* THEN mark-up is *Negative moderate*] [0.5]
   OR
[IF competition is *Moderate* THEN mark-up is *Negative small*] [0.3]
   OR
[IF competition is *Mild* THEN mark-up is *Zero*] [0.1]
   OR
[IF competition is *Weak* THEN mark-up is *Zero*] [0.05]}
   OR

{[IF OPT[1] is *Very large* THEN mark-up is *Negative big*] [1.0]
OR
[IF OPT is *Large* THEN mark-up is *Negative moderate*] [0.3]
OR
[IF OPT is *Moderate* THEN mark-up is *Negative small*] [0.1]
OR
[IF OPT is *Small* THEN mark-up is *Negative small*] [0.05]
OR
[IF OPT is *Very small* THEN mark-up is *Zero*] [0.01]}
OR
{[IF claims history is *Very good* THEN mark-up is *Negative big*] [1.0]
OR
[IF claims history is *Good* THEN mark-up is *Negative moderate*] [0.5]
OR
[IF claims history is *Moderate* THEN mark-up is *Negative small*] [0.5]
OR
[IF claims history is *Poor* THEN mark-up is *Zero*] [0.75]
OR
[IF claims history is *Very poor* THEN mark-up is *Zero*] [1.0]}

Inference Mechanism in the Fuzzy KBS

The inference for premium rating proceeds through seven steps as illustrated in Figure 7.5. The steps are described below.

1. Computing a PHI value for the project based on the user input data on project hazard attributes;
2. Computing a PSI value for the project by using the project safety attributes data fed-in by the user;
3. Deducing a risk rate for the project that causes a deviation in the mean claims unit cost as processed by the historical claims repository. The inference will be performed exploiting the outputs of the two steps above (PHI and PSI), project wage roll, and the risk rate inference expertise from the fuzzy knowledge base;
4. Predicting potential claims (C) in the project, based on the risk rate from step 3, project wage roll keyed-in by the user, and the mean claims unit cost from the historical claims repository. The C is computed as:

    C = Wage roll x Mean claims unit cost x Risk rate;
5. Deducing a mark-up rate (K) for the project, based on the mark-up parameter values keyed in by the user, and the mark-up inference expertise from the fuzzy knowledge base;

---

[1] OPT = outstanding premium target

6. Computing a risk fee for the project by using the C and the K, and presenting it to the user. The risk fee is computed as:

    Risk fee = (1 + K) x C

    Details about the C, K and the risk fee for the project in concern is saved in the WCI details repository for future use should the quotation be successful; and

7. Computing the $CCI_{contractor}$ and the SMD_{client} at the policy expiration stage, utilising the C and total actual claims (TAC) from the WCI details repository, and α from the user.

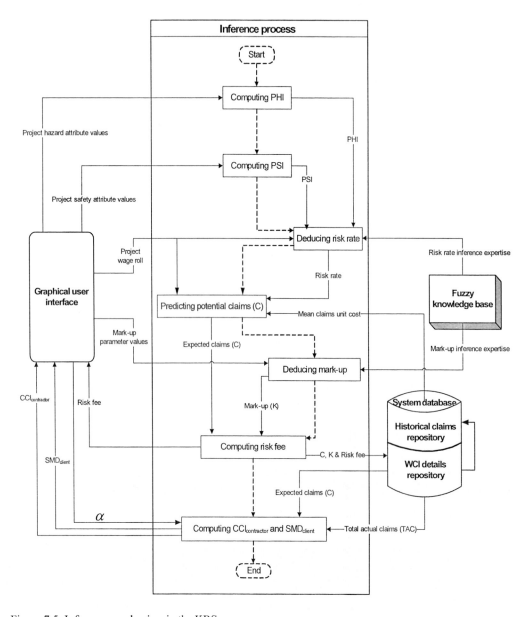

Figure 7.5. Inference mechanism in the KBS

The mathematical computations involved in the derivation of PHI, PSI, risk rate and the mark-up are described in detail in the following sections.

Computing PHI

The PHI computer estimates the project hazard intensity via the project hazard index (PHI), based on the framework for estimating PHI shown by Table 5.1 in Chapter 5. As per the framework, hazards posed by the following 11 trades have to be assessed towards computing the PHI:

1. Demolition works;
2. Excavation works;
3. Scaffolding and ladder usage;
4. False works (temporary structures);
5. Roof works;
6. Erection of steel/pre-cast concrete structures;
7. Crane use;
8. Construction machinery and tools use;
9. Works on contaminated sites;
10. Welding and cutting works; and
11. Works in confined spaces.

Nevertheless, not every hazardous trade may be applicable to a given project. Relevant trades need to be chosen and hazard rated. Hence, the PHI is derived by the following normalised formula:

$$PHI = \frac{1}{m}\left[\begin{array}{l} DMH_{score} + EXH_{score} + SLH_{score} + FLH_{score} + RFH_{score} + ERH_{score} \\ + CRH_{score} + MTH_{score} + CsiteH_{score} + WCH_{score} + CspaceH_{score} \end{array}\right]$$

Where:
$0 < m \leq 11$;
DMH_{score} = Degree of hazard contributed by demolition works;
EXH_{score} = Degree of hazard contributed by excavation works;
SLH_{score} = Degree of hazard contributed by scaffolding and ladder use;
FLH_{score} = Degree of hazard contributed by false works;
RFH_{score} = Degree of hazard contributed by roof works;
ERH_{score} = Degree of hazard contributed by erection works;
CRH_{score} = Degree of hazard contributed by crane use;
MTH_{score} = Degree of hazard contributed by machinery and tools use;
$CsiteH_{score}$ = Degree of hazard contributed by works on contaminated sites;
WCH_{score} = Degree of hazard contributed by welding and cutting works; and
$CspaceH_{score}$ = Degree of hazard contributed by works in confined spaces.

Individual trade scores will be derived based on the rating for their respective hazard attributes as per the PHI estimation framework. The algorithm exploited to derive the demolition hazard score is described as follows:

IF demolition hazard = true THEN

$$DMH_{score} = \frac{1}{3} \times \frac{1}{5} \sum_{a=1}^{3} Demolition\ hazard\ attribute\ score_a$$

ELSE $DMH_{score} = 0$

ENDIF

The coefficients of 1/3 and 1/5 are included because the hazard score for demolition works is computed by equally assessing 3 obligatory attributes on a 1-5 scale in the PHI estimation framework, and then the score is normalised to 1.00.

A similar approach is pursued to derive hazard scores for the other trades also. The algorithms used for those trades are as described below.

- IF excavation hazard = true THEN

$$EXH_{score} = \frac{1}{5} \times \frac{1}{5} \sum_{b=1}^{5} Excavation\ hazard\ attribute\ score_b$$

ELSE $EXH_{score} = 0$

ENDIF

- IF scaffolding and ladder hazard = true THEN

$$SLH_{score} = \frac{1}{3} \times \frac{1}{5} \sum_{c=1}^{3} Scaffolding\ \&\ ladder\ hazard\ attribute\ score_c$$

ELSE $SLH_{score} = 0$

ENDIF

- IF false work hazard = true THEN

$$FLH_{score} = \frac{1}{2} \times \frac{1}{5} \sum_{d=1}^{2} Falsework\ hazard\ attribute\ score_d$$

ELSE $FLH_{score} = 0$

ENDIF

- IF roof work hazard = true THEN

$$RFH_{score} = \frac{1}{4} \times \frac{1}{5} \sum_{e=1}^{4} Roof\ work\ hazard\ attribute\ score_e$$

ELSE $RFH_{score} = 0$

ENDIF

- IF erection hazard = true THEN

$$ERH_{score} = \frac{1}{3} \times \frac{1}{5} \sum_{f=1}^{3} Erection\,hazard\,attribute\,score_{f}$$

ELSE $ERH_{score} = 0$

ENDIF

- IF crane hazard = true THEN

$$CRH_{score} = \frac{1}{4} \times \frac{1}{5} \sum_{g=1}^{4} Crane\,hazard\,attribute\,score_{g}$$

ELSE $CRH_{score} = 0$

ENDIF

- IF machinery & tools hazard = true THEN

$$MTH_{score} = \frac{1}{5} \times \frac{1}{5} \sum_{h=1}^{5} Machinery\,\&\,tools\,hazard\,attribute\,score_{h}$$

ELSE $MTH_{score} = 0$

ENDIF

- IF contaminated site hazard = true THEN

$$CsiteH_{score} = \frac{1}{3} \times \frac{1}{5} \sum_{i=1}^{3} Contaminated\,site\,hazard\,attribute\,score_{i}$$

ELSE $CsiteH_{score} = 0$

ENDIF

- IF welding and cutting hazard = true THEN

$$WCH_{score} = \frac{1}{2} \times \frac{1}{5} \sum_{j=1}^{2} Welding\,\&\,cutting\,hazard\,attribute\,score_{j}$$

ELSE $WCH_{score} = 0$

ENDIF

- IF confined space hazard = true THEN

$$CspaceH_{score} = \frac{1}{4} \times \frac{1}{5} \sum_{k=1}^{4} Confined\,space\,hazard\,attribute\,score_{k}$$

ELSE $CspaceH_{score} = 0$

ENDIF

Computing PSI

The PSI computer estimates the effectiveness of the project safety management system via the project safety index (PSI), based on the PSI estimation framework illustrated by Table 5.2 in Chapter 5. According to the above framework, PSI is computed by equally analysing eight obligatory factors, viz.:

1. Project safety organisation;
2. Risk assessment and management system;
3. Safe work practices;
4. Safety training and competency of people involved;
5. Safety inspection system;
6. Machinery and tools usage and maintenance regime;
7. Subcontractors' safety systems; and
8. Emergency management system.

The formula used for PSI calculation is expressed as follows:

$$PSI = \frac{1}{8} \left\{ PSO_{score} + RAM_{score} + SWP_{score} + STC_{score} + SI_{score} + SMT_{score} + SM_{score} + EM_{score} \right\}$$

Where:
PSO_{score} = Adequacy score for project safety organisation;
RAM_{score} = Adequacy score for risk assessment and management system;
SWP_{score} = Adequacy score for safe work practices;
STC_{score} = Adequacy score for safety training and competency of people involved;
SI_{score} = Adequacy score for safety inspection system;
SMT_{score} = Adequacy score for safe use and maintenance of machinery and tools regime;
SM_{score} = Adequacy score for subcontractors' safety systems; and
EM_{score} = Adequacy score for emergency management system.

The computation methods exploited to derive individual factorial scores are described below.

Computing PSO_{score}

The adequacy score for project safety organisation (PSO_{score}) is computed by equally assessing three obligatory attributes of the factor on a 1-5 scale. Therefore, the PSO_{score} is calculated by the following single equation:

$$PSO_{score} = \frac{1}{3} \times \frac{1}{5} \sum_{a=1}^{3} PSO \; attribute \; score_a$$

Computing RAM$_{score}$

The adequacy score for risk assessment and management system (RAM_{score}) is calculated by equally assessing four obligatory attributes of the factor on a 1-5 scale. Therefore, the RAM_{score} equation is written as:

$$RAM_{score} = \frac{1}{4} \times \frac{1}{5} \sum_{b=1}^{4} RAM \; attribute \; score_b$$

Computing SWP$_{score}$

The computation of the adequacy score for safe work practices (SWP_{score}) needs to analyse three sub-factors, viz.:

- Work procedures;
- Permit-to-work (PTW) system; and
- Personal protective equipment (PPE) use.

The sub-factor score for work procedures is computed by equally assessing 13 attributes on a 1-5 scale. However, it is not necessary that all the 13 attributes will be applicable to a given project. In such cases, irrelevant attributes are marked as not applicable (NA). Thus, the following normalised equation is adopted to compute the sub-factor score:

$$WP_{sub\text{-}factor \; score} = \frac{1}{p} \times \frac{1}{5} \sum_{c=1}^{p} WP \; attribute \; score_c$$

Here, p represents the number of applicable attributes to the project for this sub-factor. If all the 13 attributes are applicable, the weightage of each attribute will be equal to 0.077 (1/13). Suppose only 10 attributes are applicable for a particular project, then the weightage will be 0.100 (1/10) to normalise the cumulative attribute scores. This will therefore maintain a consistency in safety rating and the comparison of different projects.

Akin to the above sub-factor, the equations to compute the sub-factor scores for the other two sub-factors are normalised as follows:

$$PTW_{sub\text{-}factor \; score} = \frac{1}{q} \times \frac{1}{5} \sum_{d=1}^{q} PTW \; attribute \; score_d$$

$$PPE_{sub\text{-}factor \; score} = \frac{1}{r} \times \frac{1}{5} \sum_{e=1}^{r} PPE \; attribute \; score_e$$

Where, q and r represent the number of applicable attributes to the project for the sub-factors PTW and PPE, respectively.

The three sub-factors are given equal weightage towards computing the *SWPscore.* Hence, the SWP_{score} equation is written as:

$$SWP_{score} = \frac{1}{3}\left[WP_{sub-factor\,score} + PTW_{sub-factor\,score} + PPE_{sub-factor\,score} \right]$$

Computing STC$_{score}$

The computation of the adequacy score for safety training and competency of people involved (STC_{score}) needs to analyse three sub factors, viz.:

- Safety training to management team;
- Certification of and safety training to operators; and
- In-house safety training to workers.

The sub factor adequacy scores for safety training to management team ($STMT_{sub-factor\,score}$), and certification of and safety training to operators ($CSTO_{sub-factor\,score}$) are computed by the following normalised equations since all the attributes in the sub factors may not be applicable to a given project:

$$STMT_{sub-factor\,score} = \frac{1}{s} \times \frac{1}{5} \sum_{f=1}^{s} STMT\ attribute\ score_{f}$$

$$CSTO_{sub-factor\,score} = \frac{1}{t} \times \frac{1}{5} \sum_{g=1}^{t} CSTO\ attribute\ score_{g}$$

Where, s and t represent the number of applicable attributes to the project for sub-factors STMT and CSTO, respectively.

As the adequacy score for in-house safety training to workers ($ISTW_{sub-factor\,score}$) pursues the assessment of four obligatory attributes, the equation is written as:

$$ISTW_{sub-factor\,score} = \frac{1}{4} \times \frac{1}{5} \sum_{h=1}^{4} ISTW\ attribute\ score_{h}$$

Finally, the three sub factors are equally weighted to compute the STC_{score} based on the equation below.

$$STC_{score} = \frac{1}{3}\left[STMT_{sub-factor\,score} + CSTO_{sub-factor\,score} + ISTW_{sub-factor\,score} \right]$$

Computing SI$_{score}$

The normalised equation to calculate the adequacy score for safety inspection system (SI_{score}) is written as follows:

$$SI_{score} = \frac{1}{2}\left[\frac{1}{u} \times \frac{1}{5}\sum_{i=1}^{u} Worksite\,inspection\,attribute_i + \frac{1}{v} \times \frac{1}{5}\sum_{j=1}^{v} Housekeeping\,attribute_j\right]$$

Here, u and v represent the number of applicable attributes to the project for the sub-factors worksite inspection and housekeeping, respectively. The sub-factor scores are then aggregated with equal weightage to compute the SI_{score}.

Computing SMT_{score}

The calculation of the adequacy score for safe use and maintenance regime of machinery and tools (SMT_{score}) adopts the following normalised equation:

$$SMT_{score} = \frac{1}{3}\left[\begin{array}{l}\frac{1}{w} \times \frac{1}{5}\sum_{k=1}^{w} Machinery\,testing\,\&\,certification\,attribute_k \\[2mm] + \frac{1}{x} \times \frac{1}{5}\sum_{l=1}^{x} Machinery\,\&\,tools\,\,inspection\,attribute_l \\[2mm] + \frac{1}{y} \times \frac{1}{5}\sum_{m=1}^{y} Machinery\,maintenance\,attribute_m\end{array}\right]$$

The sub-factor adequacy scores for testing and certification of machinery, inspection of machinery and tools, and maintenance of machinery are computed by evaluating w, x and y attributes, respectively. Where, w, x and y represent the number of applicable attributes for the above sub-factors in the project. Subsequently, the SMT_{score} is compiled with equal weightage to each sub-factor score.

Computing SM_{score}

The adequacy score for subcontractors' safety systems (SM_{score}) is computed by equally evaluating five essential attributes on a 1-5 scale. Thus, the equation for SM_{score} is given as follows:

$$SM_{score} = \frac{1}{5} \times \frac{1}{5}\sum_{n=1}^{5} Subcontractors'\,safety\,attribute_n$$

Computing EM_{score}

The computation of the adequacy score for emergency management system (EM_{score}) exploits the following equation:

$$EM_{score} = \frac{1}{3} \left[\begin{array}{l} \dfrac{1}{5} \times \dfrac{1}{5} \sum_{\alpha=1}^{5} Emergency\, response\ plan\, attribute_{\alpha} \\[3mm] + \dfrac{1}{5} \times \dfrac{1}{5} \sum_{\beta=1}^{5} Emergency\ response\ team\, attribute_{\beta} \\[3mm] + \dfrac{1}{5} \times \dfrac{1}{5} \sum_{\lambda=1}^{5} Emergency\ equipment\ attribute_{\lambda} \end{array} \right]$$

The EM_{score} is the equally weighted composition of the three sub-factor scores such as emergency response plan, emergency response team, and emergency equipment. Each of these sub-factors is evaluated by five compulsory attributes on a 1-5 scale.

Fuzzy Inference for Risk Rate and Mark-up

The single input - single output relations under the union rule configuration are not any different from the single input - single output rules defined under the intersection rule configuration. Therefore, they can be processed by the Mamdani inference method without any modifications (Combs and Andrews, 1998). According to Yager and Filev (1993), the Mamdani fuzzy reasoning method is a two-step inference process.

1. First, the output fuzzy set F_i inferred by the ith rule is
   $F_i = (t_i \wedge D_i)$, $i = 1$ to n
   Where t_i is the antecedent firing strength of the ith rule and D_i is the ith linguistic value associated with the output universal set; and
2. Next, the individual rule output fuzzy sets, the F_i's, are aggregated by the OR operator so that the output fuzzy set F inferred by the system is
   F = Union of all Fi's   where $i = 1$ to n
    = Union of all $(ti \wedge Di)$ where $i = 1$ to n.

Having taken these two steps, a crisp output can be calculated by defuzzifying the output fuzzy set F.

The following case example explores the inference process through the two steps above.

Case: Derive an appropriate risk rate for a construction WCI policy for the project scenario of PHI =0.90, PSI = 0.65 and Wage roll = $38 million

It is understood by studying the membership functions of the variables that the crisp value 0.90 for the PHI lies in two membership functions, known as *large(Gaussian-function)* and *very large (S-function),* each with varying membership grades. The pertinent membership grade for this crisp value in the membership function of *large* is calculated as follows:

$$\mu(x) = \exp\left(-\frac{[x-m]^2}{\sigma^2}\right)$$

Where: m = centre of the function; σ = width of the function.

The relevant values for m and σ in this instance are 0.75 and 0.075, respectively. Hence the resulting μ value is 0.02. Similarly, the pertinent membership grade for this crisp value in the membership function of *very large* is calculated as follows:

- If the crisp value is smaller than the midpoint of the membership graph, then

$$\mu(x) = 2\left(\frac{x-a}{b-a}\right)^2$$

  Where: a = lower point of the graph (0.75 in this instance) and b = upper point (1.00).
- If the crisp value is greater than the midpoint of the membership graph, then

$$\mu(x) = 1 - 2\left(\frac{x-a}{b-a}\right)^2$$

  Because the crisp value for PHI is greater than the midpoint, the second formula is applicable for this case. Thus, the relevant μ value is 0.92.

In the rule base, the relevant rules for this crisp value are as follows:

[IF PHI is *Large* THEN risk rate is *High*] [1.0]
OR
[IF PHI is *Very large* THEN risk rate is *Very high*] [0.05]

The calculated μ values will trigger the output variable's membership functions as illustrated in Figure 7.6(a) to find the areas covered by these μ values in their respective output membership functions. Since rule weights are applied, the original force of the premises is multiplied by the rule weights, thus reducing its force. This process will continue in all the variables and each variable will result in an area for the output variable. These individual areas will be aggregated to compute a single crisp value, based on the centroid defuzzification technique. Suppose the aggregated area for the above input values resembles Figure 7.6(b), the centroid technique will calculate the centre of the shaded area by the following formula:

$$Risk\ rate\ (RR) = \frac{\displaystyle\int_{i=0.25}^{2.00} \mu(a_i) \times a_i\ dx}{\displaystyle\int_{i=0.25}^{2.00} \mu(a_i)\ dx}$$

Where: $\mu(a_i)$ = weight of the area at point a_i; a_i = output value that is pertinent to the area.

Figure 7.6. (a) Output inference; (b) Output defuzzification

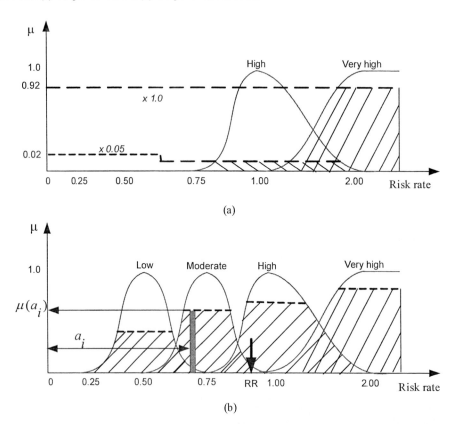

Making the Prototype of the Fuzzy KBS

The physical coding of a KBS prototype has four choices (Kamara and Anumba, 2001), viz.:

1. Programming in a procedure-oriented third generation language (e.g. FORTRAN), whereby the programmer has to describe in detail, how every task is to be carried out;
2. Programming in a problem-oriented fourth generation language (e.g. C++), wherein the programmer has to define what must be done;
3. Using a general purpose integrated package, which incorporates facilities such as word processing, spreadsheet, database, and report generators; and
4. Using a computer-aided design (CAD) tool.

The use of CAD tools eases the conception and further development of complex systems. The user is relieved of repetitive calculations and tuning tasks. Thus, the effort can be focused on more relevant aspects of system design. In the field of fuzzy logic-based systems, the need for a CAD tool is even more justified by the nature of the technology and its application areas (Baturone *et al.,* 2000). Rao *et al.* (1997) noted that the use of general purpose software, which is already familiar to users, achieves a dramatic reduction in development efforts and training time over conventional programming for systems with similar scope. Perera and Imriyas (2004) explored the potential of MS Access™ for advanced systems development, while Negnevitsky (2002) and Baturone *et al.* (2000) noted the potential of Matlab™ for fuzzy systems development. Moreover, Perera and Imriyas (2003) developed a fuzzy knowledge based system for construction cost control by using Matlab™. Hence, the proposed fuzzy KBS was prototyped using Fuzzy Logic Toolbox in Matlab™, VBA™ and MS Access™. The intermediate processing unit (IPU) and the system database were implemented in VBA™ and MS Access™ platforms, while the fuzzy inference subsystem was implemented in Matlab™ platform. Both platforms were then linked via VBA™.

Developing the IPU and the System Database

MS Access™ has seven objects to support the development of advanced systems, viz.:

1. Tables – perform the basic function of keeping files of data in a logical arrangement;
2. Queries – perform manipulations and calculations on data in tables;
3. Forms – are primarily used for data entry (inputs for the system) and information display (outputs from the system). A form can also function as a switchboard that opens other forms and reports in the system, and as a custom dialog box that accepts user input and carries out an action based on the input;
4. Reports – provide a set of effective ways to present the information the way the user wants to see it;
5. Macros – are a set of actions that can be created to automate routine common tasks;
6. Modules – are essentially a collection of declarations, statements and procedures that are stored together as one named unit to organise the VBATM code for the system; and
7. SharePoint– provides with the facilities to build shared databases that can be accessed simultaneously by many users in an organisation to enter, view and analyse data from a SharePoint site.

Basic and advanced features in Tables, Queries, Forms and Modules (VBA™ codes) were utilised to make the fuzzy KBS prototype. The development of a system on MS Access™ environment essentially requires the development of sound data tables. Hence, an entity-relationship diagram (ERD) was developed for the system as shown in Figure 7.7 to facilitate the development of data tables. For more details on how to develop ERDs, readers are suggested to read text books on relational database development.

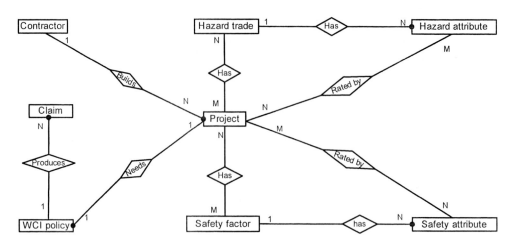

Figure 7.7. Entity-relationship diagram

The data tables that are necessary to develop the system were identified from the ERD, and described below. The fields in the parentheses indicate the column headings of tables, and the underlined field is the primary key of the data table.

1. Project *(Project Id, Project description, Client, Contractor, Duration, Wage roll)*
2. Hazard trade *(Hazard trade Id, Hazard trade description, Hazard weightage)*
3. Project - Has - Hazard trade *(Project Id, Hazard trade Id)*
4. Hazard attribute *(Hazard attribute Id, Hazard attribute description, Hazard trade Id)*
5. Project – Rated by - Hazard attribute *(Project Id, Hazard attribute Id, Attribute hazard rating)*
6. Safety factor *(Safety factor Id, Safety factor description, Safety weightage)*
7. Project – Has - Safety factor *(Project Id, Safety factor Id)*
8. Safety attribute *(Safety attribute Id, Safety attribute description, Safety factor Id)*
9. Project – Rated by - Safety attribute *(Project Id, Safety attribute Id, Attribute safety rating)*
10. Contractor *(Contractor Id, Contractor name, Contact details, BCA grade, $CLR_{contractor}$)*
11. WCI policy *(Policy Id, Project Id, Date of underwriting, Date of expiry, Expected claims (C), Mark-up (K), $CCI_{contractor}$, SMD_{client}, α value)*
12. Claim *(Claim Id, Policy Id, Date of claim paid, Description of accident, Medical claim, lost wage claim, Permanent incapacity claim, Death claim, Occupational illness claim)*

The processing methods were developed using queries and modules, based on the equations and algorithms described in the preceding section, titled Inference mechanism in the fuzzy KBS. Figure 7.8 illustrates the relationships between the data tables to process data for deriving the PHI, PSI, Risk fee (gross premium), $CCI_{contractor}$ and the SMD_{client}. For more details on how to build databases, readers are encouraged to read any book or user guide on MS Access™.

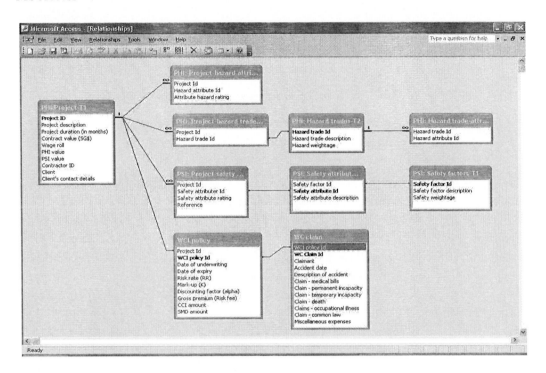

Figure 7.8. Relationships between data tables

Figure 7.9. Fuzzy system development environment

Developing the Fuzzy Inference Subsystem

As illustrated in Figure 7.9, there are five primary GUI tools for building, editing, and operating fuzzy inference systems in the Fuzzy Logic Toolbox in Matlab™, viz.:

1. FIS Editor;
2. Membership Function Editor;
3. Rule Editor;
4. Rule Viewer; and
5. Surface Viewer.

These GUIs are dynamically linked such that changes that are made to the FIS using one of them can affect what is seen on any of the other open GUIs.

The FIS Editor handles high level issues for the system: i.e., (1) how many input and output variables?; (2) what are their names?; (3) what are the implication operators?; and (4) what is the defuzzification method?. The Membership Function Editor is used to define the number and types of membership functions for each variable. The Rule Editor is for adding and editing the list of rules that defines the behaviour of the system. The Rule Viewer and the Surface Viewer are used for viewing, as opposed to editing the FIS. They are strictly read-only tools. The Rule Viewer is a Matlab™ based display of the fuzzy inference diagram. It can show which rules are active or how individual membership function shapes are influencing the results. The Surface Viewer is used to display the dependency of one of the outputs on any one or two of the inputs; i.e., it generates and plots an output surface map for the system. The development process of the fuzzy inference subsystem of the KBS is described in the following sections.

Defining the Fuzzy Inference Subsystem

This was the first step in developing the fuzzy subsystem by using the Fuzzy Logic Toolbox in Matlab™. On the top part of the FIS Editor in Figure 7.10, the fuzzy inference subsystem was described as having eight input variables namely, PHI, PSI, wage roll, overhead cost, investment income, competition, outstanding premium target and contractor's claims history, and two outputs namely, risk rate and mark-up. The inference option and the defuzzification option for the fuzzy inference subsystem were described at the bottom part of the FIS Editor.

Membership Functions Development

The second stage of fuzzy inference subsystem development was to define the membership functions for the eight input and the two output variables that were added in the FIS Editor. Figure 7.11 illustrates the steps involved in defining membership functions.

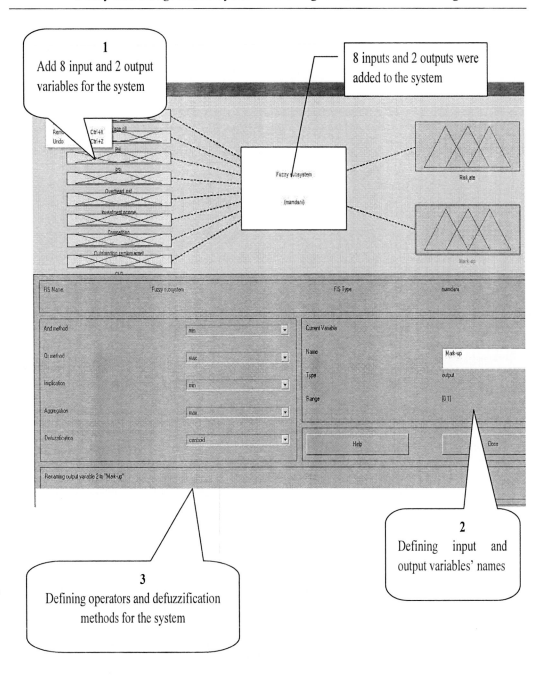

Figure 7.10. FIS Editor

Rule Base Development

The final stage of fuzzy inference subsystem development was to define the fuzzy linguistic rules in the Rule Editor. As shown in Figure 7.12, the middle part of the Rule Editor displays the input and output variables and their respective fuzzy sets, while the bottom part displays the connection options and a text box to adjust the weights of rules as they are developed. The Rule Editor allowed easy construction of fuzzy rules through the steps depicted in Figure 7.12.

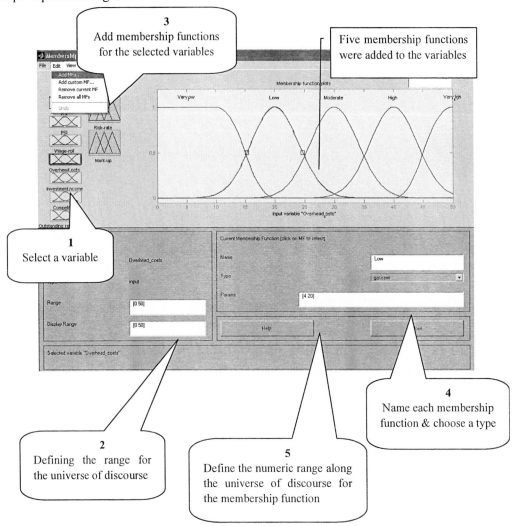

Figure 7.11. Membership Function Editor

Table 7.7. Graphical user interfaces

Interface group	Interface name	Purpose
• New Project		Booking in details of a new project when a quotation for WCI is requested
• PHI Computer	1. Hazard Trade Assignment	Linking pertinent hazard trades with construction projects
	2. Project Hazard Rating	Rating project hazards by individually analysing trades' hazards one-by-one

Interface group	Interface name	Purpose
• PSI Computer	1. Rating of Project Safety Organisation	Keying in data to assess the adequacy of the project safety organisation and responsibilities
	2. Rating of Risk Assessment and Management System	Supplying data to evaluate the adequacy of the risk assessment and management system
	3. Rating of Safe Work Practices	Date entry for safety assessments of contractors' work practices
	4. Rating of Safety Training and Competency	Keying-in data on safety training and competency of people involved to evaluate its effectiveness
	5. Rating of Site Inspection System	Feeding-in site inspection system's attribute ratings for assessing its effectiveness
	6. Rating of Machinery and Tools Use and Maintenance Regime	Supplying data for assessing safety in machinery and tools use by the contractor
	7. Rating of Subcontractors' Safety Systems	Inputting data to evaluate subcontractors' safety systems
	8. Rating of Emergency Management System	Keying-in data on a contractor's emergency management system for assessing its effectiveness
• Fuzzy Sub-system	1. Input for Fuzzy Expert	Displaying intermediate outputs which are inputs for fuzzy sub-system (PHI, PSI & wage roll)
	2. Open Fuzzy Expert	Invoking the fuzzy inference sub-system and interacting with it to derive the risk rate and the mark-up for the policy
• Underwriter	1. New WCI Policy	Keying in a new policy's basic details such as policy Id, date of underwriting and expiry, wage roll, risk rate, mark-up, etc.
	2. New Claims Details	Storing WC claims data from construction projects
	3. Update Claims Database	Appending projects' claims summary to KBS' claims repository for future use
• Print Outputs	1. Policy Details	Previewing of WCI quotations
	2. CCI Details	Previewing of incentives for contractors
	3. SMD Details	Previewing of discounts for clients

Developing the GUI

Altogether, 19 user interfaces were developed for the fuzzy KBS for data input and output display. These 19 user interfaces were clustered into six major interface groups as in Figure 7.13, namely New Project, PHI computer, PSI computer, Fuzzy Subsystem,

Underwriter, and Print Outputs. The purpose of each interface and the nature of data input are described in Table 7.7.

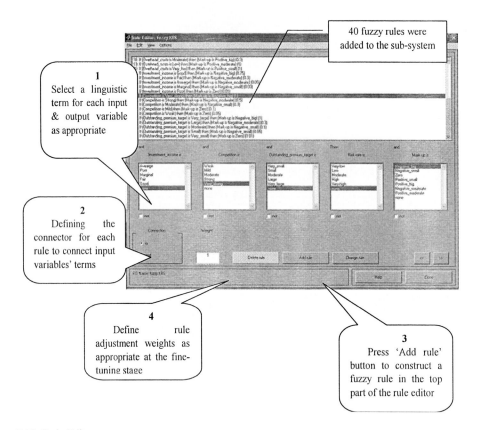

Figure 7.12. Rule Editor

Verification of the Fuzzy KBS

System verification is one of the key stages of the KBS development cycle. KBS verification refers to substantiating that a system correctly implements its specifications (O'Keefe *et al.*, 1987). It is designed to determine if the system completely and accurately implements user specifications; that is, verification determines if the system was built right (Gupta, 1992). O'Keefe *et al.* (1987) noted three common approaches for KBS verification, viz.:

1. *Predictive verification:* requires the use of historic test cases and either known results or measures of human expert performance on those cases. A KBS is driven by past input data from test cases and the results are compared with the corresponding known results;

2. *Field test:* places a prototypical KBS in the field and then seeks to perceive performance errors as they occur; and

3. *Turing test:* verifies a KBS against the human expert by comparing the human expert performance and the system performance. If the performance can be objectively measured, then statistical techniques can be used to test consistency.

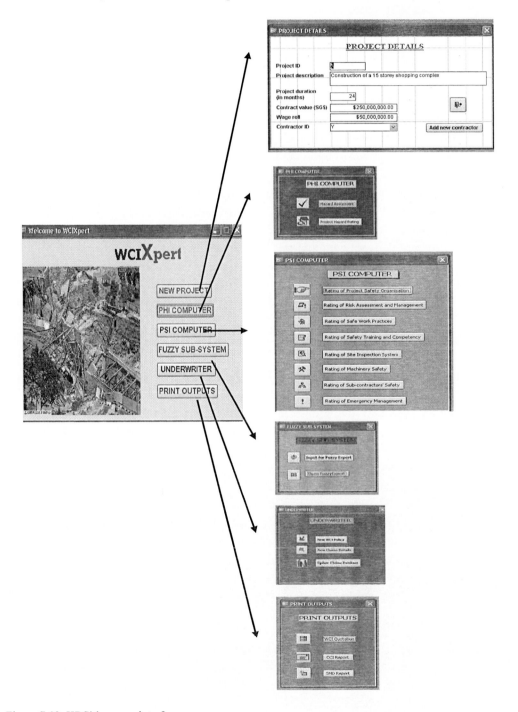

Figure 7.13. KBS' key user interfaces

It was necessary to choose a suitable verification method for the KBS whereby every approach was considered individually. Finally, the Turing test was found suitable in this study owing to the following reasons:

- In order to adopt the predictive verification method, there must be adequate past data on premiums that were derived based on the proposed premium rating model in this book. However, the Singapore insurance industry does not utilise this model but they use a benchmark approach where 1% of the wage roll makes the WCI premium for construction projects. Thus, it would not give a common basis for comparison;
- General insurance companies in Singapore were approached by the author for performing field tests of the KBS. All the companies approached refused to provide access to their premises and data for the author on account of business sensitivity; and
- The Turing test provided the flexibility that: (1) no business data from insurance companies needed for verification; (2) a hypothetical verification case was able to be developed, which embodies the proposed premium rating model; (3) underwriters were able to derive a premium rate for the verification case following the sequence explained in the proposed model in this book; and (4) the performance of experts were able to be compared with that of the KBS.

Turing Test for the Fuzzy KBS

Five underwriters from different insurance companies were contacted for the Turing test of the fuzzy KBS. A hypothetical case was developed beforehand as described in Figure 7.14. The verification case and the proposed premium rating model were presented to the underwriters at the interview sessions. The underwriters derived their answers for the case example based on the steps explained in the proposed model. Subsequently, the fuzzy KBS prototype was demonstrated to underwriters to infer a solution for the same case example. Table 7.8 shows the summarised performance of both the KBS and the experts for the same case example. The underwriters were also invited to comment on the relevance of the proposed KBS for premium rating. All five of them appreciated the scientific approach and well-thought out strategies in the KBS that can better re-engineer the WCI business in Singapore towards eliminating the current dilemmas faced by the general insurance industry.

Table 7.8. Evaluating the KBS' accuracy

Expert	Gross premium rate (% of wage roll)		Accuracy of the KBS as opposed to expert's decision (in %)
	Expert's decision	KBS' decision	
P	2.53	2.66	95
Q	2.64		99
R	2.64		99
S	2.00		75
T	1.90		73

KBS verification

A recent analysis by your company on the break-even point of workers' compensation (WC) claims in building construction projects revealed that the average break-even rate of WC claims is 2.2% of the wage roll, while the minimum is 0.03% and the maximum is 8.8% of the wage roll of a building construction project. It is noticed that the variation in the break-even rate occurs owing to three variables:

1. Project hazard level;
2. Project safety level; and
3. Project size.

The project hazard level is measured by project hazard index (PHI), the project safety level is measured via project safety index (PSI), and the project size is measured by wage roll size.

You are to evaluate the expected break-even rate in a new building project under the following scenario to decide an appropriate premium rate.

- PHI = 0.72 (where: 0 - low hazard; and 1.00 - high hazard);
- PSI = 0.64 (where: 0 - low safety; and 1.00 - high safety); and
- Wage roll = $ 43 million (contract value – $215million).

What would be the appropriate break-even rate for this project, in your assessment?

Suppose that you have to add a mark-up to the break-even rate, which you have deduced above, to compute the appropriate premium rate for the above project. Your mark-up size depends on five variables, viz.:

1. Overhead costs of your company;
2. Income rate that you can make by investing the premiums that you collect from contractors;
3. Competition level in the insurance market;
4. Outstanding premium target that you need to meet for this class of insurance for this year; and
5. Contractor's claims history (measured via contractor's cumulative loss ratio; $CLR_{contractor}$).

You are to decide an appropriate mark-up for the above policy under the following scenario:

- Overhead costs =14% of the premium;
- Investment return rate = 6%;
- Competition level = 7 (in 1 - 10 scale, where: 1 – low competition, 10 – high competition);
- Outstanding premium target = 40% of the total targeted premium volume; and
- $CLR_{contractor}$ = 0.83.

What would be the appropriate mark-up rate for this policy, in your assessment?

Figure 7.14. Verification case

The sample size of five experts with one case example was considered adequate for the verification in view of the following experiences:

- Liu and Ling (2005) verified a fuzzy system for construction bid mark-up estimation by a single expert using three case examples; and
- Tam *et al.* (2004) conducted a verification exercise of a fuzzy system for green construction assessment in the construction industry by one expert and three case examples.

The verification by five experts with one case example can be more effective in assessing the diversity in experts' intuitions and the capability of the proposed KBS in handling it, rather than utilising one expert with many case examples. The usage of a few case examples with five experts would have been much better. However, practical limitations were experienced in convincing experts to devote time for lengthy or multiple validation interviews.

Workflow Model for the Fuzzy KBS

The workflow diagram for decision-making with the proposed fuzzy KBS is illustrated in Figure 7.15, and the workflow is described below.

1. Obtaining a request for WCI quotation from a contractor or an insurance agent;
2. Obtain details of the building construction project and create a project file in the fuzzy KBS for a new WCI policy;
3. Hazard rating of the project (PHI computation) through the following sub-steps:
   a. Analysing the project scope and the vicinity based on the information furnished by the contractor or the insurance agent;
   b. Identifying pertinent hazardous trades for the project and their hazard rating attributes; and
   c. Rating the hazard intensity in each trade;
4. Safety rating of the project (PSI computation) via the following sub steps:
   a. Analysing the proposed safety management system for the project;
   b. Identifying the relevant safety factors and sub-factors for the project and their respective attributes for safety rating; and
   c. Rating the safety adequacy in each factor;
5. Inferring an appropriate risk rate for the project;
6. Predicting the potential WC claims in the project;
7. Inferring an appropriate mark-up for the policy;
8. Computing the risk fee for the policy;
9. Preparing and sending a quotation to the contractor or the insurance agent;
10. If the quotation is successful, managing WC claims data from the project during the course of construction;

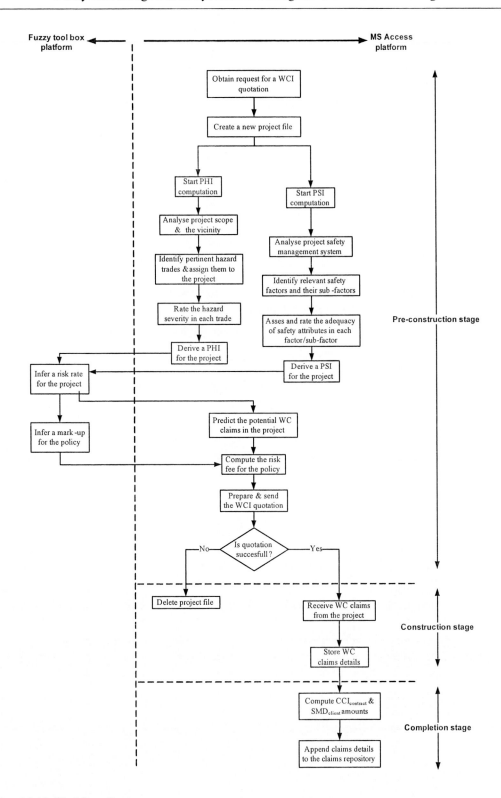

Figure 7.15. Workflow diagram

11. Computing the $CCI_{contractor}$ and SMD_{client} amounts at the completion of the project; and

12. Appending the claims data in the project to the system database for future use.

A user manual for the prototypical fuzzy KBS can be found in Appendix 2 for readers to understand the operation of the system. The user manual adopts step-by-step explanations in an easy-to-follow manner, with a demonstrative project.

Conclusion

This chapter discussed the process involved in automating the proposed WCI premium rating model into a fuzzy knowledge based system, integrating fuzzy logic and conventional computing techniques. The translation process essentially involved four sub-processes, which includes developing the conceptual model (system architecture) of the KBS, knowledge acquisition and representation, system implementation, and system verification. The system architecture established the necessary component for the KBS and their respective functions. Knowledge acquisition for developing the fuzzy knowledge base pursued a hybrid of past workers' compensation claims analysis and an interview survey. The union rule configuration method was exploited for knowledge representation, departing from the traditional intersection rule configuration method for fuzzy system. This expedited the translation process by minimising the number of rules in the rule base. The utilisation of existing software (MS Access™, VBA™, and Matlab™) shortened the system implementation time significantly, while facilitating the task. The exploitation of Turing tests provided with a flexible means for system verification.

The fuzzy KBS facilitates multi attribute inference, which usually challenges underwriters' reasoning abilities, for assessing project hazards, safety, market condition and insurers' internal factors for premium rating. While the KBS advocates real time structured assessments of various business factors discussed above, it eliminates high reliance on experienced underwriters who job hop within the insurance industry. It also captures data on workers' compensation claims and contractors' safety performance for future use. Its implementation in the general insurance industry would facilitate accident control in the construction industry, and thereby minimise losses for insurers and safeguard the interests of workers, design and project management consultants, clients, and contractors.

Chapter VIII

Concluding Notes

Introduction

This chapter brings together all of the themes and findings in previous chapters into a coherent model, and reports its applications in the construction and insurance industries. The chapter also summarises the contributions to the body of knowledge to benefit the academic community. Finally, it identifies the strong research platform that the book has established, and outlines future directions for research.

Summary

The construction industry is an integral part of the national economy of any country. It is of national significance because: (1) its contribution to gross domestic product (GDP) is relatively high; (2) it generates abundant employment opportunities; and (3) it builds a country's infrastructure and facilities for other industries in the economy, and these are the basis for a country's socio-economic development. Despite its contributions to the growth of national economy, the construction industry has been characterised to have poor OHS performance records globally. This situation has disadvantaged many parties involved in the construction of built facilities. The increasing rate of construction accidents not only wipes out the profit margin of contractors, but also degrades the quality of life of workers and their families. These eventually skyrocket the social costs associated with occupational accidents, and thereby trim down the GDP growth of the country. The insurance industries in many countries have been experiencing detrimental losses by workers' compensation insurance. An emerging trend is discernible internationally that OHS regulatory bodies are revising their Workplace Health and Safety Act to hold clients, design and project management consultants, and contractors accountable for any occupational accidents in their projects. Hence, minimising accidents and injuries in construction is of critical essence to:

- Improve the GDP growth of a country;
- Safeguard the interests, quality of life and welfare of workers and their families;
- Minimise avoidable losses to the construction and insurance industries; and
- Protect construction professionals, clients and contractors from the risks of legal proceedings, fines and imprisonments.

Since WCI is compulsory for every contractor and no project can be started on site without procuring it, this book aimed to exploit WCI for accident control. Two notions were formulated in this study in this direction.

1. The first notion stated that accidents on construction sites can be controlled through WCI if:
   (i) The premium amount for a WCI policy is significantly influenced by the effectiveness of a contractor's safety management system, which needs to be assessed in real-time to ensure that it corresponds to the level of project hazard. As per this concept, if a contractor's safety management system is robust to combat the project hazard, the contractor would get a cost effective insurance cover, which would enable the contractor to compete better in tenders. Those contractors who do not have robust safety management systems in place would be penalised by higher premiums. This approach would automatically set risky contractors aside and would motivate them to invest adequately in safety in their organisations to ensure business continuity; and
   (ii) Proper incentive systems are deployed in WCI that recognise and incentivize for the active involvement of contractors and clients in the strict execution of implemented safety systems on site that would reduce the occurrence of accidents during the course of construction; and
2. The second notion stated that the utilisation of a fuzzy knowledge based system for premium rating that encompasses modules for real-time assessments of project hazards and contractors' safety management systems will eliminate the challenges faced in multi attribute inference with subjective and imprecise data. This will also translate the new WCI model, which embodies the philosophy of the first notion, into a physical product rather than a documented model, and foster its implementation in the industry.

The existing WCI model was first scrutinised to see if it is possible to incorporate these two notions into the model as a value adding measure to the existing model. In line with this, experience modification rating (EMR) approach was found to have been used extensively for WCI premium rating. However, this model was neither found effective for construction, nor does it provide room for improvement in acquiring the two notions above. Hence, the study aimed to:

1. Develop a new WCI model that:
   a. Encompasses effective hazard assessment and safety evaluation frameworks;
   b. Facilitates effective risk control during the course of insurance coverage; and

    c.   Addresses the drawbacks of existing methods and practices.

2.   Translate the WCI model into a fuzzy KBS.

Because construction covers a wide spectrum of projects such as building and civil engineering structures, it was necessary to limit the focus of the study to a specific type of construction so the new models to be developed will be effective and pertinent. Hence, the focus of the research was limited to building construction projects.

The study evolved through the following research methods:

- The premium rating model was developed based on the findings of an extensive literature review and an interview questionnaire survey in the general insurance industry of Singapore;
- A hybrid of an interview survey and a past workers' compensation claims data analysis was pursued to develop the conceptual model of the fuzzy KBS, which was then prototyped by using Fuzzy Logic Toolbox in Matlab™, VBA™ and MS Access™; and
- Finally, the fuzzy KBS was verified by Turing tests.

Research Findings

The research study yielded two significant findings, viz.:

- A new theoretical model for premium rating of workers' compensation insurance (WCI) for building construction projects; and
- The conceptual model and the prototype of a fuzzy KBS that automates the premium model above.

As per the proposed premium model, the WCI premium for a building construction project has three components: (1) *risk fee* - paid by the contractor at the underwriting stage for the risk inherent in the project and subsequently reimbursed by the project owner via interim payments; (2) $CCI_{contractor}$ – incentive to be presented to the contractor by the insurer upon policy expiry if the actual claims in the project were below the predicted amount; and (3) SMD_{client} – discount to be presented to the project client by the insurer upon policy expiry if the client had monitored the contractor's safety system so as to minimise accidents. The *risk fee* is computed in two steps: (1) predicting the potential claims in the project by assessing the project wage roll, project hazard level and the project safety level; and (2) marking-up the predicted claims to account for the insurer's overhead costs, corporate objectives, investment income, competition and contractor's claims history. The amounts for $CCI_{contractor}$ and SMD_{client} are founded on the total actual claims amount in the project. If the total actual claims amount is lesser than the predicted claims amount, the saving will be shared by the insurer with the contractor and the client.

The fuzzy KBS emulates the human characteristic of approximate reasoning from linguistic and imprecise terms. It facilitates complex computations and inferences involved in the determination of potential claims amount and the mark-up towards deriving the gross premium at the underwriting stage, as well as the computation of the $CCI_{contractor}$ and the SMD_{client} at the policy expiration stage. The prediction of potential claims amount passes through the following steps in the KBS:

- Derivation of a project hazard index by a qualitative assessment on the project scope and vicinity;
- Derivation of a project safety index by a qualitative assessment on the safety management system;
- Inferring a risk rate for the project by fuzzy inference on the project hazard index, project safety index and the project wage roll; and
- Computing the potential claims in the project based on the wage roll and the risk rate in the project as well as the mean claims unit cost of WCI for the insurance company.

The determination of an appropriate mark-up by the KBS is performed by fuzzy inference on insurer's overhead costs, corporate objectives, investment income, competition, and contractor's claims history. Finally, the computation of the $CCI_{contractor}$ and the SMD_{client} pursues objective calculations based on the actual claims experience in the project.

Comparison of Research Findings with the Previous Technique

The effectiveness of proposed models and the EMR technique for costing the risk, mark-up adjustments, and risk control is compared below.

1. The cost of risk is termed as expected claim (C) and standard premium in the proposed model and the EMR approach, respectively. The computation methods of the cost of risk in a building project in the proposed model and the EMR approach are formulated in equations (*a*) and (*b*), respectively.

C = Wage roll x Mean claims unit cost x Risk rate ....(a)
Standard premium = Payroll unit x Manual rate x EMR ....(b)

The major distinctions between these techniques are described below.
- The *payroll unit* in the EMR approach is substituted by *wage roll* in the proposed model. The payroll unit accounts for the number of person hours of risk exposure for a particular type of work. It is calculated as:

$$Payroll\ unit = \frac{Employer's\ straight\ time\ direct\ labour\ cost}{\$100}$$

The computation of the *payroll unit* in a building project needs to consider the amount of pay for each work classification. There are a number of work classifications in a project, thus making the task tedious. However, the proposed model needs only a single piece of data, i.e. wage roll, which can easily be taken from the building cost estimate, and therefore simplifies the prediction;

- The *mean claims unit cost* in the proposed model replaces the *manual rate* in the EMR approach. The *manual rate* is calculated by using the following formula:

$$Manual\ rate = \frac{(Benefits\ paid\ for\ a\ work\ type\ +\ overhead\ cost\ for\ administering)}{Straight\ time\ payroll}$$

The *manual rate* gives a rough indication of the risk associated with each work classification. Some work classifications are more likely to result in injuries and fatalities than others. Thus, the *manual rate* varies among work classifications. The final value for the *manual rate* for each work classification is based on claims that have been filed for that work classification. The computation of the *manual rate* involves the collection and processing of claims data for each work classification in a particular state by an external body, which in turn induces insurance companies to rely on external data. On the contrary, the *mean claims unit cost* in the proposed model reveals the overall risk level associated with construction WCI business for a particular insurer and therefore simplifies the calculation process. It also eliminates the need for disclosing an insurer's claims experience to other entities and relying on any external data for premium rating. In addition, the use of a company-specific *mean claims unit cost* distinguishes one insurance company from its rivals, therefore provides it with a competitive advantage; and

- The *EMR* is replaced by the *risk rate* in the proposed model. The *EMR* accounts for the loss experience of a contractor and is used to modify the *manual rate*. It helps predict the future losses based on past experience. A contractor with poor safety records will have a higher *EMR* and pay more for WCI. However, the *EMR* is a lagging indicator. The experience period used in the *EMR* calculation process is the three-year period ending one year prior to the date that the modification becomes effective. The most recent year is not used; although there may have been an improvement in safety records, it is not accounted for the next two years. In contrast, the *risk rate* in the proposed model accounts for the project hazard level and project safety level at the time of insurance application to derive a real-time adjustment factor. Moreover, the fuzzy inference for the *risk rate* in the proposed KBS allows extrapolations with imprecise and vague data.

2. As for the mark-up adjustment technique, the EMR approach is silent with respect to the determination of the mark-up, whereas the proposed model and its fuzzy KBS

consist of a dedicated module to determine the mark-up for a WCI policy. The KBS facilitates the analysis of both subjective and objective variables for deriving an optimum mark-up for a policy; and

3. The comparison for risk control measures in the models suggests that the proposed model advocates a well-structured risk control strategy via an established incentive scheme, whereas the EMR approach does not feature any risk control strategy.

In a concluding note, the new WCI model and its KBS proposed in this book: (1) materialise the two notions that was suggested for WCI-driven accident control; and (2) overcome the shortcomings of the existing EMR approach. They also have additional features to overcome the contemporary challenges facing the current construction and insurance industries in risk management.

Practical Implications for Industries

The findings reported in this book have significant implications for various industries in the national economy as explored below.

Implications for the Construction Industry

Occupational accidents seem to be inevitable on construction sites. Various stakeholders of the construction industry are trying to control accidents through different approaches. The frameworks and strategies reported in this book will facilitate these stakeholders in achieving the safety objective. The possible directions of implications of the reported findings are described below.

1. This study suggests a cost-driven methodology for accident control grounded on workers' compensation insurance premiums for contractors. As per the proposed WCI premium rating model, the premium amount for a WCI policy is significantly influenced by the effectiveness of the contractor's safety management system, which needs to be assessed in real-time. If a contractor's real-time safety management system is robust, the contractor will get a cost effective insurance cover, which will enable the contractor to compete better in tenders. Those contractors who do not have robust safety management systems in place will be penalised by higher premiums. This approach will automatically set risky contractors aside as well as motivate contractors to invest on safety in their organisations for ensuring business continuity. The proposed new model also advocates the partnering arrangement in WCI for construction whereby a post-project discount system is introduced through $CCI_{contractor}$ and SMD_{client} to encourage the involvement of both contractors and clients in reducing claims or improving safety during the course of construction. By adopting these strategies, the proposed model pulls all the parties to a WCI with a monetary steer to ensure safe workplaces. This will eventually pave the way to

reduce construction accidents. This arrangement also functions along with the philosophy of the Workplace Safety and Health Act 2006 of Singapore.

2. The committee of inquiry into the Nicoll Highway collapse in Singapore recommended that a strict weightage system form part of the tender evaluation system (Lian, 2005). The weightage system should include non-technical and non-commercial attributes such as safety records and culture of the bidder, and its core or corporate competency. Such a weightage system should apply even if the tenderer is a joint venture or a consortium. It was recommended to clients' project managers to adopt the Quality-Fee Method (QFM) for tender evaluations, departing from the traditional lowest price method (MND, 2005). According to QFM, tenders are scored based on pre-defined weightings for both price and quality attributes. Quality attributes in a tender include safety management proposal, method statement, resources, program and innovations. Then, apply a formula approach to combine price scores and quality scores as follows (BCA, 2005):
   - The lowest price tender obtains the maximum price score and the highest quality tender yields the maximum quality score; and
   - The tender with the highest overall score would be selected.

   The effective assessment and scoring of tenderers' safety proposals is therefore a crucial task for clients' project managers to implement QFM, but it is difficult and challenging. It is inferred that the effectiveness or flaw of a safety proposal can be assessed by establishing the potential accident risks given that the proposed safety system was in place. This can be done in three steps:
   - Firstly assessing the degree of hazards in a given project;
   - Then measuring the safety preparedness of the contractor to arrest the hazards that cause accidents; and
   - Subsequently, performing a trade-off analysis between the degree of hazard and safety preparedness, and derive an accident index, which reveals the potential accident risks in the project.

   The PHI estimation framework and the PSI estimation framework reported in the book would be valuable tools to perform these tasks systematically.

3. Raising safety standards by introducing new regulations and frameworks has been a goal for the Ministry of Manpower (MOM), Singapore following a series of high profile construction accidents in previous years. Two key thrusts were recently conceptualised towards achieving this goal. These are (Loo, 2006):
   - The initiation of "The Safest Employer of the Month" award; and
   - The initiation of a system for safety rating of contractors.

   The implementation of the two systems above needs the tracking of previous accident statistics of companies, the assessments of safety conditions in their current projects via safety audits on sites, and then the rating of contractors based on these two. A decision support system could be developed by MOM to better serve this purpose. The PSI framework reported in the book would be a useful gadget that can be incorporated into the decision support system.

In overall sense, the study contributes towards improving the safety culture in contractor organisations, thereby minimising construction accidents.

Implications for the Insurance Industry

Contractors who perform construction works and whose workers are injured owing to contractors' poor safety management systems remain in safe standing via WCI. There is no significant financial burden on contractors in this regard because premiums for insurance are paid for by project owners, while the damages to accident victims are paid for by insurers. Owing to this arrangement, contractors' enthusiasm and rigour towards minimising worksite accidents seem inadequate. Hence, insurance companies are forced to assume significant financial risks. Many of the insurers who are issuing WCI policies in Singapore have experienced continuous losses and some have even given up issuing WCI policies altogether. Nevertheless, this risk could be minimised if premium decisions are integrated with robust assessments of risks on construction projects and contractors' safety management systems. Such an approach would encourage contractors to improve their safety management systems to secure cost-effective insurance cover. This, in turn, will result in fewer claims by them on insurers, leading to higher profits in insurance business. However, insurance companies in Singapore have been facing two major difficulties, which stop them from performing an exhaustive analysis before issuing WCI policies. These are:

1. Lack of a structured framework for the assessment of project risks, safety, and market competition; and
2. Lack of track records of contractors' safety performance and claims.

The WCI model reported in the book, along with the risk control and partnering strategies, overcomes the aforementioned difficulties and paves the way to reduce WCI claims by contractors, and thereby leading to higher profits in insurance business. In addition, the fuzzy KBS helps minimise insurers' financial risks in the following ways:

- The fuzzy KBS revamps the current ineffective and non-scientific underwriting practice towards minimising losses in WCI business for insurers in Singapore;
- The fuzzy KBS facilitates multi-attribute inference, which always challenges underwriters' reasoning abilities;
- The fuzzy KBS also captures data on workers' compensation claims and contractors' safety performance for future use;
- The fuzzy KBS eliminates the high reliance on job-hopping experienced underwriters in the Singapore market; and
- The KBS also serves as a good learning tool for inexperienced underwriters for systematic learning on the job.

Implications for others

The findings extend their implications for software vendors and IT consultants to a reasonable degree. The book explains in great detail the facets involved in developing a KBS for WCI. The discussions cover methodologies for the essential steps of system analysis and design, knowledge acquisition and representation, and system verification. These would be pertinent guides for IT consultants and software vendors whose prime expertise is not insurance or construction risk. Thus, the book will serve as a good reference material for software vendors and IT consultants who produce and commercialise knowledge based systems for the construction, risk management, and insurance industries.

Bottleneck for Implementation

A significant comment was made by underwriters during the KBS verification exercise on the implementation of the proposed fuzzy KBS in the industry. That is, the premium rating based on the proposed model requires a rigorous assessment of project hazard and safety on building sites. It is possibly a time consuming task for underwriters as they are well-versed in practising rules of thumb to expedite their jobs. Hence, all the five experts who participated in the verification exercise commented that the proposed KBS is less simple to operate in the current state of Singapore's insurance industry. Nevertheless, it is possible that the comment was grounded on the following issues:

1. The short duration that they spent on evaluating the proposed KBS inclined them to feel that the KBS is difficult to work with;
2. Level of IT literacy they possess; and
3. Resistance to change their traditional practice.

However, all five of them appreciated the scientific approach and well-thought out strategies in the models that can better revamp WCI business in Singapore towards eliminating the current dilemmas faced by general insurers.

Knowledge Contributions

The research study and its findings enhance the body of knowledge with the following contributions:

1. A new WCI model for construction that encompasses the following supplementary models:
   • PHI estimation framework;
   • PSI estimation framework; and
   • Partnering framework in WCI.

2. The conceptual model of a fuzzy KBS that automates the new WCI model. This gives a new dimension to the new WCI model and would foster its practical implementation in the industry. The KBS conceptual model describes:

- The system architecture that houses various subcomponents such as graphical user interface, system database, intermediate processing unit, fuzzy knowledge base, and inference engine;
- The functions and structure of subcomponents;
- The domain knowledge representation methodology in the fuzzy knowledge base; and
- The inference methods in the inference engine and the intermediate processing unit.

3. An extension to the application of fuzzy logic for construction insurance.

Future Directions

The body of knowledge evolves by research and innovations. Identifying new research gaps and addressing them is absolutely the right approach for knowledge creation and innovation. Having explored the domain of construction risk and insurance during the course of this research study, the following directions for potential research are noted:

- It will add value to the proposed fuzzy KBS in terms of its simplicity and practicability if the PHI and the PSI computation parts are fully automated to minimise insurers' involvement. The integration of virtual reality technology with the fuzzy KBS would make this possible. Hence, the following two potential areas are identified for future studies:
  1. Deriving PHIs from virtual models of buildings; and
  2. Computing PSIs from virtual site safety plans of construction sites.
- The study may be extended to cover civil engineering works (i.e. roads, bridges, tunnels, power plants, etc.) and off-shore engineering works (i.e. oil rigs);
- Future research may be carried out in the following sub-areas of the construction insurance domain:
  1. A KBS for premium rating of contractors' all risk insurance; and
  2. A KBS for premium rating of construction professional liability insurance.
- Insurance for Public Private Partnerships for infrastructural developments would be another area for exploration.

Conclusion

The book began with unpleasant images of the construction and insurance industries that struggle to combat the consequences of occupational accidents on construction sites. It ends with some insight into how workers' compensation insurance, with the support of information technology, can be made as an opportunity or a mechanism to mitigate accidents. This insight has put forward prudent solutions to contemporary issues facing the construction and insurance industries.

There has been an enduring complaint that the bridge between industry practices and theories innovated by rigorous academic research is thin. This book has clearly and systematically integrated modern theories into practice, and has made the subject evenly pertinent to both academia and industry.

As far as the academic community is concerned, there has been a need for a scholarly book on construction WCI. While this book satisfies this need, it enhances the body of knowledge with state-of-the-art risk and safety management in construction, leveraged by IT. The book also eliminates the difficulties facing the academic community in cross-disciplinary learning and applications.

Appendix 1: Survey Kit

Appendix 1.1: Interview Questionnaire Survey Form

Factors Influencing Workers' Compensation Insurance Premiums for Building Construction Projects

General Information

- *This survey assesses the degree of influence by various factors on workers' compensation insurance premiums for building construction projects. Please fill in the blanks or tick the most appropriate answer for each question from your experience/perception.*
- *The information gathered from this survey will be used to develop a knowledge based system that determines optimal premiums for workers' compensation insurance for building construction projects.*
- *Please provide accurate and complete information as this will affect the accuracy of the system that is to be developed.*
- *The data furnished will be fully confidential. It will only be used for research purposes. You will not be identified in any circumstance with any of the data that you provide.*

A. Respondent's Particulars

1. Name: ....
   Email address: ....
   Contact number: ....
2. Occupation/Job title: ....
3. Qualification(s): ....
4. Experience in construction insurance business (no. of years): ....
5. Organisation: ....

6. Industry wide, you consider your company as a:

    ☐ Small size insurer   ☐ Medium size insurer   ☐ Large size insurer

7. Number of business competitors for your company in the industry: ....

8. Date of response (dd/mm/yy): ....

B. Workers' Compensation Insurance Premium Decisions for Building Construction Projects

This section of the questionnaire assesses the degree of influence by various factors on workers' compensation insurance premiums for building construction projects. These factors are grouped under four sections: (1) Project factors; (2) Contractor factors; (3) Insurer factors; and (4) Market factors. Please answer all questions in each section from your experience/perception.

B.1. Project Factors

Please rate how the following project-related factors influence workers' compensation insurance premium rates for building construction projects.

1. Wage roll:
    1.1. How does the *wage roll* influence premium rates?

          ☐   The higher the wage roll, the higher the premium rate

          ☐   The higher the wage roll, the lower the premium rate (owing to discounts)

          ☐   No influence by the project wage roll on premium rates
    1.2. Please rate the extent to which the *wage roll* influences premium rates.
          Rating: 1   2   3   4   5   6   7   8   9   10
                      (low)   (high)
    1.3. Please explain the reasons for your answers.

2. Project duration:
    2.1. How does the *project duration* influence premium rates?

          ☐   The longer the project duration, the higher the premium rate

          ☐   The longer the project duration, the lower the premium rate

          ☐   No influence by the project duration on premium rates
    2.2. Please rate the extent to which the *project duration* influences premium rates.
          Rating: 1   2   3   4   5   6   7   8   9   10
                      (low)   (high)
    2.3. Please explain the reasons for your answers.

3. Project hazard level:
    3.1. Please rate the extent to which the *project hazard level* influences premium rates.
          Rating: 1   2   3   4   5   6   7   8   9   10
                      (low)   (high)
    3.2. Please explain the reasons for your answer.

4. Effectiveness of the *risk and safety management system* of the contractor:
    4.1. Please rate the extent to which the effectiveness of the risk and safety management system of the contractor influences premium rates.

    Rating: 1   2   3   4   5   6   7   8   9   10
                (low)   (high)

    4.2.   Please explain the reasons for your answer.

B.2. Contractor Factors

Please rate how the following contractor-related factors influence workers' compensation insurance premium rates for building construction projects.

1. Claims history of the contractor:
    1.1. How does the *claims history of the contractor* influence premium rates?

    ☐   If the claims history is bad, increase the premium rate

    ☐   If the claims history is good, you will give a discount

    ☐   Do not adjust the premium rate with respect to claims history

    1.2. Please rate the extent to which the *claims history of the contractor* influences the premium rate.

    Rating: 1   2   3   4   5   6   7   8   9   10
                (low)   (high)

    1.3. Please explain the reasons for your answers.

2. Volume of insurance taken by the contractor:
    2.1. How does the *volume of insurance taken by the contractor* influence premium rates?

    ☐   If a contractor buys all the insurance policies for a project from you, you will give a discount

    ☐   If a contractor buys only workers' compensation insurance for a project from you, you do not give any discount

    ☐   Volume of insurance does not influence premium rates

    2.2. Please rate the extent to which *volume of insurance covers taken by the contractor* influences premium rate.

    Rating: 1   2   3   4   5   6   7   8   9   10
                (low)   (high)

    2.3. Please explain the reasons for your answers.

3. Expectation of potential business from the contractor:

    3.1. How does the *expectation of potential business from the contractor* influence the premium rate?

□ If there is a large volume of potential projects with a contractor, reduce the current premium rate

□ Expectation of potential business with a contractor does not influence the current premium rate

3.2. Please rate the extent to which the *expectation of potential business from the contractor* influences current premium rates.

Rating: 1   2   3   4   5   6   7   8   9   10
            (low)   (high)

3.3. Please explain the reasons for your answers.

4. Co-operation by the contractor in assessing possible deliberate acts of workers that caused accidents:

    4.1. How does the *co-operation by the contractor in assessing deliberate acts of workers* influence premium rates?

        □ If a contractor is co-operative in risk control, give a discount

        □ If a contractor is not co-operative in risk control, increase the premium rate

        □ Co-operation by a contractor does not influence the premium rate

    4.2. Please rate the extent to which the *co-operation by the contractor in assessing deliberate acts of workers* influences the premium rate.

Rating: 1   2   3   4   5   6   7   8   9   10
            (low)   (high)

    4.3. Please explain the reasons for your answers.

5. Contractor size:

    5.1. How does the *contractor size* influence the premium rate?

        □ The larger the contractor size, the higher the premium rate

        □ The larger the contractor size, the lower the premium rate (owing to discounts)

        □ No influence by the contractor size on the premium rate

    5.2. Please rate the extent to which the *contractor size* influences premium rates.

Rating: 1   2   3   4   5   6   7   8   9   10
            (low)   (high)

    5.3. Please explain the reasons for your answers.

B.3. Insurer Factors

Please rate how the following insurer-related factors influence workers' compensation insurance premium rates for building construction projects.

1. Amount of outstanding claims to the insurer:

    1.1. How does the *amount of outstanding claims to the insurer* influence the current premium rate?

☐ If the insurer has a large amount of outstanding claims, increase the premium rates for new projects

☐ If the insurer has a large amount of outstanding claims, decrease the premium rates for new projects

☐ Do not adjust the premium rate with respect to outstanding claims

1.2. Please rate the extent to which the *amount of outstanding claims to the insurer* at the time of premium computation influences the premium rate.

Rating: 1   2   3   4   5   6   7   8   9   10
             (low)   (high)

1.3. Please explain the reasons for your answers.

2. Profit/loss experience of the insurer:

2.1. How does the *profit/loss experience of the insurer* influence new premium rates?

☐ If the insurer experiences profit, increase the premium rates for new projects

☐ If the insurer experiences profit, decrease the premium rates for new projects

☐ Do not adjust the premium rate with respect to profit/loss experience

2.2. Please rate the extent to which the *profit/loss experience of the insurer* in the recent past influences the current premium rate.

Rating: 1   2   3   4   5   6   7   8   9   10
             (low)   (high)

2.3. Please explain the reasons for your answers.

3. Investment income from underwritten premiums:

3.1. How does the *investment income from underwritten premiums* influence the premium rate?

☐ If the insurer has a high investment return from underwritten premiums, reduce the premium rate

☐ If the insurer has a high investment return from underwritten premiums, increase the premium rate

☐ Do not adjust the premium rate with respect to investment returns

3.2. Please rate the extent to which the *investment income from underwritten premiums* influences the premium rate.

Rating: 1   2   3   4   5   6   7   8   9   10
             (low)   (high)

3.3. Please explain the reasons for your answers.

4. Corporate objectives of the insurer:

4.1. Please rate the extent to which the *corporate objectives of the insurer* influence the premium rate.

Rating: 1   2   3   4   5   6   7   8   9   10
             (low)   (high)

4.2. Please explain the reasons for your answer.

5. Overhead costs:
   5.1. Please rate the extent to which the *overhead costs* of the insurer influences premium
        rates.
        Rating: 1   2   3   4   5   6   7   8   9   10
                    (low)   (high)
   5.2. Please explain the reasons for your answer.

6. Reinsurance cost:
   6.1. Please rate the extent to which the *reinsurance cost* of the insurer influences premium
        rates.
        Rating: 1   2   3   4   5   6   7   8   9   10
                    (low)   (high)
   6.2. Please explain the reasons for your answer.

B.4. Market Factors
   Please rate how the following market-related factors influence workers' compensation
insurance premium rates for building construction projects.

1. Demand for insurance (volume of business)
   1.1. How does the *demand for insurance from contractors* influence the premium rate?
        ☐   If there is a high demand for construction insurance from contractors, increase
            the premium rate
        ☐   If there is a high demand for construction insurance from contractors, decrease
            the premium rate
        ☐   Do not adjust the current premium rate with respect to demand for construction
            insurance
   1.2. Please rate the extent to which the *demand for insurance from contractors* influences
        premium rates.
        Rating: 1   2   3   4   5   6   7   8   9   10
                    (low)   (high)
   1.3. Please explain the reasons for your answers.

2. Competition among insurers
   2.1. How does the *competition among insurers* influence the premium rate?
        ☐   If the competition among insurers is high, reduce the premium rate
        ☐   If the competition among insurers is low, reduce the premium rate
        ☐   Do not adjust the premium rate with respect to competition among insurers
   2.2. Please rate the extent to which *competition among insurers* influences premium rates.
        Rating: 1   2   3   4   5   6   7   8   9   10
                    (low)   (high)
   2.3. Please explain the reasons for your answers.
                          End of questionnaire
              Thank you very much for your invaluable support!

Appendix 1.2: Interview Guideline

Mark-up Determination for Construction WCI

A. Respondent's Particulars

1. Name: ....
    Contact details: ....
2. Occupation/Job title: ....
3. Qualification(s): ....
4. Experience in construction insurance business (no. of years): ....
5. Organisation: ....
6. Date of response (dd/mm/yy): ....

B. Interview Questions

1. Overhead costs:
    a. Please indicate the overhead costs for WCI for building construction projects and their magnitudes as percentages of the premium.
    b. How is the premium rate adjusted to accommodate your overhead costs?

2. Investment return:
    a. What are the options available for insurance companies to invest the underwritten premiums and what are their rates of return?
    b. How does the investment return adjust the premium rate?

3. Competition:
    a. How is the severity of competition for construction WCI assessed by insurance companies?
    b. How is the premium rate adjusted for competition in the Singapore insurance market?

4. Corporate objectives:
    a. What are your corporate objectives with regards to construction WCI?
    b. How do you adjust the premium rate in view of your corporate objectives?

5. Contractor's claim history
    a. How is a contractor's claims history assessed by insurance companies?
    b. How does a contractor's claims history adjust the premium rate?

Appendix 2: WCIXpert User Manual

Installing WCIXpert

The following software must have been installed on your computer to run WCIXpert prototype:

- MS Access™; and
- Matlab™.

Installation Method

Adopt the steps described below to install WCIXpert on your computer.

1. Insert the CD-Rom that contains WCIXpert into your CD drive.
2. Open the CD-Rom. You will find a folder named WCIXpert.
3. Copy the folder into a preferred location on your computer.

Getting Started with WCIXpert

This section explains how you can start and exit WCIXpert. It also introduces the elements of the main window and their respective functions.

1. Open the WCIXpert folder.
2. Double click WCIXpert icon. It will open the main window of the KBS as shown in Figure A.1. If you open the system in Access 2007, VBA Macro will be disabled by default. To enable it, click on Options tab that appears on the Security Warning bar, select "Enable this content" from the Security Alert window and then click OK.

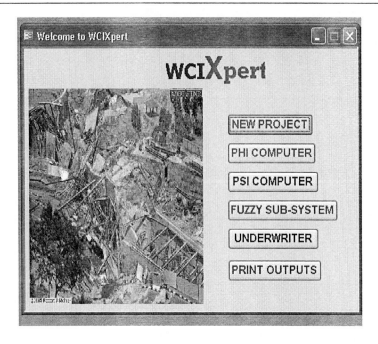

Figure A.1. Main window of WCIXpert

3. The main window contains six command buttons, which open the major interfaces of the KBS, as described in Table A.1.
4. When you have finished working with WCIXpert, click on the X button on the upper right corner of the window to exit the KBS.

Table A.1. Main window elements

Screen element	Function
New Project	Opens the interface to create a new project file
PHI Computer	Initiates the major interface of the PHI computer to determine PHI values for building projects
PSI Computer	Opens the key interface of the PSI computer to calculate PSI values for building projects
Fuzzy Sub-System	Invokes the fuzzy sub-system to infer risk rates and mark-ups for WCI policies
Underwriter	Opens up the main interface of the underwriter to create new WCI policies, store claim details on existing policies and to update the system database
Print Outputs	Opens the interface for printing outputs such as WCI quotations, and incentives for contractors and clients.

Creating a New Project File

This section of the manual explains how you can create a new project file when a contractor requests for a WCI quotation for a building project.

1. Click the *New Project* button on the main window of the KBS (Figure A.1).
2. It will open the *Project details* window as illustrated in Figure A.2.
3. Fill in all the details of the new project by passing through each textbox in the window.
4. The contractor for the project can be selected from a combo box as shown in Figure A.2.
5. If a contractor for a given project is not listed, click *Add new contractor* button to add a new contractor to the list.
6. A dialog box will appear as in Figure A.3 to record the details of the new contractor. Once you are finished with entering new contractor details, close the dialog box to return to the project details window.
7. Now select the new contractor from the list.
8. Once you are finished with keying in new project details, close the window to return to the main window of the KBS.

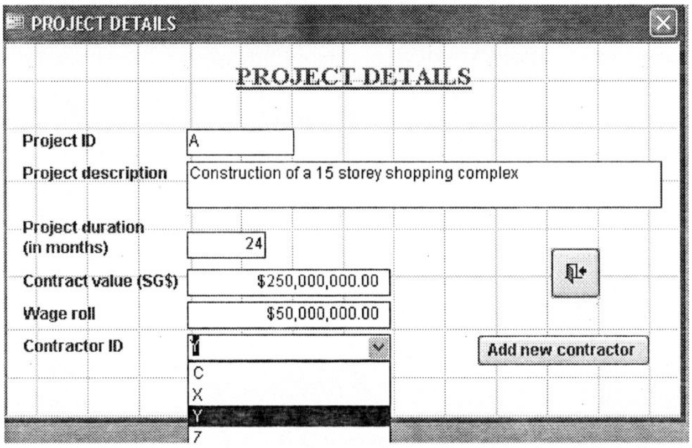

Figure A.2. Project details window

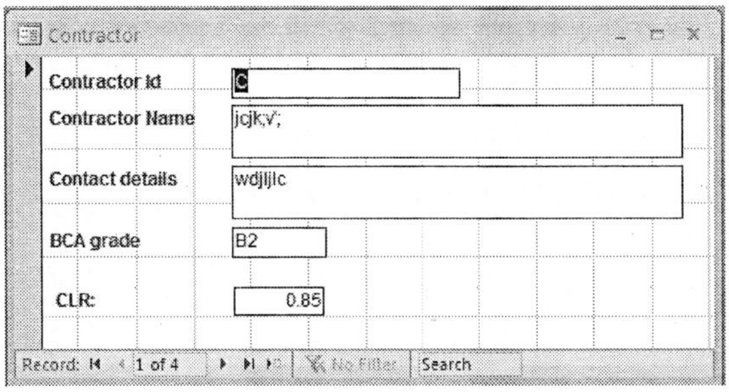

Figure A.3. Contractor dialog box

Hazard Rating of Building Construction Projects

This part of the manual describes how you can calculate PHI values for building projects.

1. Click the *PHI Computer* button on the main window of the KBS.
2. It will open the main interface of the PHI computer as shown in Figure A.4. The PHI computer interface contains two sub-interfaces for hazard rating of a building construction project.

Figure A.4. PHI computer

Hazard Assignment

This section explains how you can assign hazard trades to a new building project.

1. Click the *Hazard Assignment* button on the PHI computer interface in Figure A.4.
2. It will open the HAZARD ASSIGNMENT interface as depicted in Figure A.5.
3. There are 11 key hazard trades in building projects. But not every project will have all 11 trades. This interface allows you to assign pertinent hazard trades for a project.
4. Decide on the pertinent hazard trade Ids for the project from the list shown at the bottom part of the interface in Figure A.5.
5. Choose the Ids of the relevant hazard trades one by one from the combo box in the middle part of the interface.
6. Once you are done with assigning hazard trades for the project, close the window to return to the PHI computer.

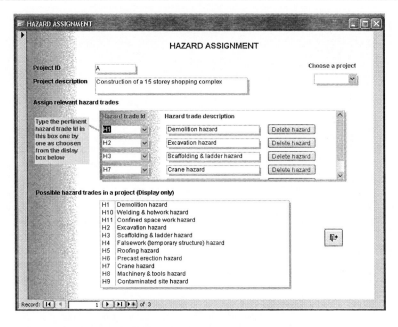

Figure A.5. Hazard assignment

Project Hazard Rating

This section explains how you can rate the degree of hazard in each trade that was assigned above.

1. Click the *Project Hazard Rating* button on the PHI computer interface in Figure A.4.
2. A macro will be triggered as shown in Figure A.6. If you are going to hazard rate a new project, click *Yes,* otherwise *No.*
3. Subsequently a dialog box, as shown in Figure A.7, will appear. Type the project Id of the project that you are going to hazard rate and then click *OK.*
4. Following that another window will appear as depicted in Figure A.8; click *Yes.*
5. The HAZARD RATING interface will now appear as illustrated in Figure A.9.
6. This interface allows you to rate project hazards by analysing each hazard trade individually. The bottom part of the interface lists all the attributes pertinent to a hazard trade (in this case it is Demolition hazard). Rate the intensity of hazard posed by each attribute by choosing an option (1 to 5) on the lower right hand corner of the interface.
7. Click the *Next hazard* button to move to the other hazard trade.
8. Close the interface to return to the PHI computer once you are finished with hazard rating.
9. Close the PHI computer to return to the main window.

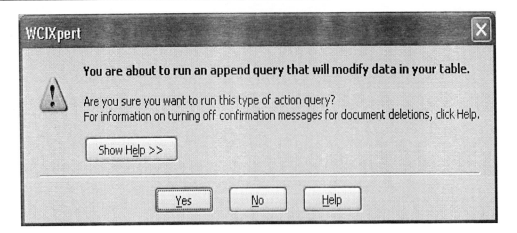

Figure A.6. PHI macro

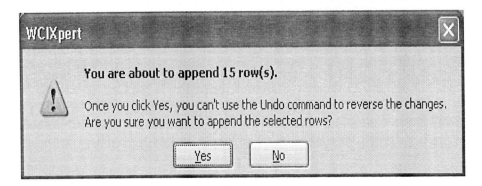

Figure A.7. PHI dialog box 1

Figure A.8. PHI dialog box 2

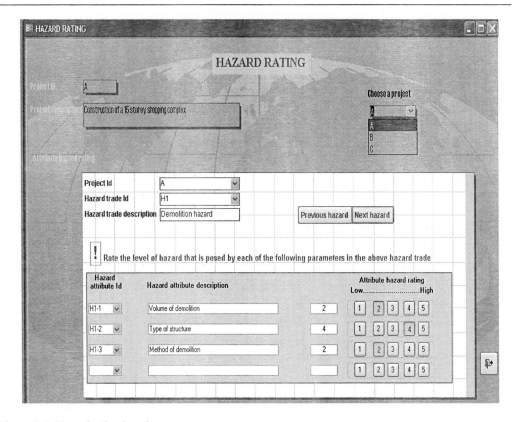

Figure A.9. Hazard rating interface

Safety Rating of Building Construction Projects

This section of the manual elaborates on how you can calculate PSI values for building projects.

1. Click the *PSI Computer* button on the main window of the KBS in Figure A.1. A macro will be triggered as shown in Figure A.10. If you are going to safety rate a new project, click *Yes,* otherwise *No.*
2. Subsequently a dialog box as shown in Figure A.11 will appear. Type the project Id of the project that you are going to safety rate and then click *OK*
3. Following that another window will appear as depicted in Figure A.12; click Yes.
4. It will open the main interface of the PSI computer as illustrated in Figure A.13. The PSI computer interface contains eight sub-interfaces for safety rating of a building construction project.
5. Click the *Rating of Project Safety Organisation* button on the PSI computer. It will open an interface similar to Figure A.14.
6. The bottom part of the interface lists all the attributes pertinent to project safety organisation. Rate the adequacy of attributes by choosing an option (1 to 5) on the lower right corner of the interface.

7. Close the interface to return to the PSI computer once you are finished with safety rating.
8. Click other buttons on the PSI computer interface to open the other interfaces one by one and follow the same method to safety rate each safety factor.
9. Close the PSI computer to return to the main window when you are finished with safety rating of all eight factors.

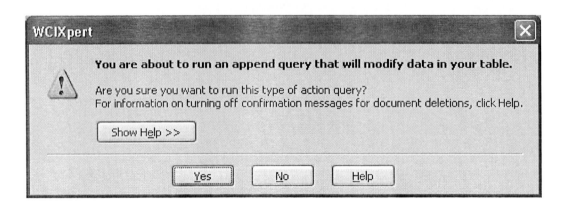

Figure A.10. PSI macro

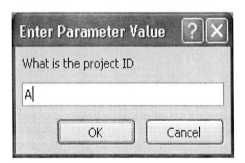

Figure A.11. PSI dialog box 1

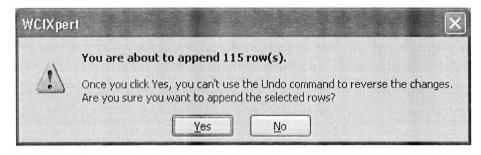

Figure A.12. PSI dialog box 2

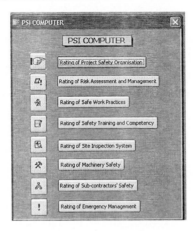

Figure A.13. PSI computer

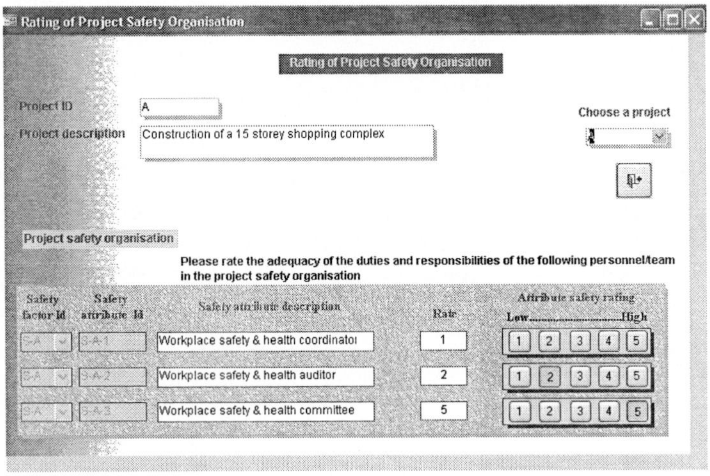

Figure A.14. PSI interface 1

Inference of Risk Rate and Mark-up

This part of the manual explains how you can use the fuzzy inference sub-system to infer risk rates and mark-ups for WCI policies.

1. Click the *Fuzzy Sub-system* button on the main window of the KBS.
2. It will open the main interface of the Fuzzy sub-system, which contains two sub-interfaces as shown in Figure A.15.
3. Click the *Input for Fuzzy Expert* button, which will open an interface similar to Figure A.16. This interface displays the inputs such as wage roll, PHI and PSI for risk rate inference by the fuzzy expert.
4. Without closing the above interface, click the *Open Fuzzy Expert* button to invoke the fuzzy expert. The KBS will open Matlab platform as depicted in Figure A.17. Type "fuzzy" in the command window space and press the Enter key.

5. Now the fuzzy toolbox window will be triggered as shown in Figure A.18. Click *File> Open FIS from disk* to open the fuzzy inference sub-system directory.

6. Choose the location of the WCIXpert-fuzzy inference sub-system on your computer and then open it as illustrated in Figure A.19.

7. The fuzzy inference sub-system of the WCIXpert will now open. Click *View> View rules* as shown in Figure A.20 to open the interface for inferring risk rates and mark-ups.

8. Figure A.21 resembles the interface for inferring risk rate and mark-up based on the user's values for input variables. The top left part of the interface displays the name of the eight inputs for the fuzzy systems. The textbox labelled "Input" at the bottom of the interface allows the user to key-in values for the inputs in the order displayed on the top part. The top right part of the interface displays the two outputs for the input values.

9. For deriving an appropriate risk rate for the policy, switch back to the *Inputs for Fuzzy Expert* interface (Figure A.16) and get the PHI, PSI and Wage roll values for the project.

10. Also obtain values for inputs such as overhead costs, investment income, competition, outstanding premium target and contractor's claims history.

11. Key-in the input values in the "Input textbox" of the interface and exit the textbox to view the results of fuzzy inference.

12. The appropriate risk rate and mark-up rate for the policy can be seen on the top right part of the interface.

13. Do make note of the output values and exit the fuzzy inference sub-system to return to KBS main window.

Figure A.15. Fuzzy sub-system

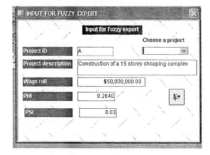

Figure A.16. Inputs for Fuzzy Expert

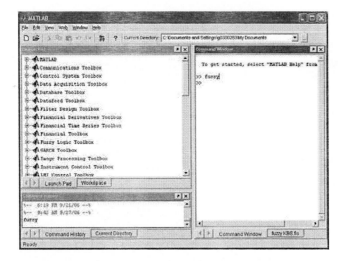

Figure A.17. Matlab platform

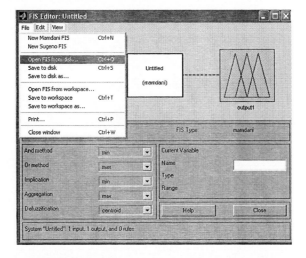

Figure A.18. Fuzzy toolbox window

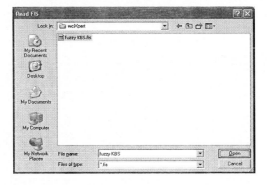

Figure A.19. Fuzzy sub-system directory

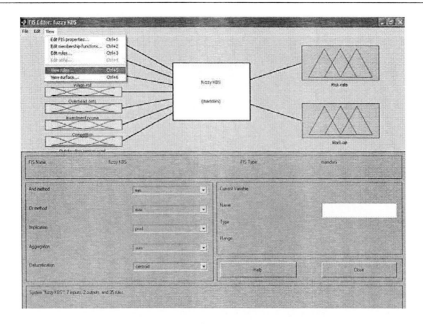

Figure A.20. Fuzzy inference sub-system

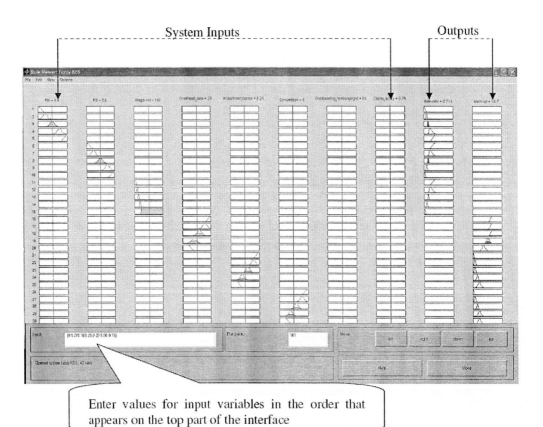

Figure A.21. Fuzzy inference Interface

Underwriting a New WCI Policy

This section explains how you can prepare a WCI quotation for a new project and print a hardcopy of it.

1. Click the *Underwriter* button on the main window of the KBS. It will open the main interface of the Underwriter as shown in Figure A.22. The Underwriter interface contains three sub-interfaces for underwriting a new policy, managing claims in the new policy and updating the claims database of the KBS.

Figure A.22. Underwriter

2. Click the New WCI Policy button on the *Underwriter* window in Figure A.22. It will open up the WCI Policy Details interface as shown in Figure A.23.

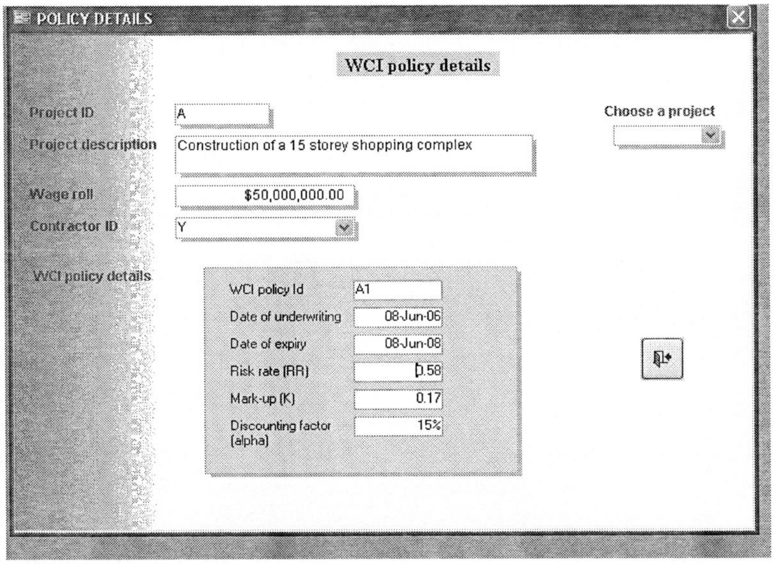

Figure A.23. WCI policy details

3. The top part of the interface displays the information about the project and the bottom gray colour part allows the user to key-in policy related inputs such as policy Id, date of underwriting, date of expiry, risk rate and mark-up rate as derived from the fuzzy inference sub-system, and a discounting factor.

4. Fill-in all the textboxes with relevant input values for the project concerned.

5. Close the WCI Policy Details interface and the *Underwriter* interface to return to the main window of the KBS.

6. Now click the *Print Outputs* button on the main window of the KBS. It will open the main interface of the *Print Outputs* as shown in Figure A.24.

7. Click the *WCI Quotation* button on the *Print Outputs* interface. A dialog box will appear similar to Figure A.25. Type the policy Id into the textbox.

8. The print preview of the WCI quotation for the above policy Id will be displayed now as shown in Figure A.26. You may print it.

Figure A.24. Print outputs

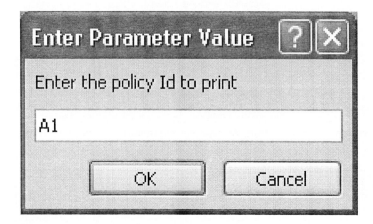

Figure A.25. Print quotation dialog box

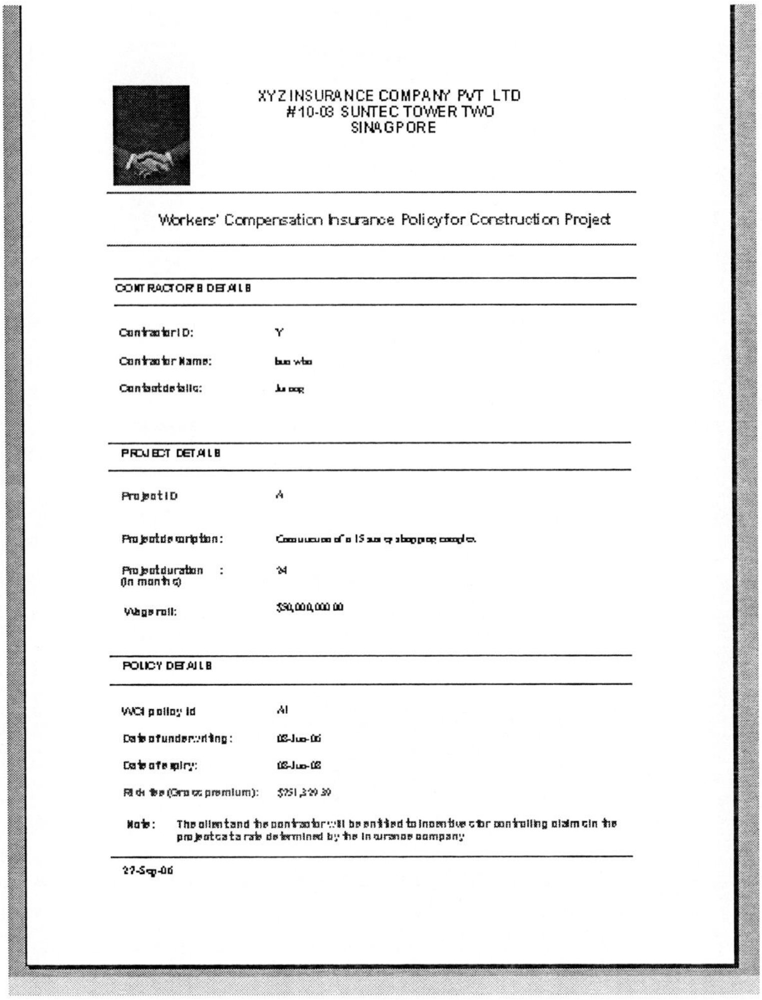

Figure A.26. WCI quotation

Claims Management

This part describes how you can maintain workers' compensation claims data for WCI policies as they emerge during the course of construction of building projects.

1. Click the *Underwriter* button on the main window of the KBS. It will open the main interface of the Underwriter as shown in Figure A.22.
2. Click the New Claims Details button on the *Underwriter* window in Figure A.22. It will open up the Claims details interface as shown in Figure A.27. Key-in the claims details to a policy in this interface as they are incurred.

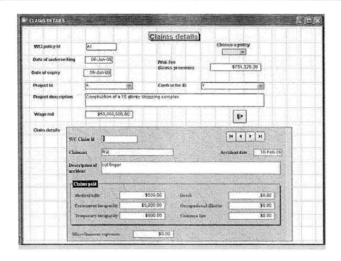

Figure A.27. Claims details

3. Upon the expiry of a WCI policy, the claims experience needs to be captured for future use. Click the *Update Claims Database* button on the *Underwriter* window in Figure A.22.
4. A macro similar to Figure A.28 will appear. Click the *Yes* button on the macro.
5. It will subsequently open a dialog box resembling Figure A.29. Key-in the WCI policy Id whose claims details will be appended to the system database.

Figure A.28. Claims management macro

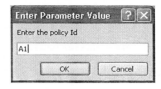

Figure A.29. Claims management dialog box

Producing CCI Contractor and SMD Client Details

This section explains how you can determine the incentives for the client and the contractor to a WCI policy at the policy expiration stage.

1. Now click the *Print Outputs* button on the main window of the KBS. It will open the main interface of the *Print Outputs* as shown in Figure A.24.
2. Click the *CCI Report* button on the *Print Outputs* interface. A dialog box will appear similar to Figure A.30. Type the policy Id into the textbox.

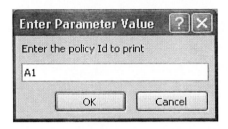

Figure A.30. Print quotation dialog box

3. The print preview of the CCI$_{contractor}$ for the above policy Id will be displayed now as shown in Figure A.31. You may print it.

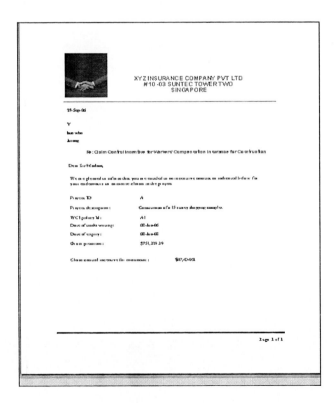

Figure A.31. CCI report

4. Follow the same steps to print the *SMD report.*

End of manual

References

Abdelhamid, T.S. and Everett, J.G. (2000). Identifying root causes of construction accidents. *Journal of Construction Engineering and Management*, 126(1), 52-60.

Arboleda, C.A. and Abraham, D.M. (2004). Fatalities in trenching operations - analysis using models of accident causation. *Journal of Construction Engineering and Management*, 130(2), 273-280.

Australian Federation of Construction Contractors (AFCC). (1987). Safety: A matter of management. *Safety Communications*. Sydney: AFCC.

Axelsson, P.O. and Fang, G. (1985). *Accidents with hand-held machineries and tools in construction work* (Report No. TRITA-AOG-0032). Stockholm: Royal Institute of Technology.

Babbie, E. (1992). *The Practice of Social Research* (6th ed.) California: Wadsworth Publishing Company.

Baturone, I., Barriga, A., Sanchez-solano, S., Jimenez-Fernandez, C.J. and Lopez, D.R. (2000). *Microelectronic Design of Fuzzy Logic-based Systems*. Boca Raton: CRC Press.

Bell, P.M. and Badiru, A.B. (1996). Fuzzy modelling and analytical hierarchy processing to quantify risk levels associated with occupational injuries-part I: the development of fuzzy linguistic risk levels. *IEEE Transactions on Fuzzy Systems*, 4(2), 124-131.

Bentley, T.A., Hide, S., Tappin, D., Moore, D., Legg, S., Ashby, L. and Parker, R. (2006). Investigating risk factors for slips, trips and falls in New Zealand residential construction using incident-centred and incident-independent methods. *Ergonomics*, 49(1), 62-77.

Berkan, R.C. and Trubatch, S.L. (1997). *Fuzzy Systems Design Principles: Building Fuzzy IF-THEN Rule Bases*. New York: IEEE Press.

Boissonnade, A.C. (1984). *Earthquake Damage and Insurance Risk*. Unpublished Ph.D dissertation, The John A. Blume Earthquake Engineering Centre, Stanford University.

Booth, P., Chadburn, R., Cooper, D. Haberman, S. and James, D. (1999). *Modern Actuarial Theory and Practice.* New York: Chapman & Hall/CRC.

Brown, C.E. and O'Leary, D.E. (1995). *Introduction to Artificial Intelligence and Expert Systems*. http://accounting.rutgers.edu/raw/aies/www.bus.orst.edu /faculty/ brownc/ es_tutor/es_tutor.htm#1-AI. [25 May 2004].

Building and Construction Authority (BCA). (2005) *Framework for Quality-Fee selection method (QFM) system.* http://www.bca.gov.sg/ PanelsConsultants/others/QFM Framework.pdf. [1 July 2006].

Building and Construction Authority (BCA). (2006a). *Annual Report 2004 – Unveiling BCA.* http://www.bca.gov.sg/AboutUs/annual_report_04.html. [11 Aug.2006].

Building and Construction Authority (BCA). (2006b). *Annual Report 2005 – Working Together.* http://www.bca.gov.sg/AboutUs/annual_report_05.html. [11 Aug.2006].

Bunni, N.G. (2003). *Risk and Insurance in Construction* (2nd ed.). London: Spon Press.

Bureau of Labor Statistics (BLS). (1996). *Fatal workplace injuries in 1994: a collection of data and analysis* (Report No. 908). Washington, DC: Department of Labor.

Bureau of Labor Statistics (BLS). (1997a). *Fatal workplace injuries in 1995: a collection of data and analysis* (Report No. 913). Washington, DC: Department of Labor.

Bureau of Labor Statistics (BLS). (1997b). *National census of fatal occupational injuries, 1996* (News release No. 266). Washington, DC: Department of Labor.

Bureau of Labor Statistics (BLS). (1998). *Workplace injuries and illness in 1996: case and demographic characteristics for workplace injuries and illness involving days away from work* (Supplemental tables, Table No. 14). http://www..stats.bls.gov/special.requests/ocwc/oshwc/osh/case/ostb 0625. pdf. [16 Feb. 2006].

Burton, G. (2005). Workers' Compensation in Australia – with specific focus on NSW. Australian and New Zealand Institute of Insurance and Finance Journal, 28(5), 14- 19.

Business Monitor. (2008). *The UK Infrastructure Report 2008.* http://www. businessmonitor.com/infra/uk.html. [11 Sept. 2008].

Canadian Wood Council. (2005). *Course of Construction Insurance Basics.* http://www. cwc.ca/pdfs/Quickfacts-Insurance and_Construction_Series_No1. pdf. [29 Sep 2005].

Carreno, L.A. and Jani, Y. (1993). A fuzzy expert system approach to insurance risk assessment using FuzzyCLIPS. In D.M. Anderson (Ed), *WESCON Conference Record*, (pp536-541). San Francisco: IEEE Service Centre

Carretero, R.C. and Viejo, A.S. (2000). A bonus-malus system in the fuzzy set theory [insurance pricing decisions]. In H.P. Del Rio & S.A. Texas (Eds), *The Ninth IEEE International Conference on Fuzzy Systems Vol.* 2, (pp1033-1036). Piscataway, NJ.USA: IEEE Service Centre.

Chen, J.J.G. and He, Z. (1997). Using analytic hierarchy process and fuzzy set theory to rate and rank the disability. *Fuzzy Sets and Systems,* 88(1), 1-22.

Chua, D.K.H. and Goh, Y. M. (2004). Incident causation model for improving feedback of safety knowledge. *Journal of Construction Engineering and Management*, 130(4), 542-551.

Clayton, A. (2004). Workers' compensation: a background for social security professionals. *Social Security Bulletin*, 65(4), 7-15.

Clough, R.H., Sears, G.A. and Sears, S.K. (2005). *Construction Contracting* (7th ed.) New York: John Wiley & Sons, Inc.

Coble, R.J. and Sims, B.L. (1996). Workers' compensation fraud in construction. *AACE Transactions*, 117(3), C&C6.1-6.

Coble, R.J., McDermott, M.J. and Carpenter, S. (1998). The liability of workers' compensation exemptions in Florida. *Cost Engineer*, 40(5), 34-41.

Combs, W.E. (1997). The Combs method for rapid inference. In E. Cox (ed.) *The Fuzzy Systems handbook* (2nd ed.). New York: AP Professional. pp 659-680.

Combs, W.E. and Andrews, J.E. (1998). Combinatorial rule explosion eliminated by a fuzzy rule configuration. *IEEE Transactions on Fuzzy Systems*, 6 (1), 1-11.

Construction Forecasting Council. (2008), *13th Forecast*. www.cfc.acif.com.au. [17 sept.2008].

Construction Safety Association of Ontario (CSAO). (1994). *Crane and rigging fatalities*. Ontario: CSAO.

Cox, E. (1999). *The Fuzzy Systems Handbook* (2nd ed.). New York: Academic Press.

Davies, V.J. and Tomasin, K. (1996). *Construction Safety Handbook* (2nd ed.). London: Thomas Telford.

DeWit, G.W. (1982). Underwriting and uncertainty. *Insurance: Mathematics and Economics*, 1(4), 277-285.

Dingsdag, D., Biggs, H. & Sheahan, V. (2006) *Safety culture in the construction industry: changing behaviour through enforcement and education*. Available at: http://2006 conference.crcci.info/docs/CDProceedings/ Proceedings/P132_Dingsdag_R.pdf [3 Oct. 2007].

Driankov, D., Hellendoorn, H. and Reinfrank, M. (1993). *An Introduction to Fuzzy Control*. Verlag: Springler.

Durkin, J. (2002). Tools and Applications. In C.T. Leondes (Ed.), *Expert Systems: the technology of knowledge management and decision making for the 21st century* (pp. 654 - 667). California: Academic Press.

Ederer. (2006). *Extra safety and monitoring for cranes and hoists*. http://www. ederer.com/x-sam.html. [4 March 2006].

Ekanayake, L.L. and Ofori, G. (2004). Building waste assessment score: design-based tool. *Building and Environment*, 39(7), 851-861.

Environmental Health & Safety (EH&S). (2006). *Confined space hazard analysis*. http:// www.ehs.uci.edu/ programs/safety/cspaceAppendixA.Pdf. [12 Mar. 06].

Everett, J.G. and Frank Jr, P.B. (1996). Cost of accidents and injuries to the construction industry. *Journal of Construction Engineering and Management*, 122(2), 158-164.

Everett, J.G. and Thompson, W.S. (1995). Experience modification rating for workers' compensation insurance. *Journal of Construction Engineering and Management*, 121(1), 66-79.

Fayek, A.R. and Oduba, A. (2005). Predicting industrial construction labor productivity using fuzzy expert systems. *Journal of Construction Engineering and Management*, 131(8), 938-941.

Fraser, L., (2007) Significant development in occupational health and safety in Australia's construction industry. *International Journal of Occupational and Environmental Health*, 13(1), 12-20.

Fredericks, T., Abudayyeh, O., Palmquist, M. and Torres, H.N. (2002). Mechanical contracting safety issues. *Journal of Construction Engineering and Management*, 128(2), 186-193.

General Insurance Association of Singapore (GIA). (2006). *Industry Statistics*. http://www. gia.org.sg/industrystats.cfm. [17 Aug.2006].

Gillen, M., Faucett, J.A., Beaumont, J.J. and McLoughlin, E. (1997). Injury severity associated with nonfatal construction falls. *American Journal of Industrial Medicine*, 32(6), 647-655.

Goh, C. (2004). Management of pains in palliative care. *Cancer Update*. www.nccs.com.sg/epub/CU/vol3-04/p2-1.htm. [20 Sept. 2006]

Groth, C. (1996). Workers' compensation. In: W.J. Palmer, J.M. Maloney and J.L. Heffron (Eds.), *Construction Insurance, Bonding, and Management* (pp125-143). New York: McGraw-Hill.

Guardati, S. (1998). RBCShell: a tool for the construction of system with case-based reasoning. *Expert Systems with Applications,* 14(2), 63-70.

Gupta, U.G. (1992). *Validation and Verification of Knowledge based Systems.* California: IEEE computer society press.

Haslam, R.A., Hide, S.A., Gibb, A.G.F., Gyi, D.E., Pavitt, T., Atkinson, S. and Duff, A.R. (2005). Contributing factors in construction accidents. *Applied Ergonomics*, 36(5), 401-415.

Health and Safety Executive (HSE). (2005). *Safety in excavations.* http://www.hse.gov.uk/pubns/cis08.pdf. [4 Aug 2005].

Helander, M.G. (1991). Safety hazards and motivation for safe work in the construction industry. *International Journal of Industrial Ergonomics*, 8(3), 205-223.

Hess-Kosa, K. (2006). *Construction Safety Auditing Made Easy* (2nd ed.). USA: Government institutes.

Hinze, J. (2005). Use of trench boxes for worker protection. *Journal of Construction Engineering and Management*, 131(4), 494-500.

Hinze, J., Bren, D.C. and Piepho, N. (1995). Experience modification rating for workers' compensation insurance. *Journal of Construction Engineering and Management*, 121(4), 455-458.

Hislop, R.D. (2000). *Construction Site Safety: A Guide for Managing Contractors.* Washington DC: Lewis publishers.

Hoonakker, P., Loushine, T., Carayon, P., Kallman, J., Kapp, A. and Smith, M.J. (2005). The effect of safety initiatives on safety performance: A longitudinal study. *Applied Ergonomics*, 36(4), 461-469.

Hsiao, H. and Simeonov, P. (2001). Preventing falls from roofs: a critical review. *Ergonomics*, 44(5), 537-561.

Huang, X. and Hinze, J. (2006). Owner's role in construction safety: guidance model. *Journal of Construction Engineering and Management*, 132(2), 174-181.

Imriyas, K., Low, S.P. and Teo, A.L. (2007a). A framework for computing workers' compensation insurance premiums in construction. *Construction Management and Economics*, 25 (6), 563-584.

Imriyas, K., Low, S.P. and Teo, A.L. (2007b). A decision support system for predicting accident risks in building projects. *Architectural Science Review*, 50 (2), 149-162.

Imriyas, K., Low, S.P. and Teo, A.L. (2007c). A fuzzy knowledge based system for premium rating of workers' compensation insurance for building projects. *Construction Management and Economics*, 25 (11), 1175 -1193.

Imriyas, K., Low, S.P., Teo, A.L. and Chan, S.L. (2006). A fuzzy expert system for computing workers' compensation insurance premiums in construction: a conceptual framework. *Architectural Science Review*, 49(3), 269-282.

Imriyas, K., Low, S.P., Teo, A.L. and Chan, S.L. (2008). Premium-rating model for workers' compensation insurance in construction. *Journal of Construction Engineering and Management*, 134(8), 601-617.

Institute of Engineering and Technology (IET) (2008). *The costs to industry of accidents and ill-health*. www.theiet.org/factfiles/health/index.cfm. [11 Sept. 2008].

Jannadi, M.O. and Al-Sudairi, A. (1995). Safety management in the construction industry in Saudi Arabia. *Building Research and Information*, 29(1), 15-24.

Jannadi, M.O. and Assaf, S. (1998). Safety assessment in the built environment of Saudi Arabia. *Safety Science*, 23(1), 60-63.

Jones, H. (2008). Construction demand still strong. *Concrete Construction Magazine*, http://www.concreteconstruction.net/industry-news.asp?sectionID=700&articleID= 651217. [18 Sept. 2008]

Kamara, J.M and Anumba, C.J. (2001). ClientPro: a prototype software for clients requirement processing in construction. *Advances in Engineering Software*, 32(2), 141-158.

Kartam, N.A. and Bouz, R.G. (1998). Fatalities and injuries in the Kuwaiti construction industry. *Accident Analysis and Prevention*, 30(6), 805-814.

Kavianian, H.R. and Wentz, C.A. (1990). *Occupational and Environmental Safety Engineering and Management*. New York: Van Nostrand Reinhold.

King, R.W. and Hudson, R. (1985). *Construction Hazard and Safety Handbook*. London: Butterworths.

Kometa, S.T., Olomolaiye, P.O. and Harris, F.C. (1995). Quantifying client generated risk by project consultants. *Construction Management and Economics*, 13(2), 137-147.

Kyodo. (1991). Foreign workers cut own fingers for money, insurers say. *Singapore suspects foreign workers*. http://www.hamline.edu/ apakabar/ basisdata/1991/02/14/0007.html. [17 Apr. 2006].

Lambrinoudakis, C., Gritzalis, S., Hatzopoulos, P., Yannacopoulos, A.N. and Katsikas, S. (2005). A formal model for pricing information systems insurance contracts. *Computer Standards & Interfaces*, 27 (1), 521-532.

Lee, S. (2006). Application and verification of fuzzy logic to landslide susceptibility mapping. *Geophysical Research Abstracts,*(Vol.8), p3243.

Lee, S. and Halpin, D.W. (2003). Predictive tool for estimating accident risk. *Journal of Construction Engineering and Management*, 129(4), 431- 436.

Lemaire, J. (1990). Fuzzy insurance. *ASTIN Bulletin*, 20(1), 33-55.

Lian, G.C., 2005 April 20. LTA acts to boost Circle Line site safety. *The Strait Times,* p.H3.

Lingard, H. and Rowlinson, S. (1994). Construction-site safety in Hong Kong. *Construction Management and Economics*, 12(6), 501-510.

Liu, M. and Ling, Y.Y. (2005). Modelling a contractor's mark-up estimation, *Journal of Construction Engineering and Management*, 131(4), 391-399.

Loo, D. (2006). Workplace safety panel sets key aims. *The Straits Times,* May 27, p. H10.

Loo, D. (2006). Workplace safety panel sets key aims. *The Straits Times,* May 27, p. H10.

Lott, R.J. (2005). *Controlling workers' compensation cost a risk management program.* http://www.healthconsultantsusa.com/Risk_Mgmt_Program_Controlling_Worker_Comp _Costs.pdf. [27 June 2005].

MacCollum, D.V. (1993). *Crane Hazards and Their Prevention.* Washigton, DC: American Society of Safety Engineers.

Ministry of Manpower, Singapore (MOM). (2008). *Work Injury Compensation Act.* http://statutes.agc.gov.sg/non_version/cgi-bin/cgi_retrieve.pl?actno=REVED-354&doctitle=WORKMEN%92S%20COMPENSATION%20ACT%0a& amp;date=latest&method=part&sl=1. [16 Dec 2008].

Ministry of Manpower, Singapore (MOM). (2006). *Workplace Safety and Health Act.* http://www.mom.gov.sg/OSHD/Legislation/Workplace+Safety+and+Health+Act.htm. [1 March 2006].

Ministry of National Development (MND). (2005) *Government response to the final report of the committee of inquiry into the Nicoll Highway collapse.* http://www.mnd.gov.sg/ newsroom/ newsreleases/ 2005/ news170505. htm. [1 July 2006].

Monetary Authority of Singapore (MAS). (2006). *Insurance Statistics- 1st Quarter 2006.* https://secure.mas.gov.sg/masmcm/bin/pt1Insurance_Quarterly_Statistics. htm. [17 Aug.2006].

National Occupational Health and Safety Commission (NOHSC). (2005) *National Standard for Construction Work.* NOHSC, Australia.

National Safety Council. (1997). *Accident facts.* Itasca, Ill.

National Statistics. (2008). *Gross Capital Stock Analysis by Type of Industry at Current Prices.* http://www.statistics.gov.uk/StatBase/TSDdownload1.asp. [12 Sept. 2008]

Negnevitsky, M. (2002). *Artificial Intelligence: A Guide to Intelligent Systems.* England: Pearson Education Limited.

Neitzel, R.L., Seixas, N.S. and Ren, K.K. (2001). A review of crane safety in the construction industry. *Applied Occupational and Environmental Hygiene,* 16(12), 1106-1117.

Newman, K.D. and Hancher, D.E. (1991). Workers' compensation issues in construction. *Journal of Professional Issues in Engineering Education and Practice,* 117(3), 228-244.

NTUC income. (2006). *Managed Healthcare System.* http://www.income.coop/ insurance/mhs/. [4 Sep. 2006]

O'keefe, R.M., Balci, O. and Smith, E.P. (1987). Validating expert system performance. *IEEE Expert,* 2(4), 81-89.

Ocal, E., Oral, E.L. and Erdis, E. (2006). Crisis management in Turkish construction industry. *Building and Environment,* 41(11), 1498-1503.

Occupational Safety & Health Administration (OSHA). (1996). *Crane and hoist safety - OSHA summary sheet for individual priorities.* USA: OSHA.

Occupational Safety & Health Division, Ministry of Manpower (OSHD- MOM). (2006). *MOM Statistics.* http://www.mom.gov.sg/Statistics/OSHD/Accidents NInjuries. [29 Sept. 2006].

Occupational Safety and Health Administration (OSHA). (2002). *OSHA Construction e-tool,* http://www.osha-slc.gov/SLTC/construction_ecat/trenching/ mainpage.html. [2 Aug 2005].

Oglesly, C.H. Parker, H.W. and Howell, G.A. (1989). *Productivity Improvement in Construction*. New York: McGraw Hill.

Ogunsemi, D.R. and Jagboro, G.O. (2006). Time-cost model for building projects in Nigeria. *Construction Management and Economics*, 24 (3), 253-258.

Parsons, T.J. and Pizatella, T.J. (1985). *Safety analysis of high risk activities within the roofing industry* (Technical Report No. NTIS PB-85163236). VA: Springfield.

Perera, A.A.D.A.J. and Imriyas, K. (2003). Knowledge based system for construction cost control. In K. Deweese (ed.), *AACE international transaction* (pp IT10.1-10.8J). USA: AACE International Inc.

Perera, A.A.D.A.J. and Imriyas, K. (2004). An integrated construction project cost information system using MS Access™ and MS Project™. *Construction Management and Economics*, 22(2), 203-211.

Phifer, R. (1996). *Reinsurance Fundamentals*. New York: John Wiley & Sons, Inc.

Pontes, J.A.P. (2005). *Assessment and control of exposure to vibration in the construction industry.* http://www.cramif.fr/pdf/th4/paris/seance_poster/pontes. pdf. [9 March 2006].

Rao, G. N., Grobler, F. and Ganashen, R. (1997). Interconnected component applications for AEC software development. *Journal of Computing in Civil Engineering*, 2(2), 82-92.

Reh, F.J. (2006). *Pareto's Principle – The 80-20 Rule*. http://management.about.com/ cs/generalmanagement/a/Pareto081202.htm. [8 Apr. 2006].

Reserve Bank of Australia. (2007). Box C: Development in the Construction Sector. *Statement on Monetary Policy – August 2007.* http://www.rba.gov.au/ PublicationsAndResearch/StatementsOnMonetaryPolicy/Aug2007/box_c.html. [07 Oct. 2008]

Rowlinson, S. (1997). *Hong Kong Construction – Site Safety Management*. Hong Kong: Sweet & Maxwell Asia.

Ruser, J.W. (1995). *A relative risk analysis of workplace fatalities, fatal workplace injuries in 1993: a collection of data and analysis* (Report No. 891). Washington, DC: Department of Labor.

Shapiro, A.F. (2004). Fuzzy logic in insurance. *Insurance: Mathematics and Economics*, 35(2), 399-424.

Shepherd, G.W., Kahler, R.J. and Cross, J. (2001). Crane fatalities - a taxonomic analysis. *Safety Science*, 36(2), 83-93.

Si, H.S., Ruxton, T. and Wang, J. (2001). A fuzzy logic-based approach to qualitative safety modelling for marine systems. *Reliability Engineering and System Safety*, 73 (1), 19-34.

Singapore Productivity and Standards Board (SPSB). (1999). *Code of Practice for Safety Management System for Construction Worksites (SS CP 79:1999)*, Singapore: Spring.

Suruda, A.J., Pettit, T.A., Noonan, G.P. and Ronk, R.M. (1994). Deadly rescue: the confined space hazard. *Journal of Hazardous Materials*, 36(1), 45-53.

Tam, C.M, Tam, V.W.Y. and Tsui, W.S. (2004). Green construction assessment for environmental management in the construction industry of Hong Kong. *International Journal of Project Management,* 22(7), 563-571.

Tam, C.M. and Fung, I.W.H. (1998). Effectiveness of safety management strategies on safety performance in Hong Kong. *Construction Management and Economics*, 16(1), 49-55.

Tan, W. (2004). *Practical Research Methods* (2nd ed.). Singapore: Prentice Hall.

Tang, S.L, Ying, K.C, Chan, W.Y and Chan, Y.L. (2004). Impact of social safety investment on social costs of construction accidents. *Construction Management and Economics*, 22(9), 937-946.

Teo, A.L.E., Ling, Y.Y.F., and Chua, K.H.D. (2004). *Measuring the Effectiveness of Safety Management Systems of Construction Firms*, Unpublished report, Department of Building, National University of Singapore.

Teo, E.A.L., Ling, F.Y.Y. and Chong, A.F.W. (2005). Framework for project managers to manage construction safety. *International Journal of Project Management*, 23(4), 329-341.

The Workers' Compensation Rating and Inspection Bureau (WCRIB) (2008a), Manual rates and rating values effective 9/1/2008. https://www.wcribma.org/mass/products/circulars/2008_circulars/c12090.pdf. [04 Dec. 2008].

The Workers' Compensation Rating and Inspection Bureau (WCRIB) (2008b), *Table of expected loss rates and discount ratios*. https://www.wcribma.org/mass/products/Rates/ERP_Table_of_ELR_and_D_Ratios_20080901.pdf. [04 Dec. 2008].

The Workers' Compensation Rating and Inspection Bureau (WCRIB) (2008c), *Table of ballast values*. https://www.wcribma.org/mass/products/rates/erp_table_of_ballast_values_ncci_20030901.pdf. [04 Dec. 2008].

The Workers' Compensation Rating and Inspection Bureau (WCRIB) (2008d), *Table of weighting values*. https://www.wcribma.org/mass/products/Rates/ERP_Table_of_Weighting_Values_20080901.pdf. [04 Dec. 2008].

Toscano, G. (1997). *Dangerous jobs, fatal workplace injuries in 1995: a collection of data and analysis* (Report No. 913). Washington, DC: Department of Labor.

Tsoukalas, L.H. and Uhrig, R.E. (1997). *Fuzzy and Neural Approaches in Engineering*. New York: Wiley.

Vaughan, E.J. and Vaughan, T.M. (1996). *Fundamentals of Risk and Insurance* (7th ed.). New York: John Wiley.

Walker, D.H.T. (1997). Choosing an appropriate research methodology. *Construction Management and Economics*, 15(2), 149-159.

Walker, M.G. and Wiederhold, G. (1990). *Acquisition and Validation of Knowledge from Data*. http://www-db.stanford.edu/pub/gio/1990/walkerDiscovery.html. [6 Oct. 2006].

Welder, arc. (2005). *International hazard datasheet*. http://www.ilo.org/public/english/protection/ safework/cis/products/hdo/pdf/welder_arc.pdf. [9 Mar. 2006].

Worksafe Victoria. (2005). *Industry standard: contaminated construction sites* (1st ed.). http://www.workcover.vic.gov.au/dir090/vwa/publica.nsf/docsbyUNID/685309488996D5ECCA25703500825779/$file/constructioncontaminated_standard.pdf. [7 Mar. 2006].

Worrall, J.D. and Buttler, R.J. (1988). Experience rating matters. In: D. Appel and P.S. Borba (Eds.). *Workers' Compensation Insurance Pricing* (pp81-94). Boston: Kluwer Academic Publisher.

Yager, R. and Filev, D. (1993). Learning of fuzzy rules by mountain climbing. In Proc. SPIE Conf. Applicat. Fuzzy Logic Technol. Boston, MA. Vol. 2061, Sept, 1993, pp. 246 - 254.

Yan, J., Ryan, M. and Power, J. (1994). *Using Fuzzy Logic*. London: Prentice Hall.

Yen, J. and Langari, R. (1999). *Fuzzy Logic: Intelligence, Control and Information*. New Jersey: Prentice Hall.

Young, V.R. (1996). Insurance rate changing: a fuzzy logic approach. *The Journal of Risk and Insurance*, 63(3), 461-484.

Young, V.R. (1997). Adjusting indicated insurance rates: Fuzzy rules that consider both experience and auxiliary data. *Casualty Actuarial Society,* 84(161), 734-765.

Zadeh, L.A. (1965).Fuzzy Sets. *Information and Control, 1965: no.*8, 338-353.

Zadeh, L.A. (1975). The concept of linguistic variable and its application to approximate reasoning. *Information Sciences*, 8:199-249 (part I), 8: 301-57 (part II).

Zadeh, L.A. (1994). Soft computing and fuzzy logic. *IEEE Software*, 11 (6), 48-56.

Index

C

S

T	**U**

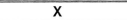